MICHEL:
THE FOURTH WISE MAN

KATHERYN MADDOX HADDAD

[A COMMENTARY IN NARRATIVE FORM

Katheryn Maddox Haddad

OTHER BOOKS BY THIS AUTHOR

HISTORICAL NOVELS & STORYBOOKSI
Series of 8: They Met Jesus
Ongoing Series of 8: Intrepid Men of God
Mysteries of the Empire with Klaudius & Hektor
Christmas: They Rocked the Cradle that Rocked the World
Series of 8: A Child's Life of Christ
Series of 10: A Child's Bible Heroes
Series of 8: A Child's Bible Kids
Series of 10: A Child's Bible Ladies

HISTORICAL RESEARCH BIBLE
for Novel, Screenwriter, Documentary & Thesis Writers

TOPICAL
Applied Christianity: Handbook 500 Good Works
Christianity or Islam? The Contrast
The Holy Spirit: 592 Verses Examined
The Road to Heaven
Inside the Hearts of Bible Women-Reader+Audio+Leader
Revelation: A Love Letter From God
Worship Changes Since 1st Century + Worship 1sr Century Way
Was Jesus God? (Why Evil)
365 Life-Changing Scriptures Day by Date
The Road to Heaven
The Lord's Supper: 52 Readings with Prayers

FUN BOOKS
Bible Puzzles, Bible Song Book, Bible Numbers

TOUCHING GOD SERIES
365 Golden Bible Thoughts: God's Heart to Yours
365 Pearls of Wisdom: God's Soul to Yours
365 Silver-Winged Prayers: Your Spirit to God's

-SURVEY SERIES: EASY BIBLE WORKBOOKS
→Old Testament & New Testament Surveys
→Questions You Have Asked-Part I & II

Genealogy: How to Climb Your Family Tree Without Falling Out
Volume I & 2: Beginner-Intermediate & Colonial-Medieval

Copyright © 2016 Katheryn Maddox Haddad
NORTHERN LIGHTS PUBLISHING HOUSE

ISBN-978-1-948462-25-9
Printed in the United States

Travels of the Magi to Sacred Libraries to find the meaning of the STAR.

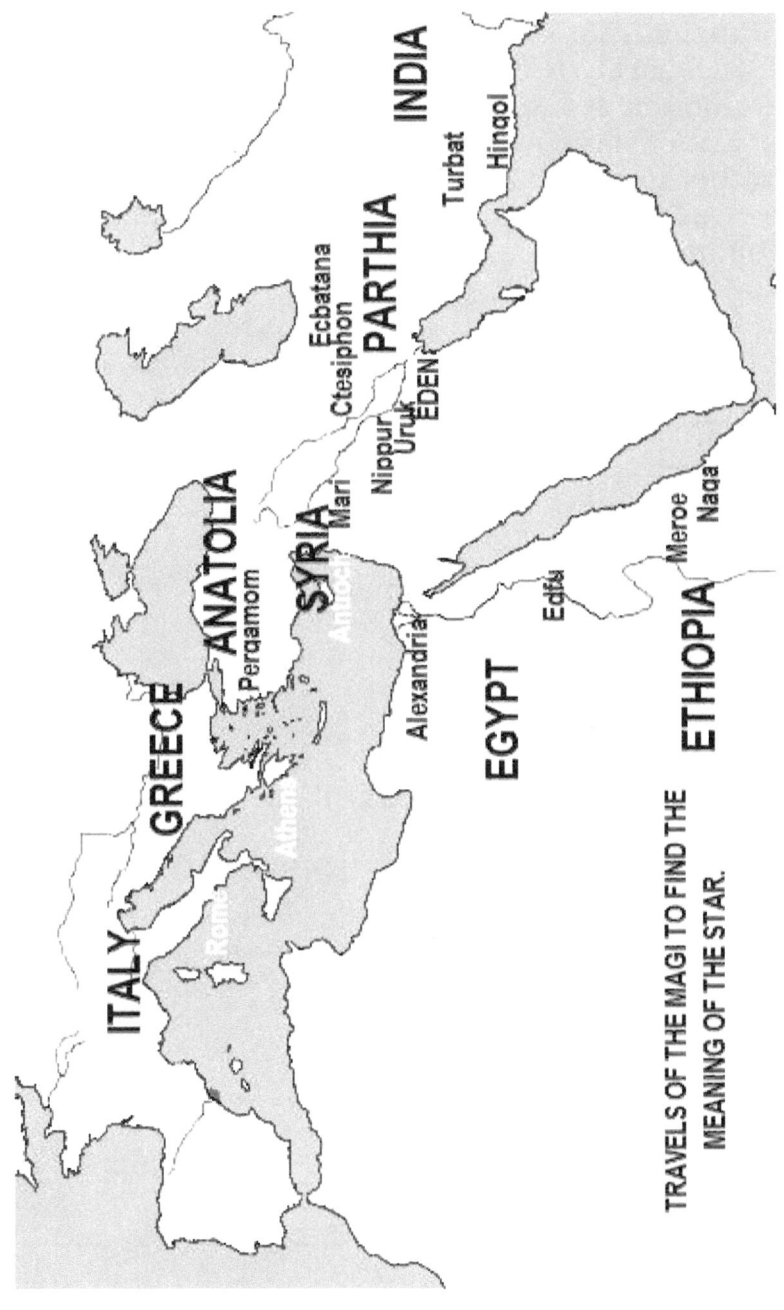

Katheryn Maddox Haddad

TABLE OF CONTENTS

1 ~ The Announcement 1
2 ~ Confusion...12
URUK, HOMETOWN OF MICHEL......................................23
3 ~ Abandonment...24
4 ~ Pursuit of Happiness 34
5 ~ Another Impossibility..44
6 ~ The Descent 53
7 ~ Ultimate Sacrifice 63
8 ~ Fatal Interruption..73
CTESIPHON IN 1867 83
9 ~ Quagmires..84
NIPPUR, HOMETOWN OF MEIRA 93
10 ~ The Decision...94
11 ~ Captive..105
12 ~ Caverns and Cliffs 115
13 ~ Near, but Far...125
14 ~ The Runaway..134
15 ~ Becalmed..144
16 ~ Warrior Queen...154
17 ~ Doomed..164
LIBRARY OF HORUS IN EDFU 174
18 ~ Confusion..175
LIBRARY AT ALEXANDRIA, EGYPT................................185
19 ~ Mourning...186
LIBRARY OF ARISTOTLE IN ATHENS 195
20 ~ Hopes...196
APOLLO'S LIBRARY IN ROME 206
21 ~ Betrayal...207
ATHENA LIBRARY IN PERGAMUM 216
22 ~ To Hope Again 217
LIBRARY AT ANTIOCH, SYRIA.......................................227
23 ~ Resurrection..228
24 ~ Trapped..238
25 ~ Escape..247
ECBATANA WITH ITS SEVEN WALLS 257
26 ~ The Impossible 258

27 ~ Discovery 268
28 ~ False Beginnings 278
29 ~ Lost.. 288
30 ~ The Premonition... 298
31 ~ Exhaustion 308
32 ~ Final Approach... 318
33 ~ The Unexpected... 328
34 ~ Destiny 338
35 ~ Meltdown 348
36 ~ Moses 358
37 ~ Recovery 368
38 ~ The Sea 378
39 ~ Eden 390
40 ~ The Eternal Child...................................... 401

Thank You 413
GET ALL 8 BOOKS IN THE HISTORICAL SERIES 414

HISTORICAL BACKGROUND................................. 415
BUY YOUR NEXT BOOK NOW 419

DISCUSSION QUESTIONS 420
ABOUT THE AUTHOR 427

CONNECT WITH KATHERYN MADDOX HADDAD......428
GET A FREE BOOK... 429
JOIN MY DREAM TEAM 429

ONE LONE STAR

One lone star, enlarged with love,
led the unknown way

To the Son who'd brought with him
Hope's redeeming ray.

Compel your eyes to venture high
above what seems to far.

Soar with Mercy's omnipotence
and dare to be that star.

Katheryn Maddox Haddad

1 ~ THE ANNOUNCEMENT

"You cannot just buy the Garden of Eden!"

"Why not?" Michel replies, looking out from the summer palace in Ctesiphon at the Tigris.

Michel is seated on a marble bench and leaning back on the west balcony wall with his hands behind his head.

"Yes," Mongol Yasib says. He pulls on his wispy gray beard. "Tell us, Dushatra, just why he cannot buy the Garden of Eden."

"It's not logical," Dushatra double checks his own beard to make sure none of the curls have come out in the evening breeze.

"Ha, ha," Indus Kumar interjects. "Since you, Dushatra, and I still have not found perfection so we can stop being reincarnated, perhaps re-establishing the Garden of Eden with all its perfection will help us on our way."

"Kumar, don't go trying to mix my religion with your's," Dushatra says, standing and pointing his finger at Kumar. "Besides, we know nothing about this garden Michel's Jews believe in."

The three friends pause and look back at Michel, who has said nothing since his announcement.

"You three don't even believe in the Garden of Eden," he finally says, still grinning, "so why should you care?"

"To be honest," old Yasib says, "we hate to see you waste your money."

"Yes, just how much is this, this garden going to cost?"

Dushatra inquires, sitting back down.

"I don't know yet. But I've got people down there trying to find the present owners."

"Where did you say it is?" Kumar asks, double checking his finely coifed beard that even the king would be proud of.

"Well, it doesn't really exist anymore," Michel says, leaning forward with his elbows on his knees. "But it *was* where the Tigris and Euphrates Rivers meet."

"Ha, ha! He wants to buy a garden that isn't there," Yasib announces.

"Probably out in the middle of the desert where no one lives," Indus Dushatra says.

"I was down there a few months ago," old Yasib says, "and you're right about that. Well, at least part of it."

"Which part?" Kumar asks.

"It's where no one lives, but not because it is desert. It is all marshland." He throws his head back and guffaws.

"So, you want to buy worthless land because it used to be a garden your Jews believe in. And how long ago was it a garden, may I ask?" Dushatra shakes his head while watching an ant skitter across the marble tiles.

"A few thousand years. Don't know exactly…"

"A few thousand years?" Dushatra interrupts. "Have you become a mad man? We're going to have to report this to King Phraattes. You may not have your head by your next birthday."

"Leave the man alone," old Yasib says. "You get too serious sometimes. Michel has his dreams. He has always been a dreamer. The king knows that. We all know that."

Michel forms a broad grin. "Indeed, I am a dreamer. Just like my ancestor, Daniel, who…"

"Not again," Kumar says with a half-grin, waving his hand at Michel, and standing. "We know all about your Daniel and his kings. The sun is low. I am going home. My wife promised to fix my favorite sauce tonight. Oh, uh, and good luck on your underwater garden, my friend."

He chuckles on his way to the steps leading to the

courtyard below. On his way down, he makes sure the hem of his silk *dhoti* is firmly tucked into his waist.

"No wife for me," Dushatra says, walking behind Kumar. "I do whatever I want."

"Nor me, but not out of choice," Yasib says as both he and Michel stand. "Her name was Ji, and she was my heart. Ah, well, appreciate your wife while you have her, my friend. Appreciate her while you have her."

"Yes, sir," Michel replies.

With that, Yasib turns, lifts his colorful appliqued scarlet skirt, and manipulates his ruby-topped cane to start down the outer steps.

Michel watches the old Xiongnu Mongol man with the top of his head shaved except for a knot right above his forehead. The hair allowed to grow from the bottom of his head is as gray as his beard.

Michel lingers on the balcony alone. He looks up into the western sky. The red sunset is too harsh on his eyes, so he turns and looks the other way. He sees a star.

"Oh, Jehovah. As sure as you made the stars, you also put a plan in my mind. Okay, a dream. You want me to restore the Garden of Eden and draw all men to it. Will you walk with us again there? Will you walk with us through the garden as you did with Father Adam and Mother Eve so long ago?"

He sighs and heads down the steps to the courtyard. At the bottom, he turns west toward the Tigris River and the Citadel of the Seleucids on the other side. The outer-most courtyard is long. It is at least one hundred man-lengths to the outer gate on the banks of the river. *I must measure it someday*, he reminds himself once again.

The great veranda housing the outer gate is said to be the most imposing in the world being ten man-length deep and fifteen man-lengths high. The walls on either side have six levels, all with barracks in them. The top of the wall over the barracks is wide enough for ten chariots to ride side by side.

Although the front is completely open to the public,

there is only a double door in the back through which the elite are allowed to exit and enter the palace grounds.

Honor guards clad in blue with gold breastplate, shield,s and cone-shaped helmets on each side of the door salute Michel and open the door to the outside for him.

Michel watches the vendors along each side wall close up for the evening and waves to his favorites. Ceiling and walls of the structure are lined with tiles of every imaginable color, though blue is more predominant than the others.

He walks out, notices the red of the sunset now reflecting in the river, and turns left toward the section of the city where high officials are allowed to have estates. He arrives at the first street but passes it. He goes on down to the fourth street and turns left again. The second estate down on the right belongs to Yasib. The third estate down on the left belongs to Kumar.

Arriving at his own estate, he knocks. The gate is covered with copper and has a silver replica of the candlesticks that stand in the Holy Place of the temple back in Jerusalem.

He hears scraping of a bar on the other side, then the squeaking of hinges as the gatekeeper opens up for his master.

"Good evening, Anu," Michel says.

"Good evening, Master," Anu says. The gatekeeper is short and bald and very attuned to his master's desires. "Welcome home. The mistress is up on the roof, and Freni will have dinner ready shortly."

Michel ascends the steps to the roof, taking off his turban as he goes, and walks over to his wife.

Meira, five years younger than her husband, having seen three decades, looks up from the rabbits she had been watching down on the ground. "Aren't they cute?"

"Aren't what cute?" he says, kissing her on the forehead. He seats himself opposite her. "I told them."

"I fear asking you for clarification."

"I don't really care what they think," Michel says. "I'm going to do it anyway. I have to. For the sake of everyone in the world who worships idols and imaginary gods. I must bring them back to Eden."

"Number one," Meira responds, pushing her black hair away from her dark eyes, "we haven't decided for sure, and number two, you had no reason to tell them. They are just co-workers."

Michel clasps hold of both his wife's delicate hands and smiles.

"Sweetheart, you may not have decided, but I have. This is something God wants me to do."

"How do you know God wants you to do it?"

"Well, I have this burning in my heart. I just know it."

Meira lets go of his hands, stands, and walks toward the steps. "You have had so many burnings in your heart over the past fifteen years, I have lost track. Each time you swore God told you to obey your burning."

"This is different, Meira."

"They all were," she says, starting down the steps.

"Okay, let's make a trip down there and see if we can find whoever owns the land where the Garden of Eden used to be," Michel says, following her down. "If we do and the owner is willing to sell it, that's our sign God wants us to buy and restore it."

"And what if we don't have the money?"

"I'll sell the estate."

She turns and stares up at her tall, handsome husband with the simple beard, high cheekbones, straight nose, and serious eyes.

Her brows furrow. "You'll what?" She walks toward the kitchen area of the courtyard, calling over her shoulder, "Never."

The evening meal is eaten in silence. The servants walk softly through the estate doing their chores and keeping their voices low. Even the moon above the wide courtyard hides behind a cloud.

The night is not spent well for either. Sometimes Michel hears Meira crying and prays to God for strength.

The next morning, no one speaks. Just before Michel

leaves, he turns to his wife, now with reddened eyes. With his heart wrenching between the two he loves most, he speaks one last time.

"If I don't do it, it won't get done. God needs me."

Michel turns toward the gatekeeper. "I will take my chariot this morning."

Anu nods to his master and walks over to another gate facing the street where the stable is. While Michel waits, he looks up into the heavens. "If Daniel is up there with you, tell him his son is taking up the banner."

Boarding the elegant silver and copper chariot, Michel clicks his tongue, and the mighty Nisean horse, king of battles, makes its way up the street. He goes past Yasib's estate and out onto the main street along the Tigris, leading to the lofty arched veranda and the palace complex.

Along the way, he sees Kumar who waves at him upon stepping aside to the curb. Michel forces a smile and waves in return.

Once through the veranda and the doors in the back, and inside the courtyard leading to the palace, Michel leaves his chariot in the hands of the royal stable and stands before the front gate into the palace itself.

Easily recognized as one of King Phraattes' honored magus, the guards with gleaming gold breastplates over their blue uniforms and pointed gold helmets open the way for Michel to enter.

He can never get used to the opulence of the grand entry hall, fully ten man-lengths wide and high, and twice that to the other end. The floor is of blue and white marble tile, with coral columns rising on each side.

The walls are colorfully frescoed with triumphs of King Phraattes since taking the throne fifty-some years earlier upon assassinating his royal father and brothers. Many a battle are depicted with the Romans to the north, while a variety of other scenes are of battles with the Indos to the south, Syrians to the west, and Chinese and Xiongnu Mongols to the east.

The scenes on the ceiling of the great hall are of King

Orodes, which Phraattes left in honor of his father, possibly to assuage the guilt he perhaps feels on rare occasion.

Separating each scene is wood molding plated with both gold and silver, but mostly gleaming gold.

Along the walls and coming down from the ceiling on chains are golden oil lamps—enough to keep the palace lit at night and kept warm on cool evenings in the Zagros foothills.

As grand as all of this is, it can never surpass the natural God-planted Garden of Eden, Michel thinks. *God, you are going to get your garden back, and the world will flock to it so you can once again walk with us in the cool of the evening.*

The magus passes the inside stairway to the observatory on the roof of the great hall, and on through an arch leading to the inner palace with the usual guards on each side. On his left is the throne room. He continues past that and finally arrives at his destination: The war room.

The golden doors with large agate handles are opened for him by doormen wearing blue multi-folded pantaloons, short matching vests wrapped both ways across their chest, and white long-sleeved and billowed shirts under that. They wear white turbans on their head attached with large rubies.

Just inside, Michel pauses to see who has arrived thus far. He moves over toward Dushatra with an empty chair beside him. He thinks back on his illustrious ancestor, Daniel. *In his day, they sat on regal cushions on their king's regal floor.*

He forces a smile. "Good morning, Dushatra. Have you heard what mood the king is in today?"

"No, but Queen Musa is said to have ordered one of her ladies in waiting beaten for blaspheming her yellow hair," Dushatra responds. "I feel sorry for anyone working for that Italian viper."

"Augustus must have sent her to the king to torment him," Michel responds with a slight grin, his head close to Dushatra's but not looking at him. "Oh, here come Kumar and Yasib."

Standing, he motions for his other two best friends to

join them. Servants clad in the same uniforms as the doormen hold chairs out for them.

"Looks like we're the last ones here," Yasib says, handing his ruby-tipped cane to the servant.

Trumpets are heard. Every one of the seventy-member council rises and bows his head to the floor.

Moments later, they hear loud footsteps leading from the private entrance and to the war-room throne. A single trumpet sounds, and everyone lifts his head, rises, and reseats himself. Michel, on one side and Kumar on the other help old Yasib up and to his chair.

"Heard any more about the Garden of Eden?" Yasib whispers while his eyes concentrate on the king. He does not receive a reply.

"I hope things will run smoothly today," King Phraattes announces, handing his alabaster staff to his closest manservant. "It has not had a good beginning."

The king does not wear a crown which would hide his black hair carefully curled and matching his short beard. Instead, he wears a long blue sash across his forehead and tied in back. A servant has held the sash out so he would not sit on it, and it flows down to the floor behind his throne. Everyone knows the coif is artificial from horsehair, thus covering his thinning gray hair.

Large bags are under the king's dark eyes. His nose is wide and long and straight with a hook on the end. His cheekbones are high, and what teeth he has left are yellow, but partly hidden by his mustache.

"First, I want to hear from my military *spahbed*. Is Suren here? Ah, there you are."

"Reports from all borders are good, Your Majesty," Suren begins, rising as he talks. "The Romans, to our north, are behaving for the time being, as well as the Syrians to our west. Our forts along those borders have reported no problems."

He pauses to allow the king to praise him. When it does not come, he continues.

"Your vassal king, Gondophares of the Indo

Southlands, is having his usual local wars to maintain his power, but I believe he will keep his disputes there and not bother us with them."

Suren seats himself.

"Not so fast, sir," King Phraattes interrupts.

Spahbed Suren rises again.

"You seem to have left out the Chinese and those pesky Xiongnu Mongols to our east."

Suren clears his throat.

"Well, Your Majesty, one of our forts along the wall between us and the Mongols did report some activity."

"How much activity, Suren? Speak up," the king bellows. "How much activity?"

"Well, a hundred of them scaled the wall we erected there and burned the fort."

The king's face turns red. "Do you mean the longest and highest wall in the world running from the Caspian up into the Pishkamar Mountains was torn down while the greatest warriors in the world slept? And you forgot to tell me?"

"Well, not exactly, Your Majesty. They scaled the wall while our soldiers slept."

An undertone of groans and snickers flows through the room except from the chair of Michel. *Oh, God, how the world needs the peace of your kingdom. Help me help you establish it.*

"But I have sent masons up to the Gorgan River to rebuild the fort," Suren adds. "Soldiers from nearby forts are already there working on the foundation."

"And I suppose that Chinese Emperor Ai has noticed a dearth of activity in our forts south of there."

"No, Your Majesty. I sent more soldiers to reinforce the troops already there."

"Sit. I don't want to hear more. But tomorrow, your report had better be one worthy of your position, or you are likely to be a meal for my wife's pets – her hungry lions.

"Next? Oh, I see you were able to make it today, Yasib, my friend," Phraattes says, his voice lower. "How are your knees? Any stronger than mine? What do you think of your Emperor Ai? Not much, I'll bet. Probably glad you're not there right now."

"Dushatra!" he continues without giving Yasib time to reply. "You're from Kandahar that ole Gondophores claims to have founded, which everyone knows isn't so. Anyway, what is your impression of him? Is he going to cause me any trouble?"

Dushatra rises. "No, Your Majesty. He is good to his subjects and loyal to you."

"I heard he's Buddhist now. Is that what you are?"

"Yes, Your Majesty, though I know your Zoroastroism is very fine also."

The king smiles, then turns his attention to Michel.

"How are the signs of the gods these days? Do you see any trouble stirring in the sky?"

"Your Majesty, Kumar was on duty last night."

Kumar stands. "All is quiet among the gods, Your Majesty. Well, there was one star that raced across the heavens, then out of sight. But I believe that was an omen of the trouble with the Xiongnu Mongols racing toward our border. The star is gone now, and we will have peace with the Mongols again soon."

"How do you do that, Kumar? And you other magi? How do you determine what the stars mean? How many are there of you?"

"Thirty-one, Your Majesty," Kumar replies.

"Yes, yes. One for each night."

Following is the treasurer's report, the palace addition report, the shipping report, the war-horse-breeding report, the mining report, and reports from mayors of various cities in the kingdom.

Some time after the sun has begun its descent from the pinnacle of the sky, the king leaves, and the assembly adjourns.

Michel and his friends file out of the palace. He says goodbye to them at the stable.

"Ha, ha. Keep us informed of the progress on your

underwater garden, my friend. Ha, ha, ha," Kumar says as he turns to walk home.

"He's a fool," Dushatra calls out as he joins his other two friends.

Michel is met by the stable keeper.

"Sir, a message was sent to you earlier today. Here is the tile it was written on. The messenger was in a hurry and said he just came up from Uruk. That's where you are from, isn't it?"

Michel takes the tile. It has only two words on it.

COME QUICKLY.

"Oh, no."

2 ~ CONFUSION

Michel boards his chariot and heads down the long outer palace courtyard to the double doors behind the grand veranda facing the Tigris. Once outside, he puts his horse into a fast trot, wishing he could go faster on the royal city streets.

"Open the gate," he calls out as he nears his estate. "Open the gate!"

Both the stableman and gatekeeper rush out to the street in time to meet their master.

Michel jumps off his chariot, his turban askance on his head.

"What is it? What's wrong?" Meira says, coming out to the courtyard from their personal library.

"Something is wrong at home. My father sent me a message. He must not have had time to explain more because all he said was to come quickly."

"What do you think has happened?"

"I don't know. Mother is gone. I have a few cousins there, but none would need me. Has Father had a bad accident? Is he unable to write? Has he contracted the same fever Mother died of?"

Michel takes off his turban, throws it onto a table nearby, and runs his hands through his thick brown hair.

"What are you going to do?" Meira asks.

"What can I do?" her husband replies, now walking in circles.

"I'll pack some food for you in a basket. Anu, will you

bring out your goat-hair tent. Or would you rather have the smaller leather one?

"Sweetheart, I need you to go with me," he responds.

"Why? You were mad at me this morning."

"If my father is dying, I do not want to face it alone. I really don't. I need you right now."

Meira steps over to her husband, puts her arms around his waist, and snuggles into his chest.

"I'm sorry I yelled at you this morning."

"Me too."

"Did I ever tell you about the happiest day of my life?" Michel asks. "It was when I was thirteen years old. My mother came to Nippur to pull me out of school because my father had come home. When I got home, there he was in his shiny parade armor from head to foot, with another set waiting for me. I was tall for my age. Once I got my armor on, Pakor helped us up onto our mighty Nisean war horses. Then we paraded through the city while my father waved a scroll of the Torah. All the pagans in the city came out and cheered us and called out, 'Great is Jehovah.' I'll never forget that day, Meira."

She pulls away and looks up into his face that reflects what she has seldom seen: Confusion. Her intelligent husband, who—although he is sometimes a dreamer who always knows what he wants and how to get there—is confused.

"When do you want to leave?" Meira asks. "I'm anxious to see my mother on the way."

"How did you manage that—stopping to see your mother?" Michel says with a grin.

"I have my ways," his wife says over her shoulder, walking toward the kitchen area of the courtyard.

"I need to go back to the palace and send word to the king. Without his permission, I cannot leave."

"I will bake extra bread to eat on the road tomorrow and the next day."

Knowing he will not be leaving until morning, Michel stops at Yasib's estate.

"I cannot come in, Yasib. But I wanted you to know why I will not be joining the other magi tomorrow."

"How long will you be gone?"

"I don't know. My father has never needed anyone. He has always done whatever he wanted whenever he wanted, even if he had to do it alone—which was most of the time."

Michel works his way over to the palace.

"You are in luck," the king's secretary and scribe says. "He is sitting in his courtyard talking to the carpenter about wood panels in his bedroom. Wait here."

Michel stares at the frescoes on the wall of the reception hall while he waits.

"He will see you now. But not for long. I think he is mad again. You'd better be careful. You know his temper."

Michel walks past the stairs to the observatory on the roof, past the throne room, past the war room, and through a wide door between frescoed columns to a courtyard resplendent with transplanted trees, a large reflecting pool, and various small exotic animals roaming around.

The king's back is to Michel. He walks around to face him and bows his head to the marble-covered pavement.

"That's fine, Michel. Now, what is so important that it cannot wait until our meeting in the morning?"

"Your Majesty, I would not disturb your business, and your repose if ..."

"Get to the point, Michel. I'm busy."

"Something has happened to my father."

"Well, what?"

"I don't know."

"Then leave."

"But, Your Majesty. He is in trouble. He could be dying."

"Who did you say your father was?"

"Nebo of Uruk, Your Majesty. He was one of your most..."

"Oh, yes. Nebo. Had to retire last year. Something about his back and not being able to ride in heavy armor any more."

"I won't be gone long, Sire. And my turn to observe the heavens does not come up for another two weeks, and…"

"Go. Get out of here. Here comes my lovely wife with her pet lion."

The two men turn and look toward a petite blond woman who looks forty years younger than the king.

"But, Your Majesty," Michel says, backing up.

"She doesn't look too happy right now," the king says. "Her pet doesn't either. You'd better leave fast."

"But…"

"Go see your father. But I want you back here in a week."

"Yes, Your Majesty," Michel says, eyeing the lion more than the young queen.

He backs away, hurries through the palace from whence he had come, boards his chariot and heads for home, thinking more now of the lion than his father.

Michel and Meira rise early the next morning. Freni, Meira's lady in waiting, is already in the kitchen area under the canopy in the courtyard, taking hot rolls out from the oven.

"The chariot is ready for you and mistress Meira, Sir," Anu announces. "I have your good leather tent and bedding on the donkey I will be riding, and fodder for the animals and cooking supplies on Freni's donkey."

Within the hour, they are out on the highway built in the Roman cobblestone fashion and wide enough for two wagons to comfortably pass each other going opposite directions.

After eight hours, they arrive in Kish.

"Sweetheart, I'd like to stop here and get a good meal at the inn, so we'll be fresh when we arrive at Nippur tomorrow. Besides, we need to talk."

Anu and Freni take care of lining up a room at the inn with a bed and plenty of space in the floor for them to sleep.

Michel and Meira settle at a table and order stew.

"If it's the Garden of Eden you want to talk about, my dear," Michel says, "I don't think we need to discuss it while we have more pressing matters to take care of."

"And that more pressing matter is what we need to talk about."

"My father? Why?"

"You were never close to your father. How many times have you told me he left you and your mother when you were three years old and was gone until you were six?"

"I know. I know. He was gone all the time. But maybe things will be different now."

"And again when you were ten, and again when you were thirteen. I thought you hated your father for abandoning you and your mother years at a time."

"Well, maybe, I was wrong."

"Will you think maybe you were wrong if he is not dying?"

"Huh?"

"We don't know what we'll find when we get there," Meira continues. "What if he's not sick? What if the message was about his house burning down or his war horses being smuggled? What if he's not sick and dying at all?"

"Oh, here is our stew. Let's eat."

No more is said on the subject. They retire to their room and try to sleep.

Morning comes, and they are on the highway again.

"I'm so anxious to see my mother," Meira says.

Soon after mid-day, the couple sees ahead of them the ziggurat with a temple at the top to Enlil, god of the cosmos subject only to An.

They enter through the northeast gate with a temple to the war god Ninurta on one side and the temple to the healing god Ninkarrak on the other side.

Straight ahead of them is the temple to Inanna surrounded by the wealthy homes of the priests in power.

They turn right past the houses and go over a bridge across the Chebar Canal. Just beyond is the palace and court of columns.

They continue on until they come to a textile-making complex where they turn left. Down, that street where the bazaar and southeast gate are, they see Atossa's house.

"I wonder if the library is as wonderful as it was when my father let me go there."

"I'm sure it is," Michel replies.

Meira looks up a high hill on the other side of the southern gate. "That's one of the city's three libraries, the one with a school attached to it. That's the one my father sent me to. I spent many happy hours there."

"Your father was a good man. Not every father would have let his daughter study at such a prestigious library. You had a tutor from there also, didn't you?"

When they arrive and knock on the gate to Meira's childhood home, no one answers.

"That's odd? Not only is my mother not here, but none of the servants seem to be either."

"Anu, will you go back to the bazaar and see if Meira's mother is there? Her name is..."

"Is it really you?"

They hear a familiar voice.

"Mother!"

Meira steps down from the chariot and rushes to her mother's arms.

"I guess I don't need to go find her mother," Anu whispers to Freni.

"Come in, my dear. Come in all of you," gray-haired Atossa says, pulling out a large key to fit in the lock on the gate.

"Where is your gatekeeper?" Michel asks.

"Don't need him anymore. I let him go work for someone else. Oh, where did I leave my basket?"

"I have it here," Michel replies, following the women inside. "Where do you want it?"

"Just under the canopy over there where I cook."

"You cook, Mother? You never liked to cook. You had the maids do it."

"Well, I don't have any maids anymore. And I only cook what I want when I want it."

Meira looks around the courtyard. "Someone needs to

pull those weeds around the reflecting pool."

"Those aren't weeds, my dear. They are my spices. Now, Michel, could your Anu get a fire going for me in the oven?"

"Mother, what's going on?" Meira asks, sitting on a bench near the pool.

"Things do not ever stay the same, dear daughter. And ever since your father passed on and I had to make adjustments, I decided to go ahead and adjust a little more and a little more until, well, here I am."

Michel walks over to the reflecting pool and sits on the edge, smiling and watching the women.

"Why didn't you tell me you were making all these, these changes?"

"Because, dear daughter, you would have rushed down here and done exactly what you're doing now. This is my life, and this is the way I like it."

"But with no one around, who do you talk to?"

"Sometimes, I talk to myself. The rest of the time, I go up to the library and let the books talk to me."

Meira is silent a moment, then smiles. "Mother, you are right. It's your life. If anything ever happened to Mi... well, I think someday I may do exactly what you're doing. Father would approve, I think."

"Your father would approve, I know."

The rest of the afternoon and evening are spent in talk. Sometimes Michel goes out onto the street and wanders into the town. On one of those trips, he meanders past the palace.

Hmmm, not as nice as ours in Ctesiphon.

The next morning, they assemble at the outer gate to resume their trip down to Uruk.

"Michel is afraid his father is seriously ill and needs him. Or has had an accident and needs him. Perhaps we can spend more time with you on our way back home."

Mother and daughter embrace. Michel and Meira board their chariot, and their servants climb onto their donkeys.

"Are you okay?" Meira asks when they stop midday to water and feed the animals. "You've been pretty quiet."

"Yes. I'm fine." He pauses. "I know we had to stop and visit your mother, especially since your father passed on just last year."

"But you're worried we won't get to your father in time."

Michel does not say anything. She takes his hand and puts her head on his shoulder. "Everything is going to be fine."

"But what if it isn't fine? What if we're too late?"

They sit in silence.

"I never told my father how much I admired him," Michel says in a soft tone. "He's so good with those war horses. And no one could ever sit on one of them with more dignity than he. And he did send money home to us all the time he was gone. We never wanted for anything. And, and, did I ever tell you there is a statue of him in one of the parks?"

"Yes, you did. But you can tell me again."

"I never thanked him for those things. He was not only a hero to the city, but he was my hero. I looked up to him."

"I know you did, dear."

"And, and..." Michel looks up at the cloudless sky. His eyes mist. "And, I never told him I loved him."

"You did in your own way, sweetheart. He knew you did."

Michel wipes away an unmanly tear. "I'm thirty-five years old, and I never told my father I..."

His lips tremble, and he says no more. Meira reaches up and pulls his face down toward hers. She kisses him on the cheek and wipes away another escaped tear."

They sit in silence.

"What was that?" Anu says, jumping up.

"They see a lone horseman rush past them with four other horsemen close behind.

"Do you think the man needs help?" Michel says, breaking free of his wife.

"Cannot tell who's in the right and who's in the wrong," Anu replies.

"Help me unhitch my horse," Michel says. "He's fast, and he's been restless hitched up to my chariot. "Let's follow them all and figure it out when they catch the man."

"Those were Akhal-Teke horses his pursuers were riding," Anu says, helping loosen the horse's reins from the chariot. "It won't take them long to catch whatever that man was riding that they were chasing."

Michel's horse duly freed, Michel mounts him and takes off after the four men chasing the one man. Its hooves pound onto the road. The cobblestones are slippery, so Michel takes his mount off the road.

He picks up speed. He sees the four horsemen ahead of him. His knees push into the side of his mount, and it gains speed. Closer his mount springs toward them, not having run as far and worn itself out.

The wind is in Michel's billowy shirt and trousers. He lowers his head and urges his mount on.

Now he is almost on top of the pursuers as they slow down.

They must have caught the man. He stays on his horse and calls over to them as they climb down from their beautiful golden chestnut steeds.

"Do you men need any help?"

"No, we're fine now. The man gave up."

"What did he do?"

"He stole our Nisean horse. That's what he was riding. It looks a lot like your horse. Anyway, we've got him, so you can go on back and resume doing whatever you were doing."

"That's a serious charge. What city are you from? Do you need me as a witness?"

"We're from a tribe over near where old Ur used to be."

"Well, if you need me to testify before your tribal chief, I'll be happy to help out."

Michel looks around for the man they captured. "Where is he?"

"We don't care about him. We just wanted our horse

back."

Michel watches as two of the pursuers walk toward their spokesman with a bulky black Nisean.

"Fine animal, isn't he?"

Michel stares a moment, then dismounts. He walks toward the captured horse, smiling.

"May I look at him? He is so much more majestic than mine. How fine he is."

Michel pats the horse and runs his hands from neck to rump on both sides.

"Yes, a very fine horse. Where did you say the thief was?"

"I suppose he's walking the way he was going before. He hasn't passed this way."

"Uh, excuse me," Michel says. "I guess I'll be going now."

Rather than remount his horse, he leads it up the road. He sees the man squatting beside the road, knees up, and back bent.

When he arrives, the man looks up. They stare at each other.

"Father?"

"Michel?"

"What are you doing out on the road like this, Father?"

"Trying to get my horse back that they stole from me."

"Then it really *was* your horse. I got a close look and found the brand. I knew it was yours. Shall we follow them and get it back?"

"How?"

"Climb up on my horse, and we'll go back to where I left Meira and the others."

Moments later, they are back with Meira and the servants.

Greetings over, Nebo looks at his son. "Well, what's the plan?"

"We hook our two donkeys to the chariot. My horse will take the lead, and they will follow. If we make enough noise, we may surprise them. Your horse that they stole cannot keep up with their Akhal-Tekes, and hopefully, they will drop the reins and keep going."

The donkeys are hitched to the chariot. Nebo and Anu ride in it prepared to yell loud enough they think there is an army after them.

Michel takes the lead, and they head down the road in pursuit. Just as they had planned, the real thieves drop the reins of Nebo's Nisean and make a run for it on their faster horses.

Once they are out of sight, Michel, his father, and Anu pull over to the side of the road. Nebo whistles, and his Nisean comes trotting over to him.

He looks over at Michel. "Well done, Son. Well done."

They catch their breath and sit beside the road. Michel turns to the older man.

"Father!"

"What, Son?"

"I just thought of something. What are you doing out of bed?"

"I get up every morning. I may be getting old, but I'm not lazy."

"But you're sick and dying."

"Huh?"

"You're sick and dying. I got your message."

"What message?"

"You sent for me. You said, 'Come quickly.'"

"I didn't send you any message."

Michel: The Fourth Wise Man

URUK, HOMETOWN OF MICHEL

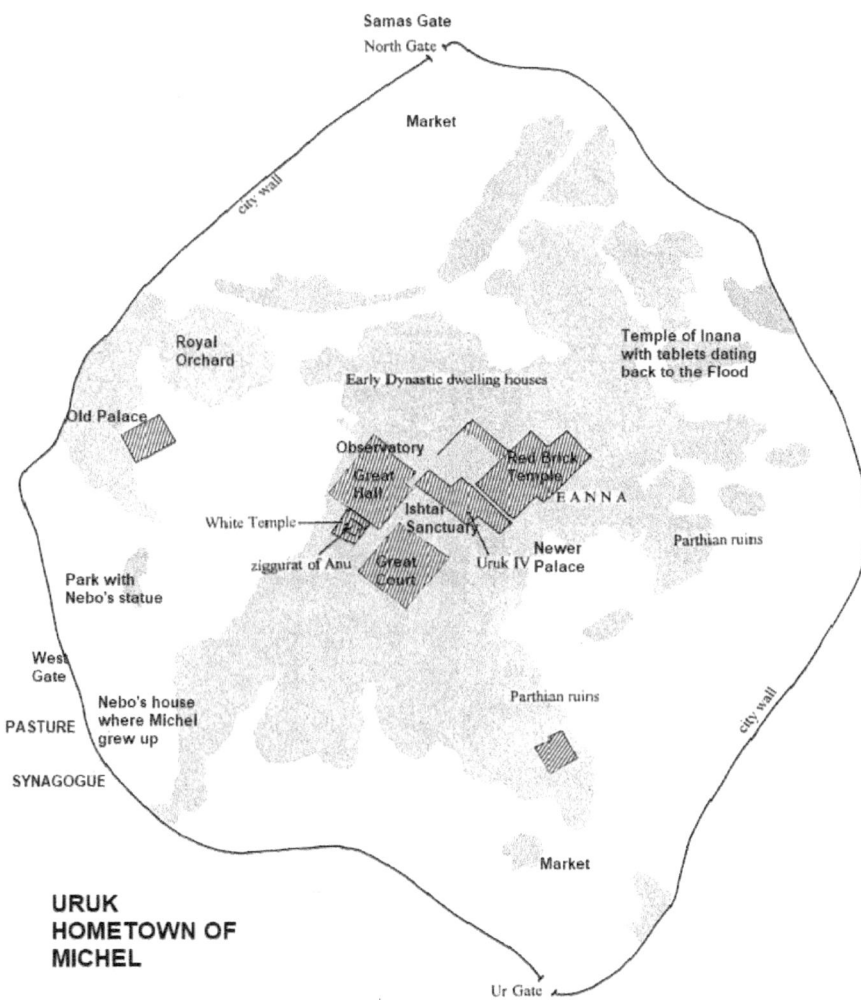

3 ~ ABANDONMENT

"You didn't? But..."

Michel stands, walks in a circle with both hands on his turban, then stops. He stares at his father.

"What is going on? The messenger told the stableman that he had just come from Uruk."

"Just because he had just come from here, it doesn't mean that's where he started. He could have started in Egypt, the Indo lands, China, or some ship."

"Oh, no. The message must have been for someone else."

Nebo stands and puts his hand on the small of his back. He walks forward, stooped.

"How long has your back been hurting? Were you in an accident?"

"More like I was in a war or two or ten. That heavy armor I wore took its toll on my back. Well, the iron armor wasn't so bad. But the ceremonial parade armor of pure gold was heavier than you can imagine."

Michel offers his father his knee to stand on while he mounts his horse, then climbs onto his own. Anu follows in the chariot pulled by the two donkeys. They return to where Meira and Freni are waiting for them.

Meira grins and walks toward them. "Is this my father-in-law? Were you the one those men were chasing?"

Nebo leans down from his horse as Meira reaches up to clasp his hands.

"I am afraid so, dear daughter. What a reversal. The scholar saves the warrior instead of the warrior saving the scholar. Ha, ha, ha."

"Anu, why don't we keep things the way they are. The two donkeys should be strong enough to pull the chariot with you and Freni in it," Michel says. "Meira, would you like to ride with me?"

Dressed in her own billowy pantaloons under her long dress slit on both sides, Meira is pulled up by her husband to sit in front of him on the steed, a descendant of Nebo's.

Nebo happily leads the way. He has a family again. Two hours before sundown, they see ahead the mound on which is the ancient city of Uruk, one of the first built after the Great Flood.

"This is the Samas Gate," he tells them as they enter from the north, "the old sun god."

They work their way up the hill on a broad street lined with columns that are decorated with multi-colored cone mosaics. They pass through the bazaar and among old adobe homes, some lived in, others abandoned and crumbling.

At the top of the hill and center of the grand old city, they see on their left red-brick walls with a temple rising up in the middle of the enclosed complex.

"That's the old temple to Eanna, god of the sky, and Inana, goddess of love. It has a library with some tablets so old, no one knows for sure how old they are. Who knows? They may have been etched by Noah himself."

Nebo leads them in a right turn. "On our left is the Great Hall used for large assemblies. On the roof is a magnificent observatory. Michel, you will want to visit it while you're here. Next to it is our ziggurat. The white structure at the top is a newer temple to the god Eanna.

"What's that over on the right?" Meira asks.

"That's the old palace. It's not in very good condition anymore. On the other side of the Great Hall is an Ishtar Sanctuary, then the new palace. It's much more modern."

At the corner—the closest they will come to the old

palace—they turn left and work their way past some fine estates and one of the city's parks.

"Oh, there it is," Michel says, pointing. "I would recognize home anywhere. The old copper gate is still the one I remember—Nisean horses embossed on it.

Nebo calls out, and a gatekeeper opens the way for them.

"Welcome back, Master," the stooped old man says. I see you have... Is that you, Michel? My, you have gotten tall. And so handsome."

Michel dismounts. He holds out his hands, and Michel takes them. "Pakor! I'm finally taller than you. I never thought that would happen."

"Well, you left home when you were fifteen to study at the library in Nippur. You were still shorter than me."

"But not for long," Michel laughs. "Mother had to have longer clothes made for me twice a year after that."

Michel looks over at his father. At the mention of his mother, his father is taking a deep breath and looking up into the cloudless desert sky. *Does he actually miss her?*

Anu and Freni have taken the supplies out of the chariot by now. "Where should we put these?" Anu asks Pakor.

"Oh. Our stable is right through these double doors. You can store them in there. And of course the chariot and animals. Then I'll show you Michel's old room. You can put their clothes in there."

"Why don't we go up on the roof," Nebo announces with a strained smile.

The three climb the long tiled steps to the roof. Benches stained a variety of colors are scattered around. Michel and Meira follow Nebo to a cluster facing each other.

"No, wait. Before you sit, come look at my pasture," Nebo says. "You can see over the city wall here. Aren't they magnificent?"

"Where did Grandfather get the first one?"

"Oh, there was no first one, Son. Our family has been breeding these fine warhorses since the days of our ancestor,

Daniel, when Cyrus conquered the Medes and Anatolians."

"Why did I never know this, Father?"

Nebo shrugs and walks over to the bench he had been heading for earlier. Michel and Meira follow him.

"Father," Michel repeats. "Why did I never know this?"

Nebo takes a deep breath, looks at the green and gray tiles covering the rooftop, and says nothing.

"You never told me because you were never here. That's why," Michel finally says. He presses his lips together and glares at the old man he had longed for so many painful years to be a real father to him.

"I never even knew you existed until I was six. Well, Mother talked about you all the time, but I only had a vague memory of a strange man in our house when I was three."

"I came home, didn't I? After our war with Marc Antony was over, I came home, didn't I?"

"Yes. Then suddenly I had to get used to seeing Mother with this strange man and neglecting me. You never once came up to me and explained, 'I'm your father. You're my son, and I'm proud of you.'"

"I *was* proud of you, Son. You had grown from just a toddler to a fine boy."

"And that's all you cared about—how big I got to be. Not how smart I was, not how well I could stay up on Mother's horse, not how well I was learning the Hebrew alphabet."

Nebo leans his elbows on his knees, clasps his hands, and hangs his head. "I didn't know they were that important to you, Son."

"Yes, you finally came home, but by then, I was old enough to go to synagogue school, and I was the one who was gone."

Nebo looks up and glares. "And I am the one who built the synagogue and the school. I am the one who sent for a rabbi from Jerusalem to serve our congregation."

"Yes, you did, Father. But now I was at school all day. And when I came home, I had to practice writing and cyphering the rest of the evening, then go to bed. You were always gone with your horses before I got up, and didn't get home until I went to bed. I hardly saw you even then."

"We saw each other on the Sabbath," Nebo says, humbled once again by his son.

"And what did you talk about after Sabbath service was over? Your war stories and your horses. Everything was always about you, Father. You never asked Mother how she was getting along or what I was learning in school. Even when Mother started coughing, you..."

Meira stands. "Okay, you two. I want to go for a walk. I heard the king has an orchard here. I would like to walk over there if we are allowed."

"Then you were gone again," Michel continues, his face now red and his eyes misty. "When Octavian lost so many troops, you up and volunteered as a mercenary for his army. Did he want you? Of course, he wanted you. You owned a mighty Nisean horse and had enough armor for you and your horse that you could serve as a *cataphract*.

"You stayed gone three years again until Octavian was declared Augustus Caesar. Three years, Father. I was thirteen years old and needed my father. But did you care? No. You decided Augustus needed you more than your own son. Your own son couldn't promote you among the ranks. Your own son could not give you a helmet of gold as a reward for your valor in battle. Your own son only needed your strong arms around me sometimes, and a lesson or two on riding those horses you bragged about all the time. Your own son only needed you to read out of the Torah with him and pray to Jehovah for him and bless him sometimes."

Michel wipes his nose with his sleeve and turns away.

"Michel, you have your father now," Meira says.

"Yes, I came home finally," the old man says hardly loud enough to be heard, "and got you into the school at Nippur."

"Yes, to just turn right around when Phraattes killed his own father to become king himself and become one of his captains. It didn't take you long to get tired of us and abandon us again. I was thirteen years old, Father."

Michel: The Fourth Wise Man

Michel stands. "I needed you, Father, but you were never there. I learned from then on that, if anything important got done in our estate, I had to take care of it myself. If I didn't do it, it wouldn't get done. Mother was sick all the time by then, I was always having to leave school and run home to take care of something, while you..."

Nebo stands and turns toward his son, now taller than him. The two men stare at each other, enshrouded by memories of what should have been but never was.

Meira stands between them. She takes her husband's hand. She reaches over for Nebo's. "Come on."

Nebo reaches out his hand to her. She gently nudges from both directions. The two broken men step forward slightly. She nudges again. Silence. Another small step. Silence. And another. The men slowly look up through red wet eyes, then fall into each other's arms.

Meira steps back and watches as two grown men who never knew how to fill each other's deepest needs groan and struggle to do what they had never been able to do before.

Their shoulders shake, their tears fall freely—tears of a thousand moments and days and years. Little by little, their knees give out, and they slump to the green and gray tiles, still clinging one to the other as though trying to merge the two into one.

Meira hears steps behind her and sees old Pakor approach them carrying a tray with pitcher and three goblets.

He sets the tray down on a nearby table, looks up at Meira with a slight grin, and whispers, "pomegranate."

He turns toward the men and announces, "Will there be anything else before the evening meal? I believe Katana is making master Michel's favorite."

The two men pull back, Michel stands, then helps his father up. They do not look at each other. Michel looks at his wife. Nebo looks at his servant.

"Uh, uh," Nebo begins. He clears his throat, "Uh, that will be fine, Pakor. Just fine."

As Pakor leaves, Meira takes hold of the men's hands

again and guides her husband to her bench and her father-in-law to his former bench. "I will do the serving. Pakor tells me this juice comes from the finest pomegranates in the kingdom. And I doubt that Pakor would lie to us."

She steps over to the table, humming a childhood ditty, and serves everyone.

"If it is still light after we eat, could we go for that walk? Uruk is old, but it is beautiful. I want to see more of it." She snickers. "I wonder if old Pakor really sneaked these pomegranates from the king's orchard."

They descend the steps and go to the grand dining hall of the estate, large enough to hold seventy people all at once, and eat with harps playing in the background.

Nebo smiles. "I hired this harpist to come for special occasions. I guess Pakor decided this was a special occasion. And, indeed, it is. My son has come home."

Michel looks at his father, smiles, and announces, "And my father has come home."

After the meal, they walk outside in the cool of the evening. The moon is bright. They walk back in the direction of the old palace they had seen earlier. They arrive at a park.

"Oh, let's walk in here," Meira urges.

"I believe this is where the statue of you was erected, Father." Michel walks ahead of them around a curved red-tiled sidewalk and calls to them. "Yes, it's here. It's right here. Come, Meira, and see this."

Meira and Nebo catch up with Michel as he stands at the base of the marble statue of his father sitting tall and straight on one of his Nisean horses, both of them clad in marble armor.

"I am so proud of you, Father," Michel says.

"What I accomplished is not near as great as what you have. An advisor to the king himself. You sit in his presence every day and provide counsel. I am proud of you, Michel."

Once again, Meira steps back so the men can draw closer and put their big arms across each other's shoulders.

"Can you imagine our ancestor, Daniel, sitting up there, Son?"

Michel: The Fourth Wise Man

"Yes. And on the ancestor of our family's Nisean."

"Remember when you taught me the Parthian shot?"

Nebo laughs. "You were always so skinny, it wasn't hard for you to twist your body all the way around and shoot arrows at men behind you."

"The hard part was keeping my balance with my knees while my horse ran in the opposite direction I was shooting."

"For your age, you did just fine."

"You learned to do the Parthian shot, Michel? You never told me that," Meira says.

"Well, I am getting a little tired," Nebo says. "You young people go on to the orchard. I have seen it before."

"No, Father Nebo. I am rather tired myself," Meira interjects. "Aren't you, Michel?"

"Oh, yes, indeed. I am getting tired," Michel says. "We have traveled nearly fifty *parasangs* in the last three days."

"Did you know that is over one hundred and fifty *milles* in Roman lengths?"

"I didn't know that, Father. You will have to tell us all about your travels tomorrow."

"And you will have to tell us all about your writings and your philosophies."

"Hey, you two. Don't forget tomorrow is the Sabbath."

"Yes, yes. We must remember the Sabbath to keep it holy."

Michel takes Meira to his old room, and Nebo goes to his.

The next morning, they sleep late.

"Oh, what does the sundial say?" Michel hears his father out in the courtyard. "Michel? Meira? Are you ready? Synagogue will start soon. We can drink a goblet of juice and be on our way. We can eat when we return."

Moments later, the three walk out through the copper gate with Nisean horses embossed on it, turn right, and out through the Hadad Gate, the gate of the storm god.

They walk up a small hill outside the city to the synagogue. The rabbi greets them.

"Rabbi Samuel, this is my son, Michel. He is one of

King Phraattes' magi."

"Well, at last, I have had the privilege of meeting the young man Nebo talks about all the time."

"And this is my wife, Meira."

They enter, and Meira walks over to the women's side.

"We have a special guest with us today, brothers," Rabbi Samuel announces. "Magus Michel, son of our illustrious *Cataphract* Nebo, is with us today. Magus Michel, would you like to come forward and read out of our scripture scroll for us?"

Michel, used to extemporaneous speeches before the king, stands and walks to the podium. He looks through the scrolls housed in teak cubicles and selects the first one. He reads in perfect Hebrew.

And Jehovah planted a glorious garden in the land of Eden for the man and woman he had made. In this garden, God provided them with every tree that was both beautiful and bore luscious fruit to eat.

Now a river flowed out of the garden, and divided itself into four rivers—the Pishon and Gihon flowed to other lands. But the other two stayed and wound around through the garden and out into our land—the Tigris and Euphrates.

Michel's eyes leave the scroll. He lifts them as though seeing a vision.

And God put Father Adam and Mother Eve in the garden he had made for them.

Michel's words are drawn out, his voice deep.

And they heard the sound of the Lord walking in the garden in the cool of the evening.

He pauses and looks over the congregation. He holds out his arms and bellows the end.

And, behold, the Lord will comfort his people. He will make the waste places like Eden, her desert like the Garden of God.

He pauses, then declares in a loud voice, "Joy and gladness will be found in her!"

Michel steps down from the podium.

Rabbi Samuel rises. "That was very interesting, Michel, adding a prediction of Prophet Isaiah to the end of your reading. Very interesting, indeed."

After the meeting, Nebo leads his family back toward home.

"Son, what did you intend for the congregation to understand from your reading?"

Michel stops walking. "Father, God wants me to restore the Garden of Eden."

Nebo stops in his tracks and stares at his son. "He what?"

4 ~ PURSUIT OF HAPPINESS

"He wants me to bring the Garden of Eden back so he can draw all men in the world back to it. Father, we will once again be able to walk the earth with God."

"Where did you get such nonsense?" Nebo shouts. "You're mad. You're insane."

Nothing more is said other than polite requests and thank you's during the noon meal afterward. Nebo walks back out to look at his horses and stays gone the rest of the day.

The next morning before daylight, Michel and Meira board their elegant chariot, their servants climb onto their donkeys, and they quietly leave the estate of Nebo, famous *cataphract* and war hero, breeder of noble warhorses, and could-have-been father.

They turn right and head south past the Great Court now turned into relaxing public baths, past the temple to death god Gareust, through the Marcet, and out the gate dedicated to Lugalirra god of the underworld.

Once outside the grand city of Uruk, Michel's childhood home, they look to their right and see on a hill the synagogue where only the day before Michel had made his dream public. The dream only believed in thus far by him and God.

Now back on the Parthian highway, they turn southeast and are quiet for a long time. When the sun is high in the sky, one wheel of the silver and copper chariot hits a large stone that had worked its way too far up from the roadbed, jarring the passengers.

"I've got to stop," Michel says.

They pull over to the side of the road. Michel jumps down and walks ten man-lengths away.

"No!" His voice is lost in the wilderness with no mountains or hills to echo his deepest thoughts. His voice is lost in a wilderness of confusion.

He lifts his head. "Jehovah! No one believes in it. No one but you and me. Give me courage to keep going. If I don't do it, no one else will. Give me courage. Strengthen my faith that you will one day return to Eden and walk there with us again."

He turns toward the highway and sees Meira and his servants staring at him. She walks forward, smiling.

"Well, good morning to you too, my husband."

Michel holds out his arms and embraces her.

Moments later, Meira pulls back. "Hey, I'm not going anywhere, so you can let go now. I have some dried figs and plenty of bread. Let's go have a little something to refresh us and be on our way to the Garden."

"You knew?"

"Of course, I knew. Why else would we be heading south instead of north back to home? Nothing down here but marshes and the Parthian Gulf, then the Indus Sea beyond that."

"Meira, I..."

She puts her finger up to his lips. "I know. I know. I'm a faithful wife to a dreamer. Now, let's go eat before our servants shrivel up from starvation and blow away."

The meal over, they resume their journey. Gradually the highway is built up higher and higher to avoid the marshes on either side that grow wider and deeper. Gradually, they progress toward the meeting of the great Tigris and Euphrates Rivers.

They notice a growing number of artificial peninsulas built off the highway every couple hours of travel, allowing for commuters to pull off and rest or even spend the night. When the sun grows low in the horizon, Michel diverts the chariot onto one of them.

"How close do you think we are?" Meira asks as they settle in their tent for the night.

"The marshes are deep enough; we are seeing boats in them. I think we'll be there by noon tomorrow. Finding it will be step one. Step two will be finding the owner or owners of the land around it."

"You mean the land under it," Meira teases.

Michel smiles. "Yes, the land under it. But, Meira, someday I'll bring it all back."

"How?"

"I'll think of something.

"Well, that's going to be a big step three. Time to go back to dreaming. Good night, my husband."

Morning comes. Meira crawls out of the tent and sees Michel walking in circles, staring in all directions.

"I didn't realize the swamps extended out so far."

"Don't worry, my dear," Meira responds. "You'll figure something out."

"You don't believe it's going to happen, do you?"

She looks him in the eyes, grins, taps her finger on the tip of his nose, and pronounces, "It will happen always in your dreams."

As predicted, they arrive when the sun is high in the sky at what Michel believes is the point where the two great rivers meet.

Meira steps out of the chariot and looks around.

"It's beautiful, Michel. Absolutely beautiful. Jehovah certainly left part of the beauty of his Garden here, even after all these centuries."

Michel spots a man in a reed boat and waves to him. The man works his way over with his pole, ties it to shrubbery along the raised highway bed, and climbs out.

Michel approaches him. "Greetings, sir. May the God of heaven bless you. My name is Michel. Do you live near here?"

"God bless you too. My name is Tajuva."

"Do you know who owns this land?"

"What land? It's mostly under water," he replies with a grin.

Michel smiles back. "I believe you know what I mean, sir. So, do you? Do you know who owns this land?"

"No. But, if you want to take a boat ride with me, we can ask around."

Michel turns toward his wife.

"Go! We'll be all right. The road's peninsula is right over there. We will pull over and wait for you. Take your time."

"Are you sure?"

"Go!"

Michel grins at his wife and follows the man into his reed boat.

Four hours later, Michel returns with a basket of fish, boiled rice, and a grin.

"I found him," he calls out as he approaches Meira and the two servants. "I found him. Oh, and here is enough fish for us to eat now and have some left to eat tomorrow. And rice. And more fodder for the animals."

Freni takes the basket from him and motions for Anu to get a fire started to cook them over.

"Well, how much money does the owner want for an underwater garden, and is he following you?"

"I don't know. He isn't here, so I have not talked to him yet."

"Well, where is he? Do you know?"

"He is a sea captain. We will have to go on down to the gulf and hope his ship is in. They say it is another half day to the coast."

Michel takes hold of his wife's hands and dances her in circles with him. She leans back as he swings, laughing with him. Anu and Freni watch and smile.

"So, where did the man take you?"

"There are some high places in the marshes with barrel-shaped reed houses on them. Where we stopped, there were several high and dry places. It was his village. He said there were villages like his all over the marshes."

"The fish is ready," Freni announces.

After the meal, the couple walks over to the edge of the raised roadbed and looks out over the water, now red with the sunset.

"I wonder why it floods here now when it obviously did not when Adam and Eve lived here," Meira muses.

"I think it was the Great Flood. Maybe land was higher here then. Or maybe the rivers flowed through ravines. Or, since the Garden was forested with delightful trees, maybe the trees kept the rivers in their separate courses. I don't know why. I did hear that it was all desert a thousand years ago. But things change. All I know is that Jehovah wants me to restore his Garden so all men everywhere can come home and walk with God again."

Michel hardly sleeps that night. Sometimes he tries to sleep. Other times he crawls out of the tent, carefully steps where his two servants are not sleeping, wanders over to the water's edge, looks up, and stares at the stars.

"Jehovah, we are close. May people of the earth who return to Eden be as the stars of the heaven. And may we finally be able to prove to all people that there is only one God, the God who made the stars of the sky and the earth below."

Morning comes, and the small group heads south on the last of the long journey.

As the sun reaches the pinnacle of the sky, they hear seagulls overhead, clanging of bells, muffled voices echoing across the water, and the smell of the salty sea.

Michel leads his fine copper and silver regal chariot down onto the docks. He pays no attention to peoples' stares.

"Uh, sir, could you tell me if the ship *Shar'n Shihab* is in port?"

"Don't know and don't care."

Michel pulls the chariot over by a warehouse. "Stay here, everyone, while I go find it."

He returns to the docks.

"Excuse me, sir. Do you know if the ship *Shar'n Shihab* is in?

"Sorry. I don't."

"Sir, do you know if the ship *Shar'n Shihab* is in?"

"Nope."

"Sir, the *Shar'n Shihab*, is it in?"

"See that tavern over there? That's where all the sea captains go. Someone in there should know."

Michel makes his way over to the tavern and enters. He looks around. Not many patrons this time of day. He spots one old man in a dark corner and approaches him."

"Kind sir. Do you know anything about the *Shar'n Shihab*?"

"Maybe. What do you want to know? Its usual cargo? Its size? Its route? What country it's from? The owner's name? The captain's name?"

"Oh, pardon me for my vague question, sir," Michel says. "Do you know the captain's name?"

"Well, it's the same as the owner's name." The old man takes a swig of his ale, puts his chin on his chest, and commences to snore.

Michel waits a moment and finally clears his throat. The old man wakes up and sputters.

"Oh, hello there, young man. What can I do for you?"

Michel sees a glitter in the old man's eye and a slight grin. "Ha, ha. You had me there. I thought you had fallen asleep. Well, as I was saying…"

"You were wanting to know the captain's name."

"Yes, sir."

"His name is Tefnak. He is Egyptian. He dresses a lot different from you Parthians, with your silly billowed pantaloons in every color under the sun. He wears simple white linen, so will be easy for you to spot."

"Oh, is his ship in now?"

"Nope. I was just saying."

"Do you have any idea when he is expected?"

"Let me see here. Hmmm." The old man holds out his hand, fingers spread, and points to each finger as he counts.

"Well?"

"Look what you made me do. I lost count. I hafta start over now."

Michel sits on the bench opposite the old man as he recounts and mutters.

"Okay. I think I've got it now."

"Well?"

"How bad do you want to know?"

Michel takes a deep breath and reaches into a leather pouch around his waist.

"Would a copper coin be sufficient?"

"Not if he's important. And he is important."

"Ten copper coins."

"Nope."

"Bronze?"

No sound.

"Silver?"

"Let me see it first."

Michel pulls out a silver coin, and the old man grabs it out of his hand, then stands. He walks toward the door."

"Hey, mister. The ship. What about the ship?"

"It should be in tomorrow," he calls over his shoulder.

Michel sits a moment longer, stares at the old man as he makes his exit, and shakes his head. "Reminds me of old King Phraattes," he mutters under his breath. "They must be related somehow." He smiles and heads for his chariot.

"I will find us a decent inn for the night," he tells Meira. "The ship should be here tomorrow."

At dawn the next day, Michel and Anu are down at the docks again.

"Now, we wait."

They watch men plod back and forth, loading and unloading cargo. They watch carts and camels being shifted around to drop off or pick up their merchandise. They watch warehousemen tug and pull and push and scrape whatever is coming in or going out.

Michel stands and paces sometimes. He crouches in his chariot and falls asleep sometimes. He talks to Anu

Michel: The Fourth Wise Man

sometimes or to his Nisean warhorse, who he knows must be humiliated back to pulling a chariot.

Two ships leave, sliding in slow motion out of the harbor and down the Parthian Gulf to the Indus Sea.

Night comes and still no *Shar'n Shihab.*

"What are we going to do, Master?" Anu asks.

"Stay right where we are."

The two men lean against the outer wall of a warehouse and try to sleep.

Just when the sky is turning the gray of predawn, Michel hears a commotion on the dock. He jumps up and approaches one of the men who is running.

"What's going on?"

"It's the *Shar'n Shihab.* Its bells are sounding distress."

Smaller boats are manned with twenty oarsmen and head for the crippled ship. Ropes are thrown down from the decks high above and wrapped around poles in the boats. Once all are secure, the boats head back toward the docks, the strong oarsmen making it possible to pull their charge to shore and safety.

Michel watches the ship all morning. He must time his approach just right. When the sun is high in the sky, he sees a man wearing a clean white *shendyt,* short and wrapped his around his hips, overlapping in the middle. His tunic is shorter than the *shendyt.* He wears a gold chain, earring, and belt.

Upon seeing the man who is most likely to be captain of the ship, Michel rushes to his chariot, where he dons a fresh green vest, his finest red turban, and a silver chain around his neck. The gold billowy pantaloons he has worn a day and night will have to do.

"Sir. Uh, sir," he calls out as he approaches the stranger. "Are you from Egypt?"

The man turns, surprised to hear a Parthian speaking in his native tongue.

"Were you calling me? How do you know Egyptian?"

"I know many languages," Michel says. "They come

easy for me and are required for my position. I couldn't help but notice your ship coming into the harbor. I admire your ability to save it after being attacked by whatever storm or enemy you faced."

"That's nice. If you will excuse me now, I am going to have something to eat at that inn over there."

"Uh, sir," Michel says, not deterred. "I have a business proposition for you that would probably help you repair your ship."

The captain stops. "Who are you? And how do you know me? You don't even know my name."

Michel smiles. "Oh, but I do know your name. You are the great Tefnak, owner and captain of the *Shar'n Shihab*. And I am Michel, magus, and advisor to Phraattes, King of all Parthia and defier of all Rome."

Tefnak stops and smiles. "Well, well, defier of all Rome, and dying to give me your money, will you join me for some repast at the inn?"

"I would be delighted, captain."

The two men, one tall and one short, but both self-assured, walk into the inn and find a table. They order their food, are brought a wooden goblet of ale, and stare at each other.

"So, advisor to kings, how are you going to make me rich?"

"You own some land I want."

"Marvelous! And what land would that be?"

"Land you own just north of here."

"I don't own any land up there."

"Well, in a sense, you don't, but in another sense you do. Your land is under water."

Tefnak slams his goblet down, throws his head back, and lets out a guffaw. "Oh, that worthless piece of whatever it is that I got swindled into winning?"

Michel smiles but does not probe.

Tefnak leans forward and whispers, "Do you want to know how I got stuck with it?"

"Uh, well, if you want to tell me," he says, not really

wanting the captain to get into a mad mood. "You don't have to."

Tefnak takes another swig of his ale and leans back, his hands behind his head.

"I won a bet. Ha! You call that winning? But that's what he called it."

"And what were you betting?"

5 ~ ANOTHER IMPOSSIBILITY

"First of all, young man, you have to understand that I have been stuck with that worthless piece of underwater land for well over twenty years. Never could find a way to get rid of it. Not a very good liar like my friend—well, my former friend."

Michel smiles, hoping the captain will not go into a tirade about the swindler.

You know I'm Egyptian. Well, you should know. I'm the only decently dressed man in this so-called inn.

"Anyway, Egypt was blessed—or was it cursed—with our own Queen Cleopatra, and her lover, Marc Antony, who appointed himself Roman ruler of Egypt, Parthia, and places in between.

"Then came a civil war when Octavian—who ruled the rest of the Roman Republic—declared war on Cleopatra, naming Marc Antony, a traitor."

"Okay, I know all that."

"You do? You must have been just a boy at that time."

"I was ten."

"Well, I was in this very port when I met the scoundrel I was telling you about. He was looking for a ship to take him to Rome so he could join forces with Octavian against Egypt. He said he didn't care which side won, but Octavian's pay was pretty good.

"He bought passage on my ship with the understanding that he would get off when we got to Eilat, the Jewish port in the eastern branch of the Red Sea. I, of course, was planning to then go up the western branch and eventually to Alexandria."

Captain Tefnak motions for the steward. "Bring us a couple bowls of stew, would you?"

"Thank you, captain," Michel says. "That is very generous of you."

"Oh, don't thank me. You're paying for it," he says, slapping Michel's hand.

"So, back to how I got swindled into that underwater land. The trip lasted longer than I thought it would because, when we got out into the Indus Sea, we got becalmed. No wind anywhere. We sat with limp sails for five days."

"That must have been frustrating," Michel says.

"It's all part of the business, son. All part of the business. Anyway, he—the scoundrel—and I got along pretty good. So, I began to bet that Cleopatra and Marc Antony would win the civil war. Of course, the scoundrel bet that Octavian would win. We went at it for a couple days, and I finally said we should make our bets official. I told him I would bet my ship against whatever he had of equal value. He said he had land covering the entire Kingdom of Eden, and he would put it all up against my ship."

"And you lost," Michel says.

Captain Tefnak glares at Michel. "I didn't lose. I was swindled."

"Yes, sir."

The stew arrives, and the men sop it with the flat barley bread that comes with it.

"So," Captain Tefnak says, his mouth half full, "why do you want my underwater Kingdom of Eden?"

"To restore it."

"Restore what?"

"The kingdom."

Tefnak drops his bread, stares, and leans back, laughing.

"Ha, ha, you want to, ha, ha, do what?"

Another unbeliever, Michel thinks. *Some day I will*

make him believe.

"I plan to restore the Kingdom of Eden."

"For who?" Tefnak says between guffaws. "The goddess Derkito with her feet turned into fins? Hee hee. Does Derkito know about this?"

Tefnak stops laughing and stares at Michel. "You're serious."

"Yes, I'm serious," Michel says, pressing his lips together and trying not to glare at the captain.

"Oh. Well, hee, hee, I guess I'm messing up a good business deal. I promise not to laugh anymore. Hee hee. Any more than I have to."

"Why don't you eat while I explain everything," Michel suggests, proud he has thought of a way to keep the captain's mouth more positively occupied and quiet."

"Good. I shall eat."

"Eden was the kingdom of my ancestors. Actually the kingdom of the ancestors of all people on earth. This is where the one God I worship—Jehovah—made man. Eden was a garden then. Jehovah wants me to re-establish his kingdom so he can walk with us again as he did Adam and Eve, the very first people."

"Well, if that's what you want to believe," the captain says between slurps. "So, it's pretty important to you."

"Very important. I plan to give my life for this project."

"Is that so? Hmmm. And how much do you think your life is worth?"

"Well, I didn't mean it that way. I just meant I will spend the rest of my life bringing Eden back and making sure it is there for all people of the world."

"All people of the world. That's a mighty dream. An expensive one too."

"Huh?"

"I tell you what, young man. I will let you have your underwater Kingdom of Eden for three hundred talents of silver. That's three hundred bricks of silver." He takes another bite of stew-sopped bread.

Michel pushes back his bench, rises, and steps away

from the table. He puts both hands on top of his turbaned head and walks in circles.

"No!"

"What do you mean, no?" Tefnak asks, sopping another piece of bread, this time in Michel's stew.

"That's, that's ten years pay for me. I could never come up with that much money."

"Okay. You haven't touched your stew. You're missing out."

"Aren't you going to counter?"

"Why? I've had that land over twenty-five years and don't have to pay taxes on it because it's underwater. I can keep it another twenty-five years."

"But you said you wanted to get rid of it."

"Oh, I do. I do. But if it's worth your whole life, maybe it will be worth someone else's whole life, once I start spreading the word how important it is to mankind."

"You wouldn't do that."

"Who says I wouldn't?"

"One hundred talents," Michel says, sitting back down and leaning on his elbows.

"Three."

"Two hundred."

"Three."

"Two fifty?"

"Three."

Michel leans back and pushes his bowl of stew over to Tefnak. He brings his hands up to his bowed head.

"Won't do you much good to pray to your God. With those three hundred talents of silver, I would be able to buy another ship. Been wanting one because of the new silk trade with China. That silk is really catching on."

Michel remains silent.

"Oh, Steward. Would you refill our goblets?"

The steward waits on the men, then leaves.

"Don't you have any rich relatives? Seems to me you would. Royalty or something? You could start out by selling that fancy copper and silver chariot and that horse. That's a

Nisean horse, isn't it? I'm done eating. Let's go look at it."

Without waiting for Michel, Tefnak takes a final gulp of his ale, draining the goblet, stands, stretches, and walks toward the door.

Michel looks up, stares a moment, and follows him out.

"Now, where is that chariot of yours? I know it was yours. I don't see anyone else out here dressed like he could afford such transportation. Oh, there it is."

Tefnak approaches the chariot but goes to the horse instead.

"Fine animal there. Not just anyone can afford a Nisean. They're the horse of royalty and mighty men of valor. Of course, you knew that."

Michel moves Tefnak's hand down from the horse. "Not my horse. I will leave you my chariot as surety that I will return with the money. If I don't, you get to keep my chariot."

"And the horse."

"No. I need the horse to get to the money and bring it back to you."

"Well, okay. You bargain hard but fine. You're in luck. My ship repairs will take a month or two. Otherwise, I would be gone from here within a week. So, if you are not here by the time my ship leaves, you forfeit your chariot. Then, when I return next year, you can try again to get my—what did you call it—Kingdom of Eden?"

The men wait while Anu unhitches the horse from the chariot and takes their supplies out of it.

Before Tefnak can change his mind, Michel climbs onto the Nisean and motions with his head for Anu to go to the inn where the women are so they can join him. He heads his horse north, hoping the captain will think Anu was just a local laborer he had hired from the docks.

When he is out of sight of the docks, he slides down and squats next to the road to wait for the others.

Michel hears a donkey's bray and stands. Soon he sees Anu leading both donkeys with the women on their backs. He has their tent and cooking supplies on his own back.

Anu stops, the women slide off the donkeys, and Michel embraces his wife.

"Anu told us what he knew. It sounds like the man is going to let you buy the land."

"That, or I lose my chariot for good. He wants three hundred silver bricks."

Meira steps back. "No, that's impossible."

"Not if I can talk my father into financing it."

"After that big argument and us slipping out of his house before he got up? He'll never do it," Meira says.

"I know my father better than you do. I think I can convince him."

"Well," she says, followed with a sigh, "I guess we'd better be on our way."

"We should be back in Uruk by the Sabbath. We will pray as we go."

"You're going to need it," Meira says.

They spend their first night at the same artificial peninsula built up next to the road they had spent coming down to Eden.

While Anu sets up the tent and feeds the animals and Freni fixes something for them to eat, Michel takes Meira's arm and draws her close to him. He smiles.

"Just think, someday soon, this will be ours. God is working things out for us. We're getting closer, Meira. We're getting closer."

Meira does not respond.

"You're not smiling. Are you sick? Hungry? What?"

"Oh, nothing," she replies.

"Tell me. Is there anything I can do to help?"

"Stop this foolishness."

Michel steps back. "What?"

"Stop this foolishness."

"It's not foolishness. You were all for it when we came down here."

"That's when I didn't think it would be possible."

"You didn't think? Where is your faith, Meira?"

"My darling husband, you have always had your dreams, and I have tolerated them. But, if you go any further with this one, you are going to ruin your life."

"Meira! How can you say such a thing?"

"Where are you going to get three hundred talents of silver?"

"I told you. My father."

"No. Don't go using him like that. You don't even get along."

"This time, it will be different. We will embark on the dream together and be true father and son."

"He won't believe your sincerity."

"I'll make him believe."

"How? How does a son force his father to believe anything?"

"God is on my side. God will help me convince him. This is all for God so we can bring all pagans in the world from worshiping non-existence gods to the one true God. This is for God."

"Are you sure?"

Meira hears Freni call to them for their meals and breaks away.

"It's for God," Michel calls after her.

Their meal is eaten in silence. Meira crawls into the tent first. Later, Michel follows.

The next morning the four rise, eat bread made the evening before, gather up their things, load them on the donkeys ridden by Anu and Freni. Michel helps Meira up onto his Nisean and climbs on behind her.

They continue on north toward Uruk. The Tigris splits off to the west and the Euphrates to the east. Gradually the earth dries out, and it is desert again.

They pass the site of the ancient and abandoned city of Ur. Ur the eternal. Ur the city of ancestor Abraham, founder of nations.

"I will bring your children back here, Father Abraham," Michel says. "You left paganism to worship the only true God thousands of years ago. Many of your children have drifted back into it, but I will bring them back. I promised Jehovah I would. I promise you, I will. I promised Daniel I would make him proud of me."

His voice is soft, and his words only heard and understood by Meira.

"We should be back in Uruk by this evening, Meira," Michel announces later on.

"Please, Michel. Don't do this. You will only make things worse."

"No, I won't. Things will be better between Father and I. We will be working side by side for a great cause. Our ancestor, Daniel, will be proud of us."

When the sun begins to turn red and gold, they see ahead of them the grand Uruk on a hill high enough that the city can be seen from far away.

They enter through the southern gate dedicated to Lugalirra, god of the underworld, and walk between the grand columns decorated with multi-colored cone mosaics in the ancient Parthian tradition. They make their way through part of the bazaar.

"Wait. I need to stop a minute," Michel announces.

He slides off his Nisean. "Hmmm. It seems my father always admired green alabaster. I need to buy a small alabaster chest and put my gold ring in it. It will be a symbol of our never-ending love for each other."

"Don't do it, Michel," Meira says, still on the horse. "He will see right through it."

"Right through what? It's a son's gift to his father to show his respect and love."

Meira sighs and looks the other way.

Michel makes his purchase and takes one of his gold rings off to put in the small box.

This time he does not remount. He leads the way, turning left now and walking into the neighborhood of the wealthy elite of the city. He knows the old palace is on the other side of the neighborhood.

He passes the western gate of Hadad, the storm god,

and finally comes to his boyhood home. He pauses and says one last prayer to the one true God.

Old Pakor answers the gate.

"Oh," he says with a half-smile, his eyes darting sideways toward the courtyard. "It's you."

"Of course, it's me, Pakor. Let me in. My urgent business is taken care of, and I am back to stay with my father a little longer, just like I intended all along."

"Uh." Pakor looks back toward the courtyard again.

"My father and I are going to have a grand time together. Just like when I was growing up. Do you remember that, Father?" Michel says, calling inside.

"Go away."

6 ~ THE DESCENT

*T*he voice is muffled. No movement on either side of the gate.

"Go away, I said," the voice growls louder.

"Uh, Father Nebo. This is Meira. Michel and I got you something special. Give us a chance to at least give it to you. Then we'll be on our way."

"Who did you say?" the voice growls.

Meira punches Michel in the arm before he can speak and glares at him. Then she smiles.

"Meira. Your favorite daughter-in-law. Well, actually your only daughter-in-law," she calls in to Nebo. And you're my favorite father-in-law. And just listen to how silly I am talking."

Meira dips her head under the arm Pakor has up to hold the gate ajar, and slides into the courtyard. Startled, Pakor takes his arm down, and the others enter all smiles.

All but Nebo.

Nebo does not rise from his seat.

Meira immediately walks over to him and kneels, smiling. She takes his hands, once mighty in thrusting the javelin at oncoming enemies, and now beginning to twist with arthritis.

Michel kneels next to Meira, then bows with his head all the way to the courtyard tiles.

"What are you doing down there, Michel? Get up. You are embarrassing," Nebo growls.

"Oh, great father," Michel begins. Meira punches him in the side before he gets any worse.

"I went on a quest. It couldn't wait, so I left as soon as God put it into my heart to do this wondrous thing."

Nebo looks over at Meira. "Do you have any idea what he is talking about?"

"Sir, you and I are descendants of Daniel," Michel continues. "He became a great man!"

"I'm already great," Nebo barks.

"Yes, you are. And I am proud to be your son. Now comes the time for you to become great on a spiritual level few men have ever reached, our Daniel being one of the chosen few."

Nebo looks over at Pakor. "Who let him in?"

Pakor shrugs his shoulders, then ducks into a side room.

Michel reaches into the pouch tied to his waist and brings out his green alabaster box. He holds it up toward his father with both hands.

"Esteemed one, I wanted to bring you something very close to me. I want you to have it. Please."

Nebo takes the box and removes the lid.

"My very own gold ring. I have worn it for many years. Now it is yours."

"It was mine to begin with, boy. I gave this to you on your thirteenth birthday."

Michel clears his throat.

"Oh, well. If you want to give it back to me, I'll take it."

"I am unworthy of it," Michel responds.

"You're unworthy of a lot of things." Nebo looks around. "Pakor! Pakor, where is my food? I'm hungry."

Michel rises. "Sir, while you eat, I long to tell you what great thing is coming your way."

"I don't need any great thing. I just need my dinner."

"Souls. I am talking about souls. No matter in the world could be greater."

Katana brings out a tray of dried figs and barley bread with a goblet of new wine. Nebo throws one of the figs into his mouth.

"Jehovah wants you and me to draw all men back to their beginnings when mankind was innocent and sinless," Michel continues. "Jehovah wants us to bring them back to the Garden of Eden so he can once again walk with them as he did our Father Adam and Mother Eve."

"I hope they're good swimmers. The Garden of Eden is under water."

"But we can take the water away, and the Garden can have a great resurrection."

"We who?"

"You and I. This is our destiny, Father. Our whole lives have been lived for this moment."

"And you're willing for us to do this impossible thing as a favor to whoever owns Eden. Your mind is in worse shape than I thought. How does the king put up with you, anyway? Get me some cheese, Pakor."

"Father, it won't be as a favor to strange owners. The owners will be us. We can own the Garden of Eden again."

"Who is we?"

"You and I, Father. God has called us to do this so we can bring pagans who worship gods that don't exist and show them the one true God."

"Well, I don't own it, and neither do you."

"But we can. Father, for just three hundred talents of silver..."

Nebo pushes the tray of food off the table and stands.

"Out! Get out of my house."

"But, Father."

"Pakor, open the gate!"

Meira steps toward Pakor.

"Now, out of here. Go."

"But, remember how we paraded together that day in our armor, you waving the scroll of the Torah, and all the pagans of Uruk began..."

"Out!"

Anu and Freni are out in the street by now.

"Come on, dear," Meira says, tugging at his arm.

"Pakor, go get my sword," Nebo barks.

"Yes, sir."

"If you are not out of here by the time I get my sword in my hand..."

"Yes, sir. I'm sorry, sir. I just wanted us to..."

Pekor appears, holding Nebo's heavy sword in both hands."

"We're leaving. We're leaving."

Pekor lays the sword on the table next to Nebo and rushes to close and bar the gate.

"Just think about it, Father," Michel calls out from the street.

Nothing.

Anu helps Meira up onto the Nisean. Michel climbs on behind her.

They head north and go past the old palace and royal orchard. They turn right at the Great Hall with the observatory on the roof, then left through the older neighborhood and bazaar, and finally out the north gate dedicated to Samas, the sun god.

No one says anything the rest of the day. The sun turns red, but they do not stop. Just as it slips below the horizon, they arrive in Nippur.

Meira calls up to the guards at the city gate, explaining who they are. The guards let them in. Her mother's house is not far from the south gate.

"We're lucky the moon is bright tonight," Meira says.

They arrive at Meira's childhood home and knock on the gate.

"Mother, it's me, Meira. Sorry, we're so late. Are you awake, Mother?"

They hear a scraping of the bar and squeaking of the hinges. Atossa opens it and smiles.

"Of course, I'm awake. I have things to do. Come in, children. Come in. You know where the entrance to the stable is, Michel. Now, you girls come join me and give me your opinion."

Meira and Freni follow her to one corner of the courtyard, where she has a potter's wheel set up.

"You're making pottery now, Mother?"

"And I'm having so much fun. So, did you have a successful trip?"

"Well, yes and no."

"I see. Well, I won't pry. Can you stay a little longer this time? I seldom get to see my daughter any more."

Michel walks over to join the women but stops at a table where several blue-glazed vases are on display.

"Is this your work, Mother Atossa?" he asks. "You must have developed a very successful business."

"Uh, Michel, come sit with us," Meira urges. When he does, she whispers to him. "Don't you dare."

"Dare what?" Michel asks.

"You know exactly what. Do not ask my mother for anything."

"Well…"

"Nothing. Is that clear?"

Michel smiles. "It never occurred to me."

Meira and Michel stay three days, enjoying the tour of all four bazaars at all four gates into and out of the city.

"Your pottery seems to have become very popular, Mother."

"And, when we get back to the house, I want you to pick out whichever vase you want. You can take it home with you."

"That is most gracious of you," Michel replies.

The following morning, Michel and Meira work their way around to the front of the library and temple to Enlil, ruler of the cosmos, and out through the north gate.

"Meira, I cannot fail at this."

She does not reply.

"I will lose everything. My friends know all about my dream of Eden and will not respect me if I fail. Even if my father does not help, he will not respect me if I fail. And God too. I will be abandoned by everyone."

57

"Then don't even start it. Just forget about it," Meira replies.

"But I have to. If I don't restore Eden so we can bring pagans back to the one true God, no one else will. It's all up to me. I cannot fail. Even while I was growing up with my mother, I knew, if things were going to get done, I had to do them myself."

They arrive back at Ctesiphon at noon the next day.

"Ah, it's so good to be home again," Meira sighs.

"I've got to go see Kumar," Michel says.

"No, Michel. We have to go to the market to restock our supply of food. Freni and I are going to need help carrying it all. It's going to take all afternoon."

Michel smiles and pushes back a strand of hair from her face. "You're right. Of course. I need to put you first."

"Well, you'd be putting us all first. We all need to eat."

The night is restless for Michel. Like so many nights of late. Wrestling as the dark hours pass. Wrestling with his dream. *Only you. Eden. No one else. Success. Abandonment. Heaven. Rejection. Garden. Pagans. Father Adam. Water. Only you. Daniel. Father. Abandonment.*

Morning arrives. Michel dons his court attire, slides up onto his Nisean, and heads toward the palace.

He arrives at the palace stable.

"I see you're back," the stable master says. "Was it bad news or good news?"

"It wasn't any news. My father lives in Uruk, and he said he did not send for me. Are you sure that messenger said he was from Uruk?"

"Well, he said he had just come from Uruk. But maybe that was just one of his stops. If I ever see him again, I'll ask where he started out."

Michel turns and enters the palace. He walks through the entrance hall with all its resplendence, meant to astound all who enter, which it does. Gold still gleaming, imposing figures on frescoes still impressing, glittering lamps still lighting the way through a paradise on earth.

He walks past the stairway to the observatory on the

roof, passes through the door on the other side, walks past the throne room, out through another door, and finally to the war room.

"Well, look who's back," Dushatra says, waving from his usual seat.

Michel smiles, waves back, and joins his friend.

"Well, did your father die?"

Used to Dushatra's cynicism, Michel smiles. "He is alive and well. I see you are still taking good care of the curls in your beard. They're perfect as always."

Dushatra flashes one of his rare smiles.

"How has the king been while I was gone?"

"Good moods and bad moods. Kind of like me. But mostly bad moods."

"Well, I could use a good-mood day today. Oh, here come Kumar and Yasib. It's a good thing Kumar is short, like Yasib. Yasib can keep up with him when they walk with each other. Greetings."

"So, how was your trip? No bad news we hope," Kumar asks.

"The trip was nothing but good news, my friends."

"So, your father was okay, after all?" Yasib asks, setting his cane aside and seating himself.

"Indeed, he was. We had a very good time together. Just like when I was a boy."

"So, you have been with him all this time?"

"No, we stopped at Meira's mother's house. And we went on down to the Parthian Gulf."

"Oh, what took you there?"

"I'll tell you later. I think I hear the trumpets. How is the king these days?"

"Same as always. Just watch your head."

The royal door is opened, and all seventy council members rise, then bow with their heads touching the royal marble floor.

King Phraattes seats himself on his throne, then looks in the direction of Michel.

"I see you're back. Was your father dead?"

"No, sir. He is well, except for the aches in his joints and back. He sends you his warmest greetings."

"I doubt that, but thank you any way. By the way, I thought you two didn't get along."

"We had a very good visit together. Things couldn't be better, Your Majesty."

"What's going on at the Mongol border?" the king growls.

Business of the kingdom continues until mid-afternoon.

"Let's go up on our balcony, gentlemen," Michel announces to his three friends, "and watch the sunset on the Tigris."

"Good idea," Yasib replies for the rest of them. "Let's do that. You can tell us all about your trip."

They ascend the steps and settle in.

"Michel, you are grinning like a crocodile. What are you keeping from us?"

"I found it."

"What did you find?"

"The Garden of Eden."

"Oh, that again. We didn't know it was lost, well other than being under water," practical Dushatra says.

Everyone laughs but Michel.

"I also found the owner."

"Someone owns it? How can you own what's under water?"

"It's not that deep. It's just a marsh."

"So, who is the owner? One of the marshmen?" Kumar asks with a grin, pulling on his half-black half-gray beard.

"A sea captain."

"That makes sense. He can ride his ship all over his land," Dushatra interjects.

"Let him talk," Yasib says. "He's always so entertaining. So, did you buy it?"

"Not yet. But, gentlemen, one day Eden will be the most sought-after place in the world. People from everywhere will flock to Eden. Eventually it will be the most powerful and most holy place on earth."

"Then, what are you waiting for? Why haven't you bought it yet?"

"I wanted to give you, my three closest friends, an opportunity to participate in its greatness."

"In other words, you want our money."

"It would be an investment. An investment in the minds, hearts and souls of mankind."

"If anyone could get to it."

"We can drain the marsh by digging deep canals for the water to go to. Then we will have bare land on which to plant our garden."

"We who? You and your father?"

"As I said, I want to give you the chance before someone else discovers its potential."

"Okay. How much is our chance going to cost us?" Dushatra asks.

"Only one hundred talents of silver."

"We cannot raise that much money."

"Each."

Silence.

They stare at their friend, the youngest of the four magi.

More silence.

Without speaking further, Dushatra stands and descends the stairs of the balcony.

Michel looks over at Kumar and Yasib. Kumar stands and silently heads for the stairs.

"Yasib. I guess it's you and me."

"No, I'm sorry, my young friend. You cannot pull us into your dream. Number one, it will never come to fruition. Number two, no one has that much money. Give it up, friend. Give it up before it destroys you."

With that, Yasib stands and shuffles over to the steps, ruby-tipped cane keeping his balance for him.

Shortly, Michel hears in the courtyard below shuffle clop, shuffle clop, shuffle clop. Yasib is gone.

He turns away from the sunset to see the same star

he had seen that night over two weeks earlier.

"Jehovah. I've lost them. First, it was my father. Now it is my best friends. You're expecting me to sacrifice too much."

He puts his hands on his turbaned head and walks in a tight circle. "Abandoned. Jehovah, don't abandon me too."

7 ~ ULTIMATE SACRIFICE

*M*ichel walks down the steps of the balcony to the courtyard below, pauses, and listens to the silence. Only the haunting sound of a harp from one of the private palace courtyards, a wolf in the distance, and the snort of a water buffalo along the Tigris are heard beyond the din of nothingness.

He makes his way to the stable. "I'm ready to go home," he whispers.

"You don't look very good, sir. Are you sick?"

"My heart is sick. That's all."

"Yes, sir."

Michel takes hold of the reins but does not mount his horse. Each step he takes is as though he is walking underwater. Each step heavy and against a tide of something. His Nisean stays close.

The sun with all its former brightness gone. His friends gone. The guards at the veranda salute. He does not acknowledge them. On the other side, he keeps going straight until he is at the banks of the great river.

He stands and watches the waves under power of the evening breeze ebb and flow, reaching for his feet.

Not much moon this night. Clouds drift between heaven and earth and hide its light. Stars mostly hidden. All but one.

He turns toward home.

Jehovah. You are expecting too much. I cannot do what I must do next. I cannot. It will mean sacrificing everything. I cannot Jehovah. Don't make me.

Somehow Michel is home. His knock on the gate is just audible. Anu, sitting on the other side waiting for him, opens it and takes charge of the horse.

With torches on the walls, Michel makes his way to the steps leading to the roof where he knows Meira will be. He sits on a bench and puts his face in his hands.

He stands in silence, looking up at the one small star. Then, with all that is in him, he shouts. "Noooo!"

It echoes from the waters of the river, bounces off the foothills of the Zagros Mountains, and gets lost in the blackness of his night.

"Darling. What's wrong?" Meira rushes over to her husband, and although he is a full hand span taller than her, she brings his head down onto her shoulder, and rocks back and forth.

"Shhh, my husband. Shhh."

Back and forth. Back and forth.

Michel raises his head, breaks from her, and stares in her eyes through the mist of his own.

"Meira. It is the last thing in the world I want to do. But I have no choice. Jehovah says I must."

She steps back from him in an effort to see what he sees. Then she does.

She steps back again. "Never. You will never sell our estate for that silly dream of yours."

She rushes down the steps. He hears a door slam below.

He stays where he is. How can he face her?

Morning comes. He hears Meira leave early as she always does to go buy what fresh fruits and vegetables they will need for the day.

When she is gone, he slips downstairs, washes, dons a clean set of silk clothes, and he, too, leaves.

He arrives at the palace and goes to the war room.

"You're late," the king growls.

Michel: The Fourth Wise Man

Michel bows completely prostrate before the king, then finds an empty chair next to the road official.

He strains to stay attuned to the proceedings. Finally, they come to an end. The king leaves. Every one of the seventy-member council leaves. Michel lingers.

When he is alone with the doorman, he requests a private audience with the king. The doorman disappears, and Michel paces.

"He said you have until the count of one hundred, and that is all."

"Thank you, sir. Is he in his courtyard?"

"Yes."

Magus Michel approaches the king and bows prostrate.

"All right. Rise and tell me something to make me smile."

"Your Majesty, a wonderful opportunity has come your way. Due to your wise planning, we have a fine highway all the way down to the Parthian Gulf. Now you have an opportunity to create a new city down there that can serve as a market city for all the wares coming into our seaport there. It will be called Eden."

"So, if I don't already own it, confiscate it for me."

"Your Majesty, it is privately owned, but I have found the owner. An Egyptian. He will part with it for three hundred silver talents."

"Out. Out! This is the work of a spy. How could you have fallen for that? Out before I have you imprisoned and hung as a co-conspirator. Out!"

Michel drops to the floor. He rises slightly and, still bowed, steps backward to the door, then disappears through it.

Once out in the corridor, he leans against the imperial wall, his eyes closed.

"Are you all right, sir?" the doorman asks.

Michel opens his eyes, and without replying, makes his way to the outer door of the palace and finally through the great veranda.

He arrives home. Meira is silent.

"I have tried everything. I even risked my freedom, my life, to approach the king himself."

She looks up. "You did what? You asked the king? You are going mad."

"One of the new magus has been looking for an estate to buy. I will go see him. Part of the arrangement will be that he allows us to rent back one of the rooms. That way, we can still be home in a way."

Meira goes to her room and bars the door.

Michel leaves and walks to the inn where the new magus is staying.

Just as the stars begin to come out, he returns home. He walks in circles in their courtyard, then sits with his face in his hands.

Meira hears the shuffling and comes out of her room. Her eyes are puffy and red. She stands before her husband and stares down at him.

He raises his head. His hair is in tangles. His short beard is full of saliva. His eyes are rimmed with red.

"I have sacrificed it all," he whispers.

He waits for his wife to approach him, but she does not. She returns to her room and once again bars the door.

Somehow morning comes. Once again, Meira leaves early to go to the food market. Once again, Michel washes, dons clean clothes, takes his horse from Anu, and leaves for work.

Somehow the day passes. The day that was never supposed to happen. The day that is really night. The first day of having nothing in the world left but his wife. Faithful Meira. Abandoned once again by his father. Abandoned by his closest friends. Now all alone except for Meira.

Late that afternoon, he makes his way home, or what used to be his home. He knows the new owner will be there, and things will be in turmoil. He arrives, but there is no turmoil. Anu sits outside his gate and opens it when Michel arrives. Inside, all is quiet.

Michel looks around. Things are different, but he is

not sure how. Things missing, he thinks. The door to his wife's room is open. He walks toward it. "Meira. Meira. I'm home, sweetheart."

He enters the room. Everything in it is gone but the bed with no coverings on it. Instead, there is a small scroll. He takes a deep breath, not wanting to read it, but having to.

I have gone to Nippur to live with my mother. We could have had a good life together.

It is not signed.

Michel sits on the side of the empty bed. He stares at the small scroll and reads it over and over. He stares at the empty ceiling. He stares at the empty floor. He stares at his own emptiness.

He does not know when it becomes dark. Upon the realization, he goes out to the courtyard where Anu has lit the torches.

"Everyone, God?" he shouts, lifting his head. "Abandoned by everyone?"

He walks in circles. "You are all I have left. Do not abandon me, Jehovah."

The next morning, Anu explains that the new owner had come by and said he would take possession today. "He said he has too many children to let you rent back one of the rooms. But you can have the stable rent-free—you and your Nisean. And me, if that is acceptable to you."

Michel tries to center his attention on Eden. It must happen. Three days go by in a strange world, with only his dream making any sense. The new family moves in.

"Anu, we must go down to find the sea captain and make the purchase. Did you buy what we will need for the trip?"

"Yes, sir. Three hundred talents of silver is the same weight as a hundred men. I bought a new, sturdy wagon and four of the largest mules I could find. Oxen would have slowed us down too much.

"Good. If we ride day and night, we should be able to make it in two days. I have made an excuse to the king about finalizing the details of selling my estate, and promised to be back with the council in four days."

"Are you sure?"

"God will make it possible."

The next morning early, Michel announces, "I must lift my eyes to a higher calling. Someday those I love and have lost will return to me."

Michel and his manservant slip out of the stable, go through the southern gate of the city, and out onto the wide Parthian highway leading to the gulf and beginning of reality. The reality of a new Eden.

"Master, it is good to hear you sing again," Anu says from the wagon, not sure about Micah's sudden mood change. "You have a fine deep voice."

"I can sing high also if you want me to," Michel says, pulling his horse to ride next to the wagon.

"I want what you want, Master."

"I have sacrificed it all. Willingly. Now the dream. This is a good and glorious day. They will be back. They will all be back."

"Yes, sir."

"Ah, it is indeed a good day."

On they ride. Stopping only to let their animals rest and give them water and a little barley as a reward for their loyalty. Always they double-check the wheels and axels of the wagon to make sure they are holding up under the weight of the silver bricks.

Back on the highway. Riding. Riding. Riding.

Night comes. On they ride. Stopping briefly to rest, then go again.

They pass a hill on the right. There are yellow lights here and there on the hill. They both know it is Nippur.

Is she asleep? Does she miss me? I must not think about it. I must answer God's call. Someday she will understand. But for now, keep going. Keep going.

The sky turns light gray. A golden red lines the horizon

on their left. A new day. The day of triumph. The day that dreams become reality. The day of God.

On they ride. Stopping. Resting. Feeding. Watering. Double checking the wagon and its wheels. Back on the highway. Steady walking, walking, walking.

"What was that?"

"What was what?" Michel asks.

"Up there. Rocks rolling toward the highway. There is someone up there."

Both men bring their animals to a halt and stare up the hill a moment. Then they hear it. The yelling. And see it. The scrambling.

"Run for it, Anu!"

Michel puts his Nisean in a gallop, kicking its sides to go faster.

Mouths agape, eyes wide, lungs pushing in and out, breath forced.

Arrows now flying. Flying over the head of Anu and his four mules, the three hundred bricks of silver and the dream of Eden.

Anu and the wagon drop farther and farther behind. Still the arrows. He ducks. He prays the mules will not be hit.

More arrows.

His mules can run no farther. Anu stops them in their tracks lest they collapse in the road, then ducks down to avoid the arrows.

Now he hears them no more. He hears no one running behind him. He peaks up.

Michel takes his horse back to Anu.

"Are you okay?"

"Yes, but those arrows. I don't know why one of them didn't get me."

"They weren't meant to get you."

"Huh?"

Michel grins and holds up his bent and ornate bow.

"You? It was you?"

"Of course. My father taught me how to shoot while

riding in the opposite direction. I brought my bow and a large quiver of arrows just in case."

"Well, I must say, your father taught you well."

"In battle, the archers would shoot their arrows at a charging army, they would huddle together with their shields up for protection. Then the *cataphract*s like my father in full armor—even their horses—would charge into them still clustered together."

"Amazing. I had heard of that. But what about riding backward?"

"That is another famous Parthian strategy, usually to pull the enemy out of the woods. The archers would pretend they were running away, the army would come out in the open to chase them, then the archers would twist around and shoot their arrows behind them, catching most of the enemy off guard and unprotected."

By this time, Michel has dismounted and Anu has climbed out of the wagon. They pull out water skins, pour their contents into leather pouches, and give their animals a well-deserved drink. When they notice breathing is slower, they untie the barley rolled up tight on the rump of their animals, and give them some energy to eat.

"Do you have any idea where we are, Master?"

"I think we just passed Uruk. We need to be on our way now. Those robbers won't be bothering us anymore."

Just before the sun goes down on the second day, they come to Michel's hallowed place.

"Eden, we will be back. You will rise again, Eden, in all your glory. Once again, you will draw all men to you, and you will once again be able to walk with the one true God."

It is dark once again. The journey is almost complete.

"No moon tonight. We'll have to depend on our animals to keep us on the road and out of the marshes. And just think, some day that water will be gone and Eden will take its place.

The end of the second night arrives just as they notice seagulls flying overhead, the smell of saltwater and seaweed, the gonging of bells, and muffled voices of seamen along the waterfront.

"Now we look for the *Shar'n Shihab*. Keep an eye for it, and pray it is still here."

The men work their way up and down the dock looking, but do not see it.

"Where is it?" Michel says, trying not to panic. "It has to be here?" Let's look again. Maybe he changed the name."

Back and forth up and down the docks.

"Sir, I just do not see it."

"Keep looking."

"Master, isn't that your chariot?"

Michel looks in the direction of the inn where he had struck his bargain with Captain Tefnak. "Yes, that's my chariot."

They ride over to the inn, Michel dismounts, and runs inside. He looks around.

"Hey Magus Michel. Good to see you again," the voice roars.

Michel sees him at the same table where they had sat before.

"I have your money."

"All three hundred bricks?"

"Yes. Where is your ship so your men can unload them?"

"Oh, I sold my ship and bought another one. I promised the owner I would have money for it by the end of the week."

"And you do. Lead the way."

Michel and Anu leave the inn and follow the captain in Michel's chariot hitched to an Egyptian horse.

They arrive at the last ship tied up to the dock.

"I plan to change the name to *Shar'n Shihab II.*"

The captain turns toward the ship and whistles. Shortly ten sailors scamper down the gangplank and begin unloading the silver bricks.

"And the deed?" Michel says, wishing he had not been the one to bring it up.

"Of course. Follow me up to my cabin."

Anu stays with the wagon while Michel goes on board. About the time the wagon is half unloaded Michel appears on the deck, waving the deed down to Anu. "Eden is mine, Anu. Eden is mine!"

The captain stands behind him grinning and shaking his head.

Anu unhitches the Egyptian horse from the chariot and hitches Michel's Nisean to it.

"Is the captain taking the Egyptian back with him?"

"No. He said he doesn't need her. Let's get some breakfast, and hire someone to wash down the animals. He was a good man to deal with," Michel says. "He even put the deed on sturdy animal parchment instead of reed papyrus. It should last many generations."

An hour later they are back on the highway.

"What are you going to do with that Egyptian horse? It's more for a woman."

Michel just smiles.

Around mid-afternoon, they are back at Eden.

They walk their animals along the waterfront looking for someone in a boat they can hail.

"We don't have time to stay long," Michel says. "But I have something here I need to take care of."

8 ~ FATAL INTERRUPTION

"I think I see someone," Anu says.

"Tajuva! Tajuva! Is that you, Tajuva?" Michel calls out.

The man in the reed boat digs into the mud below water with his pole. He turns in the direction of the two men with the wagon.

"Ha, ha!" the man says as he draws closer. "It is you, Magus Michel."

"Yes, it is me," Michel calls back with a grin of his own.

"So, did you buy us?"

"Yes, I bought you," Michel calls back, waving his parchment scroll.

"Ha, ha. Now what?"

Tajuva climbs out of his boat onto shore.

"Tajuva, I would like to hire your entire village to begin draining the marshes."

"No, Magus Michel. You cannot do that. It would destroy us. We depend on the fish in the water. And our water buffalo provide hides and meat for us. And we eat the birds that fly here. You cannot destroy us."

"Oh, I don't intend to destroy you. The water will still be here. It will just be collected into deep canals. Would that be satisfactory with you?"

"That would require much work, Magus Michel."

"That's why I want to hire your entire village. And I want you to be their taskmaster. I will pay you twice as much as I do them."

"Well, I will have to call a meeting and talk it over with them."

"I do not have time for that. I promised King Phraattes I would be back a day and a half from now. You know the villagers. You know how to motivate them."

"Well."

Michel tugs at a leather pouch around his waist and opens the flap. He pulls out two smaller pouches.

"This one is your wage. The other one you divide among the villagers. There is enough money to pay them for six months. By then, I will have more money and will return to look at their progress and pay them again. But do not pay them all at once. Pay them at the end of each week."

Tajuva pauses.

"Go ahead. Take them."

"Well."

"I'm in a hurry. Take the money," he says as he steps into his chariot. "I'll be back in six months. Make the canal travel between the rivers. I'll be back."

With that, Michel leaves, the delicate Egyptians trotting behind the chariot, and the wagon with four mules following behind him.

He stops in the road and turns around.

"You could use this wagon, Tajuva," he calls out. You can have three of the mules—one for you to ride and two to pull the wagon."

Anu climbs out of the wagon, and Tajuva runs to join them, grinning so wide evidence of the missing teeth on each side of his mouth shows. Moments later, Tajuva is on the wagon with his personal mule following behind.

Michel turns his chariot north again. Anu rides his mule on one side, the Egyptian is on his other side.

That night, they pass Uruk. Michel keeps his mind on Eden. Nothing can detract him from Eden.

There is no evidence of the highwaymen being back. They ride on.

Travel is much easier now. They travel ever north away from Michel's dream.

Will the king have forgotten my request by the time I arrive? He has so many things on his mind. Surely he will. And my friends. How am I going to make it up to them.? I've got to think of something. I have no more home to entertain them in. Perhaps I can buy each of them an astrological scroll in Nippur. Do I dare go into the city?

Mid-morning the next day, they arrive at Nippur. Michel stops.

"Master, are you going to bring your wife back with us?"

Michel sighs. "No, it is too soon. But we do need to go into the city briefly."

They circle the city so they can enter through the north gate closest to the library and farthest from Meira's mother's home.

"Anu, here is a scroll with a message on it. Take the Egyptian to that beggar over there. Tell him to deliver the horse and message to the home of Atossa. Tell him he gets a silver coin now, and another when we return in six months and verify the horse has been delivered."

"Yes, sir."

"I should not take too long at the library."

Half an hour later, Michel rejoins Anu with three parchments, each in their own leather case, and all tucked safely in his empty quiver.

By that night they are in Kish.

"We should be home by morning, in time to go to the council meeting."

It is two hours after nightfall. "Master, you look terrible. You have not slept in three days. Let's stop beside the road and rest. I will stand watch. You need to sleep a little while."

Michel looks up into the sky to determine the path of the stars. "Well, we do seem to be a little ahead of schedule. Agreed."

"Sir. Sir. Wake up, Master Michel. It is time to go."

"Oh, how long did I sleep?"

"I think a couple hours. You went into a deep sleep.

That is good. That is what you needed."

"I do feel much better," Michel responds, stepping back into his chariot.

They ride farther.

"I do feel refreshed, Anu. So... What was that?"

An explosion of light in the western sky. Light that grows large. Larger than any star Michel has ever seen. He stops his chariot and steps out.

"It's a new star, Anu. A new star. I have never seen anything like it."

"Duck. It may be a god and about to attack us," Anu warns.

"No." Michel's voice drifts away as he watches the phenomenon.

He walks in circles while gazing up.

"Look. It seems to have a tail. Like it's pointing to something. Look, Anu."

While Anu is hiding behind his mule, Michel stands transfixed, staring still.

"The light. It's not yellow. It's bright white. Is it motioning to me, Anu? Do you think it's motioning to me?"

There is no answer. Michel stares still. *How can I describe something so amazing? Jehovah, is this a sign of your approval? Is this star your very own?"*

All is black.

"Huh? What's going on? The star. It's gone. How can that be?"

Michel stares in all directions of the heavens. The star is no longer there.

"I didn't just imagine it. You saw it too, Anu."

Anu is slow to come out from behind his mule. "Master, I saw it too."

"Was the star born, then died? How could a star do that? God, where is your star?"

The night sky remains dark.

"Hurry, Anu. We've got to get back to Ctesiphon. The king is going to be calling for me."

Michel puts his horse into a full gallop, the wheels of

the chariot bouncing. Anu follows behind, his mule not able to keep up.

After an hour, Michel stops at an oasis beside the road.

"I'm sorry, friend. I know this is hard on you," he says, leading the horse to water.

He pulls out the last of the barley for the horse to eat. He watches it carefully. As soon as its breathing slows, Michel reboards the chariot and puts his horse into a gallop once more

"We've got to get to the city fast. I know it's hard, but I promise you fresh water and food when we arrive."

An hour later, the horse collapses on the road. Michel looks ahead and sees the lights of the city. He calls out, and one of the guards ever circling the wall comes down to him.

"Let me have your horse," he tells the soldier. "I've got to get to the king. Tell the man coming behind me to take care of my collapsed horse and the chariot."

With the exchange made, Michel races to the city. All guards have been put on alert since the appearance of the strange star. When Michel calls to them, they open the gate so he can enter without slowing down.

Once inside the city, he slows his borrowed horse and heads to what used to be his home. He passes Yasib's house and notices light in his second-floor bedroom. *I need to stop there. Well, I need to get rid of my money and put on fresh clothes, then go back.*

Just as he nears his house, he hears horses behind him. He turns.

"Sir, are you Magus Michel?"

"Yes. Did the king send for me?"

"Come with us."

Michel turns his borrowed horse around and follows them to Yasib's house.

"Here?" Michel asks.

"They are waiting for you."

"They are? They need me? They're no longer mad?"

By now, one of the guards is banging on the gate.

Yasib's gatekeeper opens it. "This way, Magus Michel. They are up there."

Michel dismounts and hands the reins to one of the guards. "This belongs to you."

With that, he rushes into Yasib's courtyard and up the steps to where his bed, library, and study rooms are.

"Personally, I never found much use for his Jewish religion, though. Never studied it much. But it has too many rules and regulations. Never liked anyone telling me what to do." It is Dushatra.

"Hello there, friends," Michel says, joining them.

"Uh, hello there," Kumar says.

"Yes, come in. Come in. We were hoping you were back from your trip," Yasib says. "Good or bad, at least you are back."

"We assume you saw it—the star."

"Yes, I did. I was out on the highway just south of here. I knew the king—that is, you—would need me, so rushed on ahead."

"How bad is the king?"

"What would you expect? Very bad," Dushatra says. "Kumar and I tried to calm him. All anyone knows is that a god was born."

"How many magi were there with him?"

"About ten of us. All the magi will be there in the morning."

"How did you explain to him the star disappearing so fast?"

"Well, we surmised that either the god died in infancy or went into hiding."

"Of course, he wants to know if it is a friendly god who will help protect his kingdom, or an enemy come to destroy it."

"He'll be up the rest of the night," Michel says.

"So will we," Yasib replies. "Now, where do we start? Kumar, your Hinduism is the oldest of our religions. We should start with it. We should search your scriptures for mention of all stars."

"Do you have the copies I gave you?" Kumar replies.

"Yes, hidden behind my old scrolls in the cabinet over there. We will adjourn to my study. I'll have three more tables and lamps brought in,"

He speaks to his attending servant, closes and bolts his door, then goes to the cabinet. He pulls out several scrolls, reaches to the back, and pulls out four that the other scrolls had hidden.

Just as the astrologers arrive at Yasib's study, the other tables and lamps are brought in.

The men divide up the scrolls to scan through. Everyone lapses into silence. Dead silence.

Day dawns.

"Well, we've found two references to stars," Yasib announces.

"We must be the first to appear before the king," Dushatra, a real politician at heart, explains. "We cannot look hesitant."

The four—all friends again—rush out the door. The guards are still at Yasib's gate, waiting for them with the two chariots.

They are driven to the palace outer courtyard and enter through the main front entrance. They rush through the elaborate entrance hall and past the observatory steps Dushatra had descended hours earlier to be the first to appear before the king.

The four stand near the throne room entrance and are gradually joined by most of the other magi. All look suspiciously at the others. Some take peeks at notes they have brought with them. One by one, they are recognized and given permission to enter.

King Phraattes' eyes are bloodshot with dark circles under them. The interrogations begin. And the shouting of a king who is yet to be informed of the celestial secret.

"Your Majesty, I think..." One magus begins

"Your Majesty, it seems to me..." Another magus interrupts.

"Your Majesty, we need more time because..."

"I haven't slept all night," the king bellows, "and you

bring me this drivel."

At last, their turn comes. Gray-haired Yasib approaches the throne, bowing as he goes, with the other three behind him.

"So far, I haven't heard anything that makes sense," the king says, motioning for the four men to rise and come closer.

"I'm really disgusted with the rest of the magi. Even before they start, I know they have no answers for me." He leans forward on his throne. "We're running out of time. Dushatra, are you and your colleagues ready to save our kingdom this morning?"

Yasib steps aside, letting the younger, more alert men take over.

Kumar reads the passage he had found the night before. It is in *The Upanishads* under 'Chandogya.'

'Within the lotus of the heart are heaven and earth, the sun, the moon, the lightning and all the stars.

"This, Your Majesty, means that the star we saw is a manifestation of the heart of the great god Brahman. You have nothing to worry about. You are in harmony with Brahman."

The king looks over at the other magi standing nearby. "What do you think of this?" he asks. "Do the rest of you believe this?"

One man walks forward. He is one of the new magus and not well known. Anzan stares at Dushatra with a sneer.

"Your Majesty, I am somewhat knowledgeable of Hinduism, but need time to read their writings. If it pleases Your Majesty, I will return tomorrow with an opinion."

"Tomorrow?" the king shouts. "Tomorrow? What if there is no tomorrow?"

"Your Majesty, I cannot give it justice immediately," the novice replies, not understanding how dangerous it is for him to object.

King Phraattes relents. "All right," he barks. "But you

will be here first thing in the morning. If we have a morning. Next!"

Michel has said nothing. He follows Yasib's group out to the anteroom, and attention is passed on to the next group of magi.

Yasib talks with the fifth magus, Anzan. He gives him a copy of the pertinent scroll.

Michel goes home to clean up and sleep, but sleep cannot come. Not when he knows it is true what the king had said: The world may end before morning.

He turns over and over in his bed. "Jehovah, Creator of all things and all of mankind. You are the only God. Give me an opportunity to declare you before the king. If he believes in you, perhaps, just perhaps, many others will come to you and your glory."

Morning. Back in the palace and to the throne room, the four are called forward to hear rebuttals by Anzan, critic of the Hindu opinion of the star. They do not like what they hear.

"Your Majesty," he begins, scroll in hand. "The same passage these men quoted yesterday about the star has some contradictory statements in it. It says that the great god Brahman thought to himself, 'Let me be many.' If Brahman, the great Self, the Essence of the Universe, voluntarily and happily divided himself up to be many, why do the Hindus consider themselves evil by being separated from Brahman, but good by becoming one with Brahman?"

The king takes a sip of wine from his silver chalice.

"Furthermore, Your Majesty, if a person must renounce all relationships and wealth, why does this passage say that being cows and horses, elephants and goats are poor existences? They have what the good Hindu wants: No wealth and relationships. Why would Hindus consider it punishment to be reincarnated as an animal?"

King Phraattes leans forward in his throne.

"In addition, this passage talks of a sage seeing the dead—his fathers, mothers, and brothers of previous lives in the spirit world. How can this be possible since Hindu scriptures say everyone is continually reincarnated? The spirit world would be empty with everyone reincarnated or absorbed into the Essence of the Universe, Brahman."

The king shifts and leans on his arm.

"And finally, Your Majesty, it says that, when we move about in our dreams, we enjoy sensuous delights and are clothed in glory when we experience the Self, the Brahman. That, too, is contradictory. In order to be joined with the Self, one must renounce all desires and delights of the senses."

Kumar shifts from one foot to the other and lowers his eyebrows, glaring at his antagonist.

"I do not see how Hinduism could have the answer for you. Therefore, the star being a manifestation of the great god Brahman's heart could not be true."

"Gentlemen," King Phraattes replies, turning his attention to Yasib and his three colleagues, "Do you have a rebuttal?"

"Yes, Your Majesty," says Kumar. "In *Brihadaranyaki*, it says this:

Among the gods, he who awakened to the knowledge of the Self became Brahman. He it is who dwells in the sun, in the moon, in the stars.

"This is just further proof that the star is a good omen. An omen that your kingdom is in harmony with Brahman."

Once more, King Phraattes turns to the critic. "Any comments?"

Once more, the contending magus requests the scroll and permission to return the next day with his reactions. The scroll and time are begrudgingly granted.

CTESIPHON IN 1867

9 ~ QUAGMIRES

Still, Michel has said nothing. Again the sleepless night.

"Don't they realize, Oh Jehovah, that the gods are not playing games with them? Don't they realize those are no gods at all?"

He steps outside the stable where he has been sleeping. Out in the street, he paces. He returns inside, climbs back into bed.

Back up again. Back out in the street.

Michel looks up into the sky. "If, Jehovah, you would just explain the star to me tonight, I could prove to them in the morning that you are the only true God."

"If there is another morning." It is Anu. "Go back to your bed, Master."

Morning and once more to the palace. Once more, a rebuttal by the young Anzan.

The throne room is now empty except for guards, personal servants, and the five magi.

"Your Majesty," Anzan begins. "This passage quoted yesterday says we must live a life of renunciation of wealth, desire, and relationships in order to lose our individuality and become one with the god Brahman. This is inconsistent with their teachings that, if we live bad lives, we are reincarnated as small animals or even unthinking objects such as rocks."

The king says nothing.

Emboldened, the young magus continues. "Since rocks automatically have an existence of renunciation and no thoughts of their individuality, wouldn't being a rock be considered a reward rather than a punishment? Wouldn't a rock be closer to being one with Brahman, the Essence of the Universe, than a human?

"Furthermore..."

King Phraattes interrupts. "I've heard enough. None of this reincarnation thing makes sense to me."

"Your Majesty," Dushatra interjects, "if you will give us a little more time, we will search through the documents of the Buddhist religion. There are references to stars there."

"Since when did you become Buddhist?" the king asks.

"Your Majesty, I've always been Buddhist. It is no disrespect to your Zoroaster religion. I was just born that way."

"Oh, I forgot. Very well. It looks like the gods have given us somewhat of a reprieve. But for how long? I will give you two days. No longer. After that, you will be executed or banished. I haven't made up my mind yet." The king's voice drifts away.

"We are certain there is no imminent danger to you, sir," Dushatra continues. "Therefore, we are asking for a week, so we may be better prepared than previously."

"Are you willing to lay your life on the line like this? Are you willing to give your life for that star?" the king asks.

A week later, Yasib, Dushatra, Kumar, and Michel arrive back at the throne room. They wait nervously among the growing crowd in the corridor. Awaiting their turn, they listen to the low conversations of each magus near them, secretly hoping all the others will be wrong, and only they right. They can hear through the closed door as one by one the king shouts, impatient with each magus and his postulations.

"You're an idiot! Do you expect me to believe that? Leave. And don't come back. If I ever see you again, you will be fed to the lions," they hear as the door to the throne room is opened, and the dejected magus rushes out.

King Phraattes' anger grows with each interrogation. Eventually, it is their turn.

"Well, Yasib, I see you are back. What foolishness are you going to tell me?"

"Your Majesty, as you know, I am old. Though my mind is as sharp as it ever has been, my voice is weak. Therefore, once again, I defer to my younger colleagues," Yasib explains.

"Guard, bring a chair for Yasib," the king calls out. Turning to Yasib, he adds, "You were a good friend to my father. Sit and rest while I listen to your friends. Perhaps, under your guidance, they will make sense."

Dushatra steps forward. "I bring you the wisdom of the compassionate Buddha."

"Compassionate? What does compassion have to do with anything?" King Phraattes is back to his old self.

"My kingdom is about to come to an end, and you talk about compassion. Forget it. I don't want to hear any of your foolishness. Leave me." The king's face grows red with anger.

In desperation, Dushatra raises his arms heavenward. "Truth. I bring you truth," he shouts. "Truth reveals all secrets. Truth is stronger than all things. Truth will bring us freedom from the threat of the star. Truth will bring our kingdom everlasting happiness."

The king unexpectedly smiles at the expert politician and lets Dushatra continue.

"Your Majesty, from the *Sutta Pitaka* we found this statement in CHAP. fifteen called 'Happiness.' 'One ought to follow such a good and wise man, as the moon follows the path of the stars.' This means that you are a good and wise king as long as the moon follows the path of the stars."

King Phraattes takes his chalice filled with wine on the table next to his throne and throws it at the magus. "I am not a fool, Dushatra. Your explanation is no explanation at all."

Ejo has been standing at the back of the group of four

magi. He steps forward.

"Your Majesty, may I speak?"

Dushatra turns and stares at the stranger in disbelief. *Must be a spy.* He cannot admit someone came in with his team without anyone knowing it. He remains quiet.

"I have studied the Buddhist religion. It is full of flaws. I would like to study this passage and return later to explain the contradictions I am sure I will find."

"I suppose you want your week. As though I have all the time in the world. Are the Medes rebelling again? How about the Indios? What is that star a sign of? I demand to know." He stands and struts before his throne.

"Guards!" the king shouts. "Arrest Dushatra and his friends."

Yasib stands. "Your Majesty. Please. They are doing better than any of your other magi. They are close. I know they are close. Under my guidance, Your Majesty, they will discover the secret of the star."

Realizing Dushatra and his colleagues have slipped through his fingers, the king motions the guards back to their posts. He allows the five magi to leave unharmed and orders the next magus to enter and give his postulations as to the secret of the star.

Michel's friends go home. Michel goes to the stable that is now his home.

"I was wanting to make some drawings of the way I want Eden to look when we are done exposing it to the sun again, Anu. That star is interrupting the process. That star is ruining everything."

"I am sure the king will be satisfied with your next explanation, and you will be able to return to your dream of Eden."

A week later, Yasib and his group show up again at the throne room. The king is astonished. Admiration for their courage and audacity makes him allow their entrance and an audience. The magus who had challenged the Buddhist interpretation of the star is there too. It is he who begins the discussion.

"Buddhists..." Ejo begins. "Buddhists," he repeats, "state the highest good is unity with Nirvana, personal annihilation, unity with the Essence of the Universe. On the other hand, Buddha said this:

There is one sole Truth, and apart from consciousness, no diverse truths exist. We must remain free from lusts and dogmas.

"But then in *Sutta-Nipata* Buddha said he had preached the Truth. How can someone preach something that is only consciousness?"

Dushatra presses his lips hard against each other.

"Furthermore," the critic continues, "in his *Sutta Pitaka* Buddha says this:

A wise man rejoices always in the law.

Later he talks about the sinner following false doctrine. What law and doctrine can he refer to if there is only one truth, and that is consciousness?

"And one last comment, Your Majesty. In the *Spirit of Theravada Buddhism* in CHAP. eight, 'Majjhima-Nikaya,' it is said that Buddhism makes no claim to the exclusive possession truth. If there is no exclusive truth, then there is no truth. So how can anyone's statement be known to be true?"

King Phraattes stands, then paces. He looks at Dushatra, Kumar, and Michel. Though Michel, once again, has said nothing, he is still part of the team.

"You are a bunch of idiots. You're supposed to be telling me the secret of the gods, and you don't even know what truth is."

The king looks over at Yasib, who he has allowed once again to be seated near him. "Are you sure you want to claim these men?" He looks back at the other three. "Get out of my sight!"

Dushatra and his colleagues, feeling grateful the king has forgotten his execution threat, bow to the floor then partially rise and back slowly away from the throne, heads bowed in submission until they reach the doorway. Yasib is the last to leave.

Hurrying out of the palace, they talk. "We must keep searching," Yasib tells the others. "This time, we will pursue my holy writings, the scriptures of Zoroaster. And this time, we will do it right." Yasib leads the way out of the palace grounds.

"Come to my house, and I will give each of you a different book of Zoroaster to study. We'll meet at the end of two weeks and compare notes. We must be more thorough."

I certainly hope so, Michel thinks as he turns toward home and the stable. *That star could not have appeared at a worse time. At first, I thought it might be God's star, God's sign to me that restoring Eden is what he wants done so he can walk the earth there again. But it is nothing but a nuisance.*

Two more weeks. Searching. Searching for a star that was and no longer is. Searching, perhaps, for a god that was and no longer is. Finally, they come back together. They compare notes. Each prays to his preferred god for the king's good graces. They head for the palace.

"Your Majesty, Yasib, Dushatra, Kumar, and Michel wish an audience. They have found the secret of the star."

Michel knows they are taking a chance. The emperor could turn them down if he is in another bad mood, and they could be executed for their impudence.

But King Phraattes' fourteen-year-old son is on a smaller throne next to his proud father. They are laughing at something. The king looks up at the guard announcing the magi's presence in the corridor, and the purpose of their mission.

"Star? What star?" the king responds to the guard. "Oh, yes, the star. That was over a month ago. Well, these magi are harmless enough."

He looks at his son. "It'll give young Phraattes some experience in how to deal with the magi." He pokes his son with his elbow. "Besides, I like them," he says with a wink.

"They're the only ones with the nerve to stand up to me."

To the guard, he waves and says, "Send them in."

"Your majesties," Yasib begins, "we believe we have found the secret of the star. It is found in the beliefs of the Zoroasters. I know you will be pleased because this is the religion of the Parthians and of Your Majesty."

"Go ahead," the king responds while his son hands him a cluster of grapes.

"In *The Yasna* 12,1 it says the Glorious Beings are clothed in the light of the stars. As you know, each of the gods is clothed with a star. The writer of this scripture said he was a praiser of the Bountiful Immortals and Ahura Mazda, and sacrifices to them.

"I made a list of the Bountiful Immortals as I found them in *The Yasna,*" Michel interjects, not believing what he is about to say: "The sun god, the god of truth, the rain god, god of the earth, the god of metals, the god of best righteousness, the god of the air and the guardian god of dead souls."

"I went through *The Vendidad*," Kumar adds. "I found the god of good mind and guardian of sheep and cattle, the god of fire..."

The king whispers to his son, and the two laugh. Things are not going well.

Dushatra interrupts. "Your Majesty, Tishtrya, the rain god, is identified with the star Sirius. As you know, Sirius is the brightest star in the heavens. The new star we saw must have been the son of Tishtrya."

"So, what you're trying to tell me, gentlemen," the king interjects, poking his son and giving him a wink, "is that the rain god had a son, but the son did not live. If the son did not live, that means you are predicting a drought this year."

"No, Your Majesty. That is not the meaning at all. When the new star appeared, it..."

"What did I tell you, Son? These magi expect me to believe all this. Now, as you know, I do believe in deity. I believe in as many gods as the next man. But there are only so many you can believe in.

"Gentlemen, you are lucky I am in a good mood. Today is my son's birthday. You are thenceforth exiled from my kingdom."

"Your Majesty," Dushatra hurriedly interjects, convinced even their lives are on the line, "I must strongly object to your treatment. We are your priests. We are doing the best we can to watch for the welfare of both you and your kingdom. We are the only intercessors you have between yourself and the gods."

Two powers have locked horns. The head of a kingdom on earth. The heads of kingdoms in the heavens. Who is stronger?

Furious, the king stands. "The only way you will be allowed back into my kingdom is that you present me an interpretation that is provable. Provable! Do you hear me? Provable!"

"But Your Majesty…"

He looks at Yasib. "I have had it with you and your so-called protégés. If I ever see any of you again, you will be executed immediately. Now out. Leave me. It's my son's birthday." He motions for the guards to escort them from the palace.

The four magi bow to the floor, then, standing stooped, make their ways backward until they reach the exit from the throne room. Soldiers escort them through the outer courtyard and out into the street.

"It is finally time to investigate the Jewish religion," Michel says. "We should have no trouble finding the meaning of the star there. Then we can get back to other matters."

"That is out of the question," Dushatra objects. "That religion makes no sense. We will systematically study the religions of all the nations west of us, the nations in the direction of the star."

"In that case, we must go down to Nippur," Michel replies with a sigh. "The oldest and greatest libraries in the world are there."

"They have more than one library?" Yasib asks.

"They have three," Michel continues. "There are over fifty-thousand ancient tablets there, some governmental, but mostly sacred."

"That isn't out of Parthia. We're exiled, you know." Kumar says.

"It's on our way out of Parthia," Michel says.

"Isn't your wife down there, Michel?"

Yasib interrupts Dushatra. "Uh, gentlemen, we need to get some rest and make arrangements for our trip."

"Yes, Meira is there with her mother while I develop the land, well, while I make arrangements for another home for her. Did I tell you I gave her a fine delicate Egyptian horse when I returned from my last trip?"

Michel walks home. *Will I be able to see her while I am there? Will I be able to convince her to return to me as soon as I have finished restoring Eden? Oh, God, why did that star have to appear and interrupt everything?*

Michel: The Fourth Wise Man

NIPPUR, HOMETOWN OF MEIRA

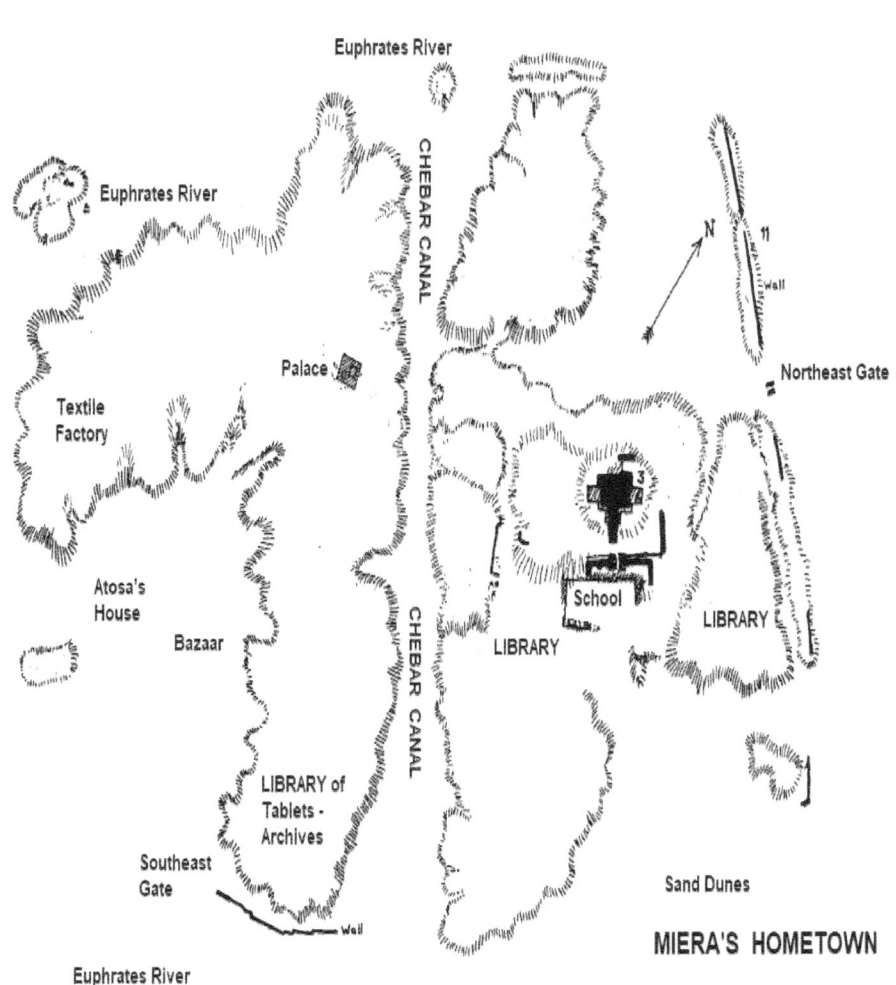

10 ~ THE DECISION

*T*he journey takes them two days. The magi have decided to ride desert-hearty camels.

It has now been six weeks since the elusive star was spotted and interrupted Michel's plans for Eden. The four magi have vowed to stay in Nippur until they find the explanation of the star. They must. Their only alternative is permanent exile from Parthia. Or execution if they return with the wrong answer to the celestial secret.

They enter through the northeast gate between the temples to Ninurta and Ninkarrak and proceed up the main street until it stops in front of the temple of Inana.

"Which way now?" Kumar asks Michel.

Michel looks both ways trying to remember where everything is. They turn right, go a little way, then left on the street that goes between the side of the temple and the wealthy priest houses. He continues until he reaches a branch of the Chebar Canal.

Just as they approach the bridge crossing the branch of the main canal, he stops.

"Gentlemen, if you will look over to your left, you will see the library attached to the temple to Inanna. That is Nippur's first library.

"Nippur has more than one?" Kumar asks.

Not answering, Michel turns right onto a street parallel to Chebar's branch and proceeds to its intersection with the main Chebar Canal. They cross the bridge and turn south alongside the main canal. Once again, he stops.

"Gentlemen, on your left is Nippur's second library. It has a school attached to it. If you will now look to your right, you will see the third library."

Knowing they are now near the southwest gate, and Meira and her mother are a few streets on the other side of it, Michel leads them back to an inn close to the intersection of the main and branch canals.

I wonder what Meira is doing right now. Does she sense that I am this close to her?

After stabling their camels and settling in their room, Dushatra, Kumar, and Michel walk around the city. Yasib stays back at the inn so he can nurse his aching joints and retire early.

The three sit in a park then walk through the bazaar.

Michel finds a silk scarf that would look perfect on his wife and buys it. The others pick up a few souvenirs themselves. There are some dates at one of the booths, and they all buy a few to eat as they walk.

Finally refreshed enough they think they can relax sufficiently to go to sleep, they return to the inn.

Morning comes, and they divide up.

Dushatra goes to the temple library, and Kumar goes to the library closest to the south gate. Michel and Yasib go to the library with the school attached.

This is the school my Meira attended. These are the writings she read through. I wonder if she ever comes here now.

Their work is slow. Although there are many modern scrolls, he and Yasib head for the ancient cuneiform tablets in back rooms piled on shelves. The librarians are surprised they can read the old cuneiform script until old Yasib explains the retinue of investigators that has just arrived in the city is from the magi council of King Phraattes.

Yasib settles down in one room and Michel in another.

I have been distracted from restoring Eden for over a month because of the interrupting star. If only they would listen to me and investigate the ancient Jewish writings, I'm sure they would figure out the meaning of the star, and I could return to more important things. Maybe they're still mad because I asked them for money.

One by one, the four search the writing of ancient religions on the tablets for any significant mention of a star.

A week passes. Together, the four have managed to read about ten an hour, so fifty to one hundred tablets a day.

"We have investigated the most sacred of the holy writings. No mention of a star," Dushatra says. "Perhaps there is a mention in the lesser sacred writings."

Another week. Back and forth to the inn. Each has read nearly one thousand tablets, and still no significant mention of a new star.

"We have now investigated writings referring to Anu the god of heaven and Ea the god of waters and a host of others. Nothing to do with a special star," Kumar tells the others.

Another week. "There must be ten thousand tablets in the three libraries," Dushatra says. "But we cannot leave without investigating them all."

"Will our money hold out?" Kumar asks.

"It has to," Michel says. "You know we cannot return home without declaring with absolute provable certainty they know the meaning of the star.

Three weeks.

"We have investigated Baal Marduk," Michel says. "No star. And I found writings on Sin, the god of the moon, and Shamash, the god of the sun. We have read the sacred writings of every god represented in this city, in Kish, Uruk, and even old Ur and Babylon that were abandoned long ago. Nothing about a star."

Four weeks. The old clay tablets are fragile. Sometimes they have to brush years of accumulated dust from the sand dunes blowing across the city. Sometimes they find only half a tablet and must search among the shelves for the other half.

Michel grows discouraged again. *If they would only investigate the Jewish holy writings, they would have their answer. God, help me convince them. And show me the answer too. Then I can get back to the more important things—resurrecting Eden to draw all men back to you there.*

"Well, we found Nabu, Nergal, and Ninim," Yasib explains, "but everyone knows these are gods of planets and not stars."

"We have read through the ancient sacred hymns and prayers, omens and incantations, astrological texts and medical advice," Michel says. "I have even read their mathematical, historical, and linguistic tablets."

"We cannot give up. If we do, we'll never see home again. We can never give up. As long as there is breath in us," Kumar declares, "we cannot give up."

Michel nods in agreement. "But, if you'd just…"

"Not now, Michel," Yasib says.

The next day while breaking their fast at the inn, Kumar makes an announcement. "I have now gone through all the ancient tablets in my library."

"I have in mine also," Dushatra adds.

"Then we'll have to switch to reading the ancient scrolls, Yasib announces, "We will have to investigate gods of the Grecians who came here four hundred years ago."

Dushatra slams his fist down on the table. "No. No! Enough of this."

"What do you mean, Dushatra?" Kumar says. "You yourself said we cannot stop the search. We'll be in exile until we find the meaning of the star."

"You are correct. But we must do it right."

"What do you mean?" Yasib asks.

"We make a world tour of all the great sacred libraries."

"Huh?"

"I have been investigating them. We can start down in Indo-Parthia, then go across to Egypt, up to Rome, then Athens, then Anatolia, and finally to Syria."

"No. We cannot do that. It would take us over a year to travel that far," Michel objects. "If you would just investigate the Jewish holy writings, I know the answer will be there."

"Michel, your holy writings are inferior," Dushatra says

"We don't know our way around in those places," Yasib says.

"I have thought of that too," Dushatra explains. "We send messages back to Magi Hophni, Demetrius, Katazuli, and Borseen to come join us and share in our reward when we return with the answer. Hophni is from Egypt, Demetrius from Rome, Katazuli from Anatolia, and Borseen from Syria. They will be our guides when we are in their homelands."

Silence.

"I don't know," Kumar says. "Who is going to pay for this journey?"

"Don't we all have enough to pay ship passage as far as Egypt? If anyone is short, I have a little extra. After that, we will work our way from place to place. We can take turns tutoring, scribing, translating, or whatever we can find to do for some pay."

Silence.

"It will work, gentlemen."

"But a whole year?" Michel objects.

"You and your Eden are going to have to wait."

Michel jerks his head back and looks around. "You all knew I bought it?"

"Of course we knew. We've been friends for too long."

"But..."

Yasib smiles. "We are used to your dreams. We were just mad at you wanting us to help pay for it. We got over it."

"How am I going to pay my workers?" Michel asks.

"As we said, your Eden will have to wait."

"Well, I say we give it a try," Kumar says. "There is a caravan that goes to Ctesiphon every couple of days. Hopefully, we will hear back from Hophni and the others within a week."

"I hope the rest of you don't mind, but I sent word to them two days ago," Dushatra says.

"Then it is settled," Yasib says. "We will find the meaning of the star, and the eight of us will share the honors King Phraattes bestows upon us when we return with the answer."

"A year is a long time," Michel objects.

"You claim Eden has been there thousands of years," Dushatra says. "It will still be there when we return."

The next day when the magi begin their wait, Michel purchases a basket with several small blank scrolls in it and takes it to a plaza along the canal. He sits cross-legged on the ground and writes.

My darling, Meira. I have been in Nippur at the library several days. I have respected your decision to stay with your mother while I have no real home to offer you, so have not tried to bother you.

Did you see the star that night? Even though the king only claims to believe in the one Zoroaster god, everyone knows he believes in all the others too. He is demanding to know if a god was born that will destroy him. He has banished my friends and I until we find the provable meaning of the star.

I fear we will be gone from Parthia at least a year. Wait for me, my darling. I will come back for you, and you will have a home again.
By the way, did you receive my gift? The delicate Egyptian is a lady's horse, and that lady is you.

Michel rolls the scroll up, seals it, numbers it, and puts it in the basket the scrolls came in.

"I think I'll go on down to Eden and check things out," Michel tells Kumar that afternoon.

"No, you cannot do that. If the other four magi arrive in a couple days, everyone will have to wait for you. Just stay here."

The next morning Michel returns to the park and pulls out another blank scroll.

My wife and my love. You always knew there were two I love more than any other in the world—God and you. When God comes first in my life, what I have for you is a hundred times more than it would have been without God. I promise you Eden someday. Some day you and I will walk through God's resurrected Eden just as our parents Adam and Eve did. And once again, we will walk with God on earth. Believe it, my darling. Please believe it.

He rolls up his scroll, seals it with his insignia ring and wax, and numbers it.

The rest of the day, Michel walks over to the other libraries he had not worked in, looks around a while, and leaves. He walks over to the palace on the hill near the northeast gate, sits in the reception park in front of it, and watches important people come and go.

The next morning he writes again.

Meira, why did that star have to appear when it did? It is ruining everything. If Eden became the destination of pilgrimages for pagans throughout the world, we could teach them about the one true God. Perhaps God will walk the earth with them in Eden. Why did the star have to show up? How could God have let it appear and interrupt everything?

I bought you a scarf the other day. I shall roll it up inside here. It reminds me of your laughter.

That afternoon Michel finds a public bath. He indulges himself and feels refreshed.

"You men should try it while we wait," he tells the others later.

Evening and morning.

"Hophni is here," Kumar says at the inn where everyone is having a noon refreshment.

Hophni grins at everyone.

"I went over to the north gate this morning as usual, and guess who had just arrived?"

"At least I don't have to be the youngest anymore," Michel says as he embraces his Egyptian friend and pounds him on the back. Did Kumar get you and your camel settled in?

"Just now."

"Doesn't look like your white *shendyt* got too dirty out on the trail," Yasib says. "You Egyptians wear such boring clothes. No color."

"Looks like you put on a little weight while we were gone," Kumar teases. "Well, it looks good with your magnificent dark skin."

"Hey, it's all muscle," Hophni responds. "So what's going on down here since King Phraattes exiled you?"

"We have not proven anything among the most ancient gods. We must seek the answers elsewhere," Yasib says.

"So we are going to travel to each civilized nation to see if their gods hold the meaning of the star," Dushatra says.

"Of course we could avoid all this if they'd just examine the Jewish holy books," Michel adds.

Everyone laughs.

"So, did you talk to the other three before you left Ctesiphon?" Kumar asks.

"Yes, and we all liked the idea. They will be here in the next day or two," Hophni says.

The next morning after Michel writes to his wife, he joins the others at the north city gate to watch for their friends.

When the second caravan of the day arrives from the north, Demetrius and Katazuli are among the travelers. They climb down off their camels.

Demetrius, wearing his usual tunic and toga, stands out among all the Parthians he is surrounded by. He takes their stares in stride. Though on the short side, he is handsome with high cheekbones, slightly wavy black hair, and blue eyes.

He raises his hands as though beginning a great oration and declares, "We were flattered to have been invited to join the most elite among the king's magi."

Hittite Katazuli, almost as tall as Michel, but fifteen

years his senior, shakes sand out of his red hair. "It's a good thing we were in that caravan. I had to fix someone's broken leg when they stepped in a gopher hole along the way."

"Good to have you both," old Yasib says. "So, when is Borseen going to be here? Or did he turn down the invitation? You know how suspicious Borseen is."

"And arrogant," Hophni says. "He is so young, he still thinks he can conquer the world. Uh, no offense to you, Michel."

The seven magi walk over to the inn, showing the sights along the way to the two most recent additions to their investigative team. They stable the two additional camels and arrange to rent a second room.

"I'll take you to the three libraries tomorrow," Hophni says. "They showed them to me yesterday, and I want to go back and look around some more."

The following day, Michel walks once more to his spot in the park along the Chebar Canal.

My darling wife. This may be my last letter to you in a while. Borseen, the young Syrian, will probably join us tomorrow. Then our team will be complete, and we will leave here. We will be taking a ship to Egypt. Perhaps I will be able to send a message to you from Alexandria.
Do not lose hope while I am gone. God will protect me while we are distracted by the star. Until then, walk with God in your soul, and someday you and I will walk with God in the resurrected Garden of Eden.

"There you are, Michel," Kumar says. "Borseen has just arrived. We are leaving within the hour."

"What kind of mood was he in?"

"Well, carrying that sword he always wears along with his dagger, people seemed to be staying clear of him."

Michel laughs. "Yes, that's our Borseen. Well, I will get this basket delivered, then pick up my luggage and camel at the inn. Is that where everyone is meeting?"

"Get there as soon as you can," Kumar calls over his shoulder.

Michel picks up his basket with the numbered scrolls in it. He takes a deep breath and heads down the street he had longed to walk along but had stayed away from.

I do not trust anyone else to deliver them. I won't try to talk to her and upset her. I wonder what she is doing right now?

He walks through the bazaar watching for pottery booths. He does not see any and decides he does not have time to look for them in another section.

I wonder if her mother has taught her how to make pottery. Maybe they have formed a partnership: Her mother making the pottery and Meira painting designs on them. Meira always was good at drawing things on clay tiles. And she designed an elegant mosaic for our courtyard.

He sees her mother's house ahead of him. He presses his lips together and looks up into the sky. He says a prayer for his Meira and for the star and the new Garden of Eden, and the libraries they will be going to and the ships they will be sailing, and back to Meira.

He walks to the gate and sets the basket down. He lets go of the handle, knocks hard on the gate, and runs behind a nearby cart.

The gate opens. Meira steps outside, looks both ways, sees no one, and picks up the basket with her delicate hands. She goes inside and shuts the gate.

Michel smiles to himself. *She is exactly where she said she would be. I will be back for you in a year, Meira. I will be back.*

He returns the way he came and arrives at the inn. He puts his belongings and a supply of barley on his camel's rump, gives it plenty of water, fills his waterskin, and mounts his ride.

The eight magi of Phraattes, mighty King of all Parthia, ride out the south gate of Nippur and head for the world.

"On our way down to the gulf to catch the ship, I want to stop by Eden to pay a little more to my workers."

"We're not going that way," Egyptian Hophni says.

"We aren't?"

"Don't you remember? Dushatra and Kumar are leading us down to the Makran Desert and Mountains in

Indus."

11 ~ CAPTIVE

The eight magi take the Parthian highway straight east in the direction of the Zagros Mountains.

"What we really needed to do is keep going east all the way to Taxilla," Dushatra says. "My King Gondophares has made sure the great library is protected. Ancient writings of the Buddhists are there. I visited it a few times since it is not far from my hometown, Kandahar."

"Sounds like we should start there," Demetrius says.

"Too far. Much too far. It would take us two weeks to get there. And another two weeks to get back. Plus research time," Michel says.

"You have many of those writings in your private collection, don't you?" Yasib asks. "You certainly made a viable presentation to the king."

"Yes, I do. And that is why we do not need to go there."

"Dushatra and I have decided to go straight down the coast of the Parthian Gulf to a couple of ancient holy places of both the Buddhists and Hindus," Kumar explains. "This is my territory, so I am taking over now."

By the time the sun has turned red, they have arrived at the Kur River.

Each man pulls out either a small goat-hair tent or a leather tent. The leather tents keep the cold wind out while they are in the mountains.

"You know, we could have gone down through Eden and Uruk to get to the Parthian Gulf. We didn't have to go this way," Michel says as they sit around a fire before retiring.

"Sorry, Michel," Kumar says. "We admire what you are wanting to do, but it's too swampy down there."

"You are becoming obsessed with Eden," Yasib adds with a grin. "We are your friends and are going to protect you from that obsession. Now, you young ones can sit up all night if you want to. My bones are tired, and I am going to let them sleep now."

Morning. They break camp and move on east. By mid-afternoon, they arrive at the Karum River. Their camels are ready to load up on water once more, so the men dismount and eat whatever dried fruit or cheese they have left in their supplies. An hour later, they cross the river and stop outside the city gate into Ahvaz.

"Sir," Kumar calls over to one of the guards on duty, his bronze conical helmet gleaming in the sun. "Could you tell us of a good inn where we may spend the night?"

"Where is your caravan from?"

"We are ambassadors of King Phraattes."

"That's what I thought. When you enter the city, turn to your left. That is the better part of town. Of course, if you want fresh food, you will turn right where the merchants are."

As they enter the city, Borseen pulls up beside Kumar. "Are we going to have to go through this every city we go to?"

"If we want the protection and goodwill of the city fathers, we will," Kumar says. "Now, get back in line, Borseen. And put that sword away."

They find an inn Kumar approves of, stable their camels, and rent two rooms.

"I, for one, am going over to the bazaar to buy more food to take," Katazuli says. "We never know how far apart the cities are going to be."

"That's where we're all headed, my Hittite friend," Hophni says.

Michel: The Fourth Wise Man

The next morning at dawn, they leave out the south gate of the city and follow the Karum river.

"I heard it is going to replace Susa someday as a winter palace," Roman Demetrius says, pulling his toga closer around him in the cool morning.

"Not any time soon," Yasib says. "At least, that's my opinion."

"It's getting cold up here."

"This river originates in these mountains," Kumar explains. "It splits up here and will take us back down toward the coast of the gulf."

About noon, they cross the Zohreh River. Five hours later, Kumar stops them for the night.

"Where are we?" Yasib asks.

"We're half a day ride from Bushire on the Mand River. It's a little swampy down there because the city is surrounded by two branches of the river. It would be better for us to go down there in full daylight."

Michel tries to put his dream of Eden in the back of his mind. It is a constant struggle.

At noon the fourth day, they spot seagulls and hear the signal bells of ships. Demetrius smiles. "Sounds like Rome," he tells the others.

"Part of the king's navy is down here," Michel says. "I wonder if there are any merchant ships from Egypt with them."

"We need to stop here to replenish our food again," Kumar says.

"I don't eat much. You men go on. I want to see if I can find a captain friend," Michel says.

Michel heads his camel down toward the shore. He sees a corral and pays a man to watch his animal while he walks down to where the ships are moored and reads the name of each merchant ship. None has an Egyptian name or even looks Egyptian.

"Here's one!"

Before Michel can react to the voice behind him, a sack is shoved over his head, his hands tied behind his back, and his ankles chained.

"Huh? What's going on here? Stop. Let go of me. You made a mistake."

"Shut up," his assailant growls, pushing him down the dock.

Michel tries to orient himself. He thinks he is going in the same direction he had been walking before. *The naval ships are there.*

"Stop. You've got it wrong. I am not a spy," he shouts from under the sack.

"We don't care what you are. We just need to meet our quota so we can get outa here."

Michel is forced to his left, then trips."

"Watch it there, fella. This gangplank is kinda narrow. Don't want you falling into the drink and drowning."

"Huh? Stop," Michel shouts as he senses he is on an upward incline. "You don't know what you're doing. I'm…"

"I know. You're not a spy. That's nice."

No longer on the incline. Michel feels swaying under his feet and staggers.

"Whoa, there, sailor. You're going to have to get used to this," the voice says. "Sir! I have brought you another one. How many does that make?"

"That makes one hundred sixty-six. We need one hundred seventy rowers to leave and get back out to sea."

"Okay, sir. I'll go back down and find us another."

With that, Michel hears the gangplank rattle. He wonders if he is standing alone now.

"All right," a third voice says. "Get him below."

Realizing he is near a man with authority, Michel calls out from the sack over his head.

"Sir, I am Magus Michel, personal advisor to His Majesty Phraattes, King of Parthia, and of the seas."

"No government official would be down here walking around without personal guards. Where did you get those clothes? Stole them, didn't you?"

"They're mine. Sir, I have money. I will give you my money if you'll let me go."

"Get him below with the other oarsmen before I start believing his ridiculous story. Oh, and take whatever money he has on him."

Michel feels himself stepping forward, then falling.

There is a banging overhead. His left shoulder suddenly feels as though lightning has hit it. His left leg is twisted under him and feels like fire with an elephant sitting on it.

He hears scuffling next to him.

"Do you think he's dead?"

"Hey, fellow."

"If he's dead," the second voice says, "they still won't have met their quota, and we can stay here in port."

"Once we're out at sea, our chances of escape are gone. Hey, fellow. You alive?"

Michel groans.

"I guess he's alive. Too bad."

"Fellow, I'm going to take that sack off your head. Don't be scared. I'm not trying to decapitate you or anything."

After a tugging at his head and twisting his neck, the sack is off, but Michel still has trouble seeing.

"Where am I?" he groans.

"Below deck," he hears. "You've been kidnapped just like the rest of us. There was some kind of epidemic while they were out at sea from what the other oarsmen tell us. They managed to make port, but cannot leave until they are fully manned."

"This is a warship," the second voice says. "Do you think you can sit up?"

Michel pushes up with his arms, despite the pain in his shoulder, then lies back down. "My leg."

The first man takes Michel's left foot and brings it around, so it is straight.

"Ahhhggh."

He feels around the leg. "Maybe you cracked it a little. Or maybe it got your ankle. Try to sit up again."

This time Michel manages to sit up. He grasps the

hands of the other two men as he tries to stand.

"Ahhhggh."

"Well, sit back down. Nothing anyone can do about it, even if you did break it somewhere. You don't need your legs down here. You'll be sitting and rowing. Better hope your shoulder isn't bad. If it is, they'll probably pull you out of here and throw you overboard."

"My name, my, my, my name is Michel. I am a personal consultant to King Phraattes."

"Maybe you are, and maybe you aren't. Doesn't matter down here."

"My friends. They'll come after me," Michel groans amid his pain.

"You'll have to have a whole army of friends to get you off a warship. By the way, I am Givv."

"My name is Tus," the second man says.

"Well, Givv and Tus, I plan to do a lot of praying now."

"Us too. But our gods seem to be busy doing other things. How about yours?"

Michel hears two voices off in a distance, then blackness. And silence. All he is aware of is rocking, rocking, rocking. And now and then heavy footsteps overhead.

Once he thinks he hears someone say it is night. The footsteps have stopped. All that is left now is the rocking, rocking, rocking.

Michel dreams he is on a reed boat where the Tigris and Euphrates Rivers meet. Meira is in the boat with him. Her legs look like a fishtail and she dives into the water. When she comes back up, she has a twig between her teeth. The twig has tiny blossoms on it and two pieces of fruit.

He hears footsteps again. The hatch opens, and another man with a sack over his head is thrown down.

"Hey, fellow," he hears Givv say. "You alive?"

The pain in Michel's shoulder and leg continue, only now, the pain is hot. He feels his leg where it hurts the most—it is swollen—and lies back down onto the cold, wet planks.

"Four more, and we're gone for good. We'll never get

off this ship alive."

Heavy footsteps again all day. Then they stop again. It is the second night.

He dreams of Meira again. Only this time, she is a peacock up in a tree in the Garden of Eden. She is singing a beautiful song. Then she stops and flies down to the ground with a loud thump.

"Michel, Michel," he hears. It is not Meira's voice. Michel opens his eyes.

"Michel." A man is whispering. "Are you down here?"

"Huh? Borseen? Is that you, Borseen?" Michel whispers. "Over here."

Michel tries to crawl over to the other magus. "Did they get you too? What are we going to do, Borseen?"

"We're going to get out of here."

"We cannot. They've got us trapped down here to be their oarsmen."

"You've sure got that wrong, Michel. Follow me."

"I cannot walk."

Michel looks up and sees stars.

"Hey, Katazuli, hand me a rope," Borseen says with his Syrian accent. "There should be some laying around the deck."

Shortly a rope is thrown down, and Borseen ties one end around Michel's chest.

"Okay, Katazuli. Pull him up."

"No."

"No?"

"What about these other men?"

"Hey, we don't want to go," an oarsman says from deeper along the hull.

"Huh?"

"We were hired. We're getting paid. You last guys are the only ones who are slaves. We like our job. Take Givv and Tus."

"Yeah, take us," Givv says.

"Okay, climb out after me," Borseen says. "Now, Katazuli, get Michel out of here."

Michel positions himself directly under the hatch the best he can and holds on to the rope over his head to try to help.

"He's too heavy," Katazuli calls down. "Wait, I'll wrap the rope around this pole for more traction."

Givv and Tus get behind Michel and push up on his legs. Soon Michel's head is above the hatch. Katazuli, with his long Hittite arms, grabs him under the shoulders and pulls him up the rest of the way.

He sits on the deck while the other three men follow him up. For the first time, he sees that Borseen has a long curved dagger in his hand.

"Quickly," he says, still whispering.

Katazuli leads the way to the side of the ship. Michel looks around. "Where is everyone?"

"We'll tell you later," Katazuli says as he pushes Michel over the side, head first.

"Hey, wait."

Arms reach up and catch Michel. The strong arms of Hophni. Hophni teeters a little.

"We've got him, Hophni. Lower him down." It is Kumar.

The next thing Michel knows, he is in the bottom of a rowboat at Kumar's feet.

"Get down here, you men, and let's make our escape." It is Dushatra's voice.

"No."

"What do you mean, no?"

"There are two more."

A leg is thrown over the edge of the ship, and another one with it. Givv jumps down into the boat, followed shortly by Tus. The boat rocks.

"Hey, sit still," Dushatra warns.

Last Hittite Katazuli and Syrian Borseen.

"Go!" Borseen barks.

Dushatra and Demetrius grab their oars while the other rescuers push on the side of the ship to break away.

Swish.

Michel: The Fourth Wise Man

Swish.
Swish.
The strokes of the oars synchronize, and silently, the crowded rowboat slips parallel along the shoreline.

"Where are we going? The dock's that way?" Michel asks.

"Shhh."
Swish.
Swish.
Swish.
On down the shoreline.

They hear no more bells or voices on docks, and the only noise is that of the seagulls. They head toward shore.

Thump. A scraping sound.

All the men jump out of the boat. All but Katazuli and Michel.

Katazuli backs up to Michel. "Hang on to my neck."

With Demetrius and Kumar steadying the boat, Katazulli climbs out with Michel on his back. He wades ashore with the rest of the men and lets go of him in the sand at the feet of Yasib.

"What under the great cosmos of the universe were you doing, Michel?" Yasib pronounces.

"I, uh...I, uh..."

All but Michel, Givv, and Tus break out in guffaws of laughter.

"Well, while everyone is recovering from your narrow escape from a living death, let me look at that leg of yours," Katazuli says.

"We can always depend on you, Katazuli. But how did you know? And how did you get past the ship?"

"When you didn't come back after we were through buying our food for the next couple days, we sent Borseen after you," Kumar begins.

"When I got down to the docks, someone slipped up behind me and tried to throw a sack over my head. But I was too quick for him. I pulled out my sword, turned around and swung at him. By the time I got the sack off my head, he was ten man-lengths away.

"I stood there watching him to see which ship he would be boarding, or if he just took off to a warehouse or some other hiding place. It was a ship all right.

"I walked over to one of the better-dressed men on the docks and asked him about that ship. He explained they were short of men because of an epidemic at sea. Well, I knew what that meant, and knew that's what had happened to you."

Michel lies where he is while Katazuli wraps bands around his ankle.

"It's not broken, but is probably cracked enough to keep you from walking a week or two."

"I'll look around for a branch to make a crutch for you," Demetrius says.

"I saw some good crutches at the bazaar," Hophni says, trying to scrape mud off his white kilt.

"Cannot go back there. Whatever Demetrius makes for him will be fine."

"Well, anyway," Katazuli says, finishing up Michel's bandages, "when Borseen told us what probably happened, we knew we had to get on board that ship. Of course, I knew exactly how we were going to do it."

"You have Katazuli to thank, not only for fixing your ankle but for using his magic on the guards of the ship," Yasib says.

"What magic?" Michel asks.

"Opium, of course," Dushatra says. "We bought some filled wineskins at the bazaar, poured more than a few drops of opium in each of them, and offered it to the guards. They were out within moments."

"And you know the rest," Katazuli says to Michel. "Now, who are your two friends, and what are we going to do with them?"

12 ~ CAVERNS AND CLIFFS

"I'm Givv."

"I'm Tus."

"Where do you live?"

"We live in Turbat in the Makran Desert just on the other side of the Makran Mountains."

"Well, that is our destination, sirs," Kumar says. "You may accompany us. But do you have any transportation? We have to stay on our mission."

"They can ride my camel," Michel says. "That's the least I can do for them."

"Well, I guess that means you'll be riding with me," Yasib says.

"If you don't mind, friend."

"Of course, I don't mind. You can tell me all about your underwater garden on our way," he says with a snicker.

"His underwater what?" Borseen asks.

"We'll tell you later," Kumar says. "We need to get on the highway. "Would Givv and Tus feel comfortable taking the lead?"

"Yeah, we can do that," Givv says. "We know the way blindfolded."

"When you get us to the foothills of the jMakrans, it should be safe to stop and get some sleep," Kumar says.

"The Makrans don't have many foothills. They just suddenly sprout up out of the desert."

"Okay, everyone. Mount up and follow our new guides," Kumar says. "Let's get out of this cursed place."

The caravan of now ten men leaves the coast and continues on south, dodging the numerous tributaries of the swampy Mand River.

By the time the sky begins to turn a light gray, they are on higher ground.

"We may as well stop now," Kumar says. "We're too far away now for those sailors to follow—that is, if they have awakened yet." He chuckles to himself.

"So, are we in the foothills yet?" Dushatra asks.

"We told you, there are no foothills. But, we are on a little higher ground and won't be bothered with that Mand any more."

"Then, we stop and sleep awhile."

"In this heat? I'm perspiring already, and the sun isn't even up yet," Katazuli says.

"Haven't you adjusted to being away from the mountains around Anatolia?" Hophni teases.

The camels kneel and let their passengers off. Michel leans on his new crutch as he slides off the camel while Yasib stands ready to help him to a good spot to rest. He throws a rug down for each of them.

The men sleep on and off until the sun is bright in the sky.

"Well, let's get going," Kumar says. "So, what's ahead for us?" he asks their guides.

"We should be in Gamaroon by tonight. Then we start over the mountain passes tomorrow.

The caravan moves slowly.

Michel begins singing.

"What are you singing about?"

"Oh, it's one of the psalms of David, one of our famous Jewish poets and songwriters. He was our king too."

"A singing king," Yasib reflects aloud. "An interesting concept."

"Doesn't your leg hurt?" Demetrius asks.

"That's why I'm singing. Gets my mind off the pain."

As promised, they arrive in Gamaroon just as the sun is setting.

"Oh, no," Michel says.

"Oh, no is right," Demetrius says. "This is another seaport. No navy here yet, but they might just get desperate enough for more oarsmen that they come down here."

"Givv? Tus? Would it be feasible for us to bypass the city before it is completely dark?" Kumar asks.

"We can try. We'll go another hour until dark. After that, it's the mountains. They are too high to travel without daylight."

"Then take us as far as you can."

The night is moonless. They stop after only half an hour. "We can go no farther. Too dangerous," Tus says.

The caravan stops, one of the men starts a fire with his bow drill and a few twigs off desert shrubs. The others wander around, hoping to find something larger to keep it going, but with no luck. They let the fire go out.

"Don't worry. We can eat without light," Yasib says. "What are you doing, Dushatra?"

"I'm trying to remember exactly where the star appeared. It was the most amazing phenomenon I have ever observed. Just amazing."

"If only it hadn't appeared when it did," Michel says. "It interrupted everything."

"Not to change the subject, but you didn't buy any food back in Bushire," Yasib says. "Are you okay?"

"I have some bread left. I'll be all right."

The ten men gradually stop talking and lie on rugs on the ground without the shelter of tents.

"Oh! I see what you meant last night," Hophni says the next morning. "Those mountains just rise up out of the desert. Some of it is straight up."

"Just follow us," Givv says. "We know where the passes are."

"Aren't you glad I convinced the king to amass a herd

of Mongol Bactrian camels?" Yasib calls out as they wind around another outcrop of rocks going straight up. "I grew up near the Caspian Sea, where they roamed wild. They are sure-footed and can stand both heat and cold. Not like those puny Dromedary camels over in Egypt."

"Hey, our Egyptian camels are perfectly fine," Hophni objects.

"Yes, as long as you are on flat land, and the temperatures are not too extreme."

"Shhh. What was that?" Demetrius says in a loud whisper.

"What was what?" Michel asks.

"There it is again."

"Oh, it's just a lynx. They're small. They won't attack us."

They continue to climb. The men try not to look down though sometimes their instincts make them look anyway. Always they wish they hadn't.

"All right. This is as high as we go," Givv calls back to the others. "Why don't you let your animals rest and come look at the view."

The magi climb off their animals and walk to where Givv is standing.

"Oh. That valley. It's amazing," Hophni says.

"Never saw anything like it," Michel says, leaning on both his crutch and Yasib.

"Once we get out of these mountains, we will pick up the Dasht River," Givv explains. "It will take us the rest of the way to Turbat."

"Well, my lungs aren't as good as they used to be. I need to be down there," Yasib says.

It takes the rest of the day. But late in the afternoon, they arrive down in the valley.

"Do you want us to take you on to the city in the dark?"

"No, we need to rest and be fresh in the morning so we can present ourselves respectfully tomorrow," Dushatra says.

"Are those date palms I see?" Hittite Katazuli asks. "Why don't you climb up there and drop enough down for our evening meal?"

"Stand back," Syrian Borseen says, taking a running leap at the bottom of one of the trees.

An hour later, everyone is sufficiently filled on dates.

"Tomorrow in Turbat we feast on cheese and barley bread and any other delicacies they have for us," Demetrius declares.

"And tomorrow we search for Buddhist writings," Dushatra says.

Morning comes. The caravan reassembles and heads up the Dasht River with faithful camels who have been rewarded with enough water to keep them happy several more days.

They arrive at the city gate, and Givv leads them through. "There is an inn down this street. I think you'll like."

"What were all those tombs along the river?"

"No one knows."

"Will I be permitted to examine them?" Dushatra asks.

"I don't think anyone cares. They are old."

When they arrive at the tombs the next day, the magi stop and wait for Dushatra. He climbs among the rocks into which the tombs have been hollowed out.

He stays in each one different lengths of time. Michel assumes it is because of the size; from the outside, it is hard to tell.

Dushatra works his way down, in and out of the tombs, climbing, slipping, jumping across crevices, and boulder to boulder. Sometimes standing, sometimes crawling, sometimes bent, sometimes stretching.

Michel and the others pull out something to eat, or take a nap, or talk to their camels, or pace, or just stare.

"I did not find anything," Dushatra says, walking back to the group sweating and with dirt all over his now torn billowy pantaloons and sleeveless vest.

"No tablets, no parchment scrolls, no writing on the

walls, no statues, nothing but scattered shards of pottery with nothing etched or painted on them.

"I don't understand it. Did those people—whoever they were—use this as their necropolis, their burial ground away from their village? Where was their village? Were they nomads? Were they Buddhists, Hindus or animists, or maybe even wandering Jews?"

Givv walks up to Dushatra and extends a sympathetic arm across his shoulder. Dushatra shrugs it off and walks toward his camel. "I just don't understand it."

He turns back to Givv. "Is there any place else we can search?"

"If you would tell me what you are searching for, I might be able to help you," Givv says.

"Sacred writings referring to a star, especially the birth of a star," Kumar explains.

"Why?"

"Our king is demanding to know if his kingdom is in danger. And—well, you may as well know the rest—we have been exiled until we find the provable answer," Yasib explains.

"Tus, do we know of any place that might have writings or symbols of a star?"

"What about that old fortification? It's just north of here a short way."

"Dushatra, do you want to try there?" Kumar asks.

"Yes. I know the Buddhists lived around here somewhere. This is as far west as they went, but they definitely were here. If I can find ancient writings heretofore unknown, they will reveal the meaning of the star. I'm sure of it."

Within a few moments, the caravan has reassembled and backtracked to an ancient fortification far enough off the road, no one had noticed it.

"Maybe now we can find the meaning of the star so we can go back to more important things," Michel says as they reach their destination.

Besides an eroded but high rampart, there are the

remains of tall conical shaped buildings that look like they had been the walls of the fort.

The magi walk around among the ruins and do their own investigating.

"Dushatra!" Demetrius calls out. "Come look engraved on this wall."

Dushatra runs over to the conical building Demetrius is in. He inspects the etchings. "They're just scrapes."

"But one looks like a star," Demetrius says.

"There is no writing with it. This fortification is obviously very ancient—one or two thousand years perhaps. I am surprised any part of it is still standing."

"Well, should we try somewhere else?" Kumar asks.

Dushatra shakes his head, looking down at the ground. He walks slower now—partly because of the oppressive heat, and partly because of hopes unfulfilled.

"He got me!"

Hophni jumps, then sits on the ground holding his foot and rocking.

"He got me!

"Who got you?"

"A scorpion."

Michel hobbles over with his crutch and kneels so he can see the foot.

"Katazuli!" he calls out. "Katazuli! Where are you? Hurry, Katazuli!"

"He's not here," Yasib says.

Michel looks at Hophni. "Lie down."

"No, I always heard you need to sit up to keep the poison from rising."

"Would it help if I wrapped your foot up?"

"No. Nothing is going to help. I am going to die."

"Katazuli!" Michel calls out again. "Where is Katazuli?"

The magi scatter, all calling their healer's name.

"I'm going to die," Hophni moans. "I'm going to die."

"Katazuli won't let that happen. He trained at the temple of Anatolia's healing god. The priests know a lot about healing. Everyone took their sick to these priests. They taught Katazuli, and..."

Hophni leans over and wretches.

"That's good, Hophni," Michel says.

"No, it isn't. I'm going to die."

"But you probably spit the poison out just now."

"No," Hophni groans, tears flowing down his beardless face. "I'm going to die."

Michel moves his crutch to an upright position and pulls himself up. "Katazuli! Where are you, Katazuli?"

He shuffles around the encampment. "Katazuli! Oh, Jehovah, bringing him back to us. He wasn't bitten too, was he? Where could he be that he doesn't even hear us? Jehovah, protect him and nudge him somehow. Send him back to us. Don't let Hophni die. Katazuli!"

"Over there! I see him coming up the hill," Syrian Borseen shouts.

Two of the magi rush toward Katazuli while Michel returns to Hophni. "He's on his way."

He kneels next to his wounded friend. "Hophni? Hophni? Don't die. He's on his way." He taps Hophni's cheek with his open hand. "Wake up, Hophni. Wake up."

He slides around so he can lift Hophni's head and put it on his lap. "Come on, Hophni. Don't die. Katazuli is almost here. Hang on, friend. Hang on."

"Where was he bitten?" Katazuli asks, rushing over and kneeling. "Someone go to my camel and bring me that leather pouch."

"In the foot," Michel explains. "He was bitten in the foot."

"Bring me my pouch, someone. Hurry!" he calls out. "That's good that you have his head up."

Someone arrives with the pouch. Katazuli pours its contents out onto the desert floor. He finds a small cup and hands it to Yasib nearby to fill halfway with water from the skin he has around his waist.

Katazuli pours the crushed leaves into his hand and then into the cup of water. He mixes the leaves in with his finger, then puts it up to Hophni's lips.

"Come on, wake up, Hophni," Michel says. "Wake up so you can drink this. Come on. Help us out."

Hophni groans, his eyes still closed and voluntarily opens his mouth slightly.

The herbal mixture is poured, a few drops at a time, into Hophni's mouth.

"Now we wait," Katazuli says.

"What did you give him?" Michel asks.

"Leaves from the mongoose plant. It is an old Indus cure. And it works."

"Do you hear that, Hophni?" Michel says. "It works. You're going to be all right. Hophni?" Michel looks up at Katazuli.

Katazuli feels his patient's face. "It is warming up again. He is sleeping now. That is the best for him."

"How long will we have to stay here?" Kumar asks.

"He should be able to travel again tomorrow. Maybe if Michel rides with him instead of Yasib, he can keep close watch on him."

The magi set up camp, which consists of taking supplies off their camels and spreading out a rug and whatever else they want. They mostly lean back on rocks and think about the elusive meaning of the strange star.

"Uh, is there anywhere else around here we can look?" Dushatra asks Tus while watching Hophni sleep. "Anywhere at all?"

"What about Gandakahar?"

"What did you say?" Dushatra says, jerking his head up to look at Givv. "That's where I am from—Khandahar. Is there another city by that name?"

"It's not really a city," Tus explains. "It is a tribe of people, the Kahars. Ganda is another tribe of people. In Gandakahar, the people intermarry."

"Oh. Well, where do they live?"

"In Gondrani. It is about a day and a half ride south of here."

"Are those people Buddhists?"

"I do not know. But there are a couple of caves up in

the hills that I heard a holy man lives in. Do you want to see them?"

Dushatra looks around for Kumar.

"What do you think?"

"Is it near Hinglaj? That's where I want to go," Kumar says.

"The two places are right across the mountains from each other."

Michel spends the rest of the day and all night sleeping next to Hophni. Katazuli sleeps on the other side of his patient. He gives him water with honey in it periodically during the night.

The following morning, Katazuli walks over to Kumar and Dushatra. "He says he thinks he can travel today."

"If you agree, then we should load up our supplies and be on our way," Dushatra says. "Are you sure Hophni is going to be okay?"

13 ~ NEAR, BUT FAR

A day and a half later, the caravan reaches Gondrani in the foothills of the Makran Mountains, despite Givv's denial that the range has foothills.

By the time Michel settles himself and Hophni in the shade of a boulder, Dushatra is gone. He looks around and sees his friend climbing up a sharp limestone incline. Above Dushatra is a single cave that seems to have been man-made, though Michel cannot be sure.

The magi sit, stand, pace, wander, and do whatever they can in the heat while their friend searches for the meaning of the elusive star.

Michel tries to sleep as much as possible, hoping that will help heal his leg. He encourages Hophni to do the same.

"I found it! I found it," Dushatra shouts.

Michel is awakened from one of his naps with the Buddhist running toward them.

Everyone but Michel and Hophni stands.

"A prophecy of the star?" Demetrius asks.

"Well, not that. But I did find proof the Buddhists settled here a while. Well, not many. The cave had several rooms in it, and I found evidence of an entire family being there. But mostly, I saw a statue of Buddha himself."

"Were there any writings?"

"The man who had lived there was a hermit monk—well, except for his family. But I found some writings indicating he wanted more Buddhists to follow him here. Maybe even start a monastery."

"And the star?"

Dushatra stares at Kumar, presses his lips together and shakes his head. "Nothing about a star," he says in a muffled voice. "I was certain there would be, but I was wrong."

Kumar smiles. "Then we cross the mountains and search for Hindu writings."

"Wait. Before we cross the mountains, you might want to fill your water skins and the bellies of your camels," Givv says. "Over here is a step-well."

"A what?"

"It's a well so deep, you need to go down steps to get to the water."

The magi lead their camels as they follow Givv and Tus.

"These steps are wide enough, our camels should be able to go down there with us," Borseen says.

"Well, I'm staying up here with Hophni," Michel says. "Yasib, would you fill Hophni's and my water skins for us?"

Michel waits at the top of the well and dozes. Hophni does the same.

"I found something," he hears Kumar call out, running up the steps to the surface. "I found something."

"Not already," Dushatra says. "I've been everywhere and didn't find anything close to what I was looking for until the end."

"So, what did you find, Kumar?" Katazuli asks.

"I found statues in niches in the wall of the well. I found Chandra of the moon, Surya of the sun, and all the planets. But I guess none are of stars."

"I'm sorry," Michel says.

"I guess we need to go ahead and cross the mountains," Kumar says.

"Okay," Givv announces, "let's do it."

An hour later, the caravan has been reformed, and the procession of magi on the move again, searching for the meaning of the star.

As long as they follow the wadi, travel is smooth. Then come the mountains. The uncrossable mountains they are about to try crossing.

They had better be good guides, Michel thinks.

The range is like solid-rock waves that the Parthian Gulf on the west side of the mountains keeps pushing in. Wave after wave.

Givv and Tus lead their camels back and forth, back and forth to go around the waves. For every rocky wave they pass, there are five more.

The trail is gravely, the going slow as the camels by instinct put one wide foot down, then the other, and the other. One slow step at a time. Back and forth. Back and forth.

"This is the Hingol River we are about to cross," Tus calls out. "It originates in a spring somewhere up here. Up away farther, we will pick up one of the Hingol's branches and follow it down the other side."

The magi follow their guides with continued hopes and prayers to their respective gods that they know where they are going

"Here is the branch," Tus announces. "We'll go down into the gulley with it."

"We need to stop," Yasib calls up to their guides "My joints are hurting so bad, I cannot sit any longer. I'll bet Michel and Hophni would like to stop too."

"Well, it does grow dark sooner in the mountains," Givv says. "Kumar? It's your decision."

"I guess we need to stop. Besides, I like the cooler air up here. But we leave at daylight tomorrow."

Once again, the caravan breaks up, camels kneel, men slide off their mounts, grab their supplies, and stumble over loose rocks to find a smooth place to lay their rugs out.

"Is our entire quest going to be like this?" Borseen asks Demetrius. "At this rate, it will take us five years to go to all the major sacred libraries. The library in Antioch, Syria, is the last one on our list. I don't see how you are going to last."

"These old men seem to think we have nothing better to do," Demetrius responds. "The king didn't exile us. He only exiled Yasib, Kumar, Dushatra, and Michel. Why should we help them?"

"Maybe we'll meet some beautiful women," Borseen suggests with a wink.

"That, my friend, would make all this tedium worth it."

"Hey, everyone. Time to get up. Rise, everyone. Rise!"

Morning has come too soon. Kumar walks among the sleep rugs kicking whoever is on them.

The camels have spent much of the night getting their fill of water and are ready to go.

Within the hour, everyone has refilled their water skins and washed at the Hingol River edge, loaded up their supplies, and climbed onto their mounts.

"I would say going down the other side will be easier," Givv says, "but the mountains do not end until they are almost in the waters of the Parthian Gulf."

Back on the trail, they make their way west toward the majestic Hindu shrine.

"Look over at Kumar," Michel tells Hophni. "He can hardly sit still."

Late afternoon comes.

"Well, we're here," Tus announces.

Everyone stops and looks around.

"Here, where?" Michel asks. "Just more mountains."

"What in the world is this?" Kumar asks.

"Look down there in that gorge," Tus says.

"I don't see anything," Borseen says.

"Me neither. We're not fools, you know," Demetrius says.

"Look again. Follow that cliff over there way down to the bottom. Don't you see it?"

"See what?"

"The cave."

"What cave? Oh, I think I see it now. It's like one of the gods put his hand down there, slid it in, then back out, and left a dent." It's Dushatra.

"Yeah, I guess that describes it. But that dent is much bigger than you think. See those people down there?"

"Those are people? I thought they were ants."

The two guides laugh, then start down a side trail to the bottom of the gorge. As they draw closer, they see people just inside the shallow cave on their haunches praying.

"That is a Hindu shrine. I know it now," Kumar says. "It is more holy than a shrine built with hands. Oh, thank you. Thank you."

Kumar's camel kneels, he slides off and runs toward the wide yawning cave opening. By the time the others arrive, he is in prayer.

"Oh Hingula Devi, she who holds nectar in herself and is power incarnate. She who is one with Lord Siva. To her, we pay our respects."

His friends stay where they are while Kumar finds a monk. They talk a while, then Kumar and the monk disappear farther back into the cave.

Evening comes. A monk approaches the caravan. "Since he is one of the elite magus of King Phraattes, we are allowing him to read our sacred books. It will probably take him the rest of today and all day tomorrow."

"We will wait," Dushatra replies, "just as he waited for me."

"Uh, how far is it from here to the Parthia Gulf coast? We're almost there, aren't we?" Michel asks the monk.

"Well, it is half a day away—an hour to get to the main part of the river, and two or three to follow it the rest of the way to the gulf."

The magi move over to the river, clear off rocky places, and put down their rugs and supplies.

"What are you doing, Michel?" Hophni calls to him. Why aren't you sitting down and resting that leg?"

"My ankle is fine now."

Hophni and the others watch Michel walk in large circles around the grounds in front of the vast cave.

"Katazuli, should he be doing that?" Yasib asks.

"As long as it doesn't cause him any pain, he should do at least some exercises, so his muscles don't shrivel up."

"Muscles do that?"

"Of course, they do."

Borseen looks up into the sky. "Those clouds are sure stirring around up there. As restless as Michel."

That evening, Kumar returns to his friends and tells what he has learned so far.

"But what about a reference to a new star, or any kind of star?" Michel urges.

"So far, nothing. But I am certain it will be in there."

"If you men would give in and read the Jewish sacred writings, you would find the meaning of the star," Michel urges once again.

"Your religion is inferior and narrow-minded. You only believe in one god. What good is that?"

Michel falls asleep thinking about Eden. He dreams he sees the star again, but it is falling through the sky. It plunges into the waters of the marsh and settles at the bottom where once Adam and Eve had walked with God. He stirs when he thinks the star has gone out. But suddenly it bursts out of the water, brighter than ever.

It is morning.

Jehovah. This is not right. I should not be running after an elusive star. I should be helping you restore Eden.

Michel walks over to the river bank and cleans up. He returns to his rug, looks around, and gathers everything up.

"Uh, Hophni, I think I'm going to take my camel for a walk."

"Okay, Michel. Have a good time."

He taps the camel's knees with his crutch, the camel kneels, Michel loads everything on it and climbs on himself.

Other than Hophni, no one sees Michel leave.

Jehovah, forgive me. You put your trust in me.

His camel is surefooted. With its wide feet and toes that separate to accommodate rocky surfaces, he gives Michel a steady ride.

I have let you down. I have let down Archangel Michel,

Michel: The Fourth Wise Man

after whom I was named.

The clouds stir overhead. An unusual early-morning breeze stirs up.

I have let my ancestor Daniel down. I have let Meira down.

He reaches the main Hingol River. It is wider than Michel had expected. He orders the camel to kneel and climbs off. They both go to the river and drink their fill.

Michel looks up into the sky, enjoys the cool breeze growing stronger as he nears the gulf, then remounts his camel.

And I have let down the people around the world believing gods that do not exist, postponing them returning to Eden. How many will die while I search the world for an answer to something Satan has sent to distract me?

He hears seagulls squawking overhead and looks up. They dart between clouds and soar above them, then dive to someplace along the shore to scrounge up dinner.

Forgive me. Oh, forgive me. If I don't do this, it won't get done.

He rides the last hour humming a hymn David had composed at one of his own low times. The clouds continue to churn overhead. The wind picks up a little more. Oh, how good it feels.

I have not been much help to them. I don't believe in any of their gods. They all know that. So, actually, I have not been any help to them. They don't listen to me when I speak of our divine plan. Well, they listen, but only with their ears. Not their heart.

The camel steps out onto the beach.

"Just as I had hoped," he says aloud. *Ships. Merchant ships, not military ones. And luxury barges. What are those barges? The barges of nobles by blood, heroes by action, and imitators who wish to buy their way to world renown.*

Michel orders his camel to kneel and takes his belongings off of it. Now the camel is back on his feet. Michel pulls the reins around to the front and leads his animal to a corral.

"Sir, how much would it cost for me to board my animal with you for a week?"

"A silver coin," comes the reply.

Michel pulls the silver coin out and hands it to the proprietor. "My friends are up at the shrine right now. When they arrive, you will recognize them. All our camels are tackled the same and have the same rugs and muzzles on them. The riders will be richly dressed, though their clothes may be a little dirty and torn after going across the desert and the mountains."

"Yes, sir. So you want me to hand your camel over to them."

"That's right."

Michel takes all his supplies off the camel and puts them on his back. He walks down the docks slowly, looking at each ship and trying to determine what it is carrying. He makes his final decision.

"Sir, might you be taking your ship up to the northern gulf coast in Parthia?"

"No. Just came from there."

"Sir, might you be taking your ship up the gulf?"

"No, I just stopped to pick up cargo. I'm headed for China."

"Sir, if you are going up the gulf, I would like passage for myself."

"Sorry, I don't take passengers. Why don't you take one of those barges? They never leave the gulf. I'm sure their owners will want someone to add to their entertainment."

"Sorry, sir. But I have serious business to take care of. I need speed and reliability."

"Oh, you do? And how much are you willing to pay so you can take care of your serious business with speed and reliability?"

Michel walks up the gangplank.

"Halt. You do not have permission to come on board."

"Will this buy me permission?" Michel holds out ten silver coins in the palm of his hand.

"Oh, well, in that case, I do believe I am going up the

Michel: The Fourth Wise Man

gulf. Just came from there, but perhaps I forgot something in Uruk."

"Yes, sir," Michel says. "Are you the captain?"

"I am, sir," the man says, reaching over and taking the ten silver pieces.

Michel steps on board and looks around.

"If the wind is with us, it should take us about four days." The captain looks up.

"I see you have a tent with you. You can set it up in front of my bridge. Or you can go below and not need a tent."

"Yes, sir," Michel answers. "I appreciate this."

"Oh, don't appreciate me yet. Those clouds up there have been building up all morning. You understand that, if we get into a storm, you will be expected to help man the oars below or throw water overboard. So, if you have a rope, keep it handy. You may have to tie yourself to a pole if the weather gets ugly and my ship turned into a toy boat at the mercy of the gods."

He turns to his first officer. "Put those down in the hold," he says, then turns back to Michel.

"I shall pray that the storm passes us by, I will arrive on time, and you will be able to resume your trip," Michel says. "I pray to the only true and living God. I am on a very important mission for him, and know he will hear my prayers."

"Whatever you say, my new friend. Let's hope your God is stronger than all those other gods. The ship is already rocking, and we haven't left port yet."

With that, the captain leaves Michel to settled in on his own.

Satan, get away from Eden. You took Adam and Eve. I will stop you.

He looks around, shifts his supplies off his back, and walks toward the bridge.

Well, here we go. By not paying for passage all the way to Egypt, I have enough to pay my marsh workers.

Michel stops and squats on the deck near the bridge. *Or did they take the money and desert me and the mission?*

14 ~ THE RUNAWAY

*M*ichel mindlessly ties his rope around his waist. He leans his head back and looks up at the clouds. Clouds which had been so friendly this morning. Clouds which had been so welcomed then.

Rain. Rain for the dying desert. Rain for the thirsty mountains. Gentle rain arranged for by a gentle God.

Bells are rung, signaling the sailors to begin the casting-off routine. Uncoil the ropes from the pilings. Weigh anchor. Unfurl the sails. Sailors rush around the deck doing their jobs.

Michel pays little attention as the ship makes its way out into the main waterway. His mind has already transcended all the libraries and ancient tablets, deserts and mountains, wells and caves, monks and artificial gods.

He closes his eyes and sees a world more real, more important, more ethereal than a world turned upside down by a silly star that had appeared at the wrong time, teased chance observers, then gone back to its old nothingness.

Oh, Jehovah, help me. He puts his face in his hands. *Help me guide the lost to the protection of your Eden.* He lifts his head to stare into the angry sky. *They are lost and do not know it because they do not know you.*

Thunder explodes behind him. Lightening crashes into the churning waves just ahead. Michel struggles to not notice what is challenging his plans. Impudent thunder again. Invasive lightening again.

The ship rolls from side to side as the captain tries to head his vessel directly into the storm. Before Michel knows it, he has been tossed to the railing of the ship. He grabs it and hangs on. The gale whips around and forces the ship over onto its other side. Michel's body follows unwillingly.

He remembers his rope. As the ship lists again to the opposite side, he lunges at the mast, hangs on to it with one hand, and ties the other end of his rope to it the best he can.

He struggles to stay near the mast. He clings to it as the storm collides with itself around him. His two worlds mesh together, and he struggles to understand. What is he clinging to? The mast or the storm?

The water. Friend to take him where he must go, or foe to force him away? Carrier or destroyer of utopia?

Still the storm. Still the water and wind, lightning and thundering. Rolling. Crashing. Threatening Promising.

The mast! Falling. Down and down. Closer. Michel leans back and ducks. He falls. He slides across the deck. The rope is not attached. Was it ever really attached?

Torrents.

Pounding. Thrashing. Pummeling.

Sliding. Out of control. Rushing to nowhere.

Now flying. Now dropping. Now sinking.

Water. Again the enemy. Deceptive water disguised as a flower giver, now a life taker.

Down. Down. Down.

Breath. Out of breath.

Breathe. Don't breathe.

Fight. Don't fight.

Kick at the water. Struggle. Live.

Live like Eden must live. Live like the dream must live.

Black.

Fight for light and life

More crashing. More banging.

No light. Bad light. Good light.

Then.

Nothing.

No sound.
Rumble gone.
Crashing gone.
Tall waves gone.
Alone in the night.
Alone in the waters of the Parthian Gulf.
All alone.
Live.
Live for Eden.
Live for Meira.
Live for what once was and should be again.
A star.
A single star.
Peeking out from behind an angry cloud.
More and more, the anger stirs and rushes away.
More and more, the star winks and sings and laughs.
Michel remembers.

He looks around the waters surrounding him for something to let him know where he is. And where shelter is.

Shelter? Too late for shelter. Not too late.
Kick. Reach. Kick. Reach.
Call out. "Hello! Hello! Can anyone hear me?"
Again.
And again.
"Hello! Hello! I'm here. In the water. I'm out here. Hello."
Swallowing water. Gagging. Choking. Sputtering.
"Hello! Anyone? Hello! I'm here. I'm here."
God, do you hear me? God, are you here?
"Anyone?"
The star. Did you send the star to me? The star just now? The star to give me hope?
"Hello!" It is not Michel's voice.
"Hello?"

He sees a pin of light. It is above him. "Hello," he shouts again.

"Hello?" the voice echoes.

The pin of light grows. Like the star had that night.

"Hello. We hear you. Call to us again."

"Hello!" Michel shouts as loud as his voice will allow. "I'm down here."

The light descends lower and lower.

No. Don't go. Don't leave me alone out here. Stay with me, light. Stay with me.

The light moves toward him. Closer. Closer.

"Hello!" Michel says, waving in the darkness, but not knowing at what.

"Call again. We're almost there. Call again."

"Here I am," Michel responds. "I'm over here. Keep coming. Keeping coming. I'm over here!"

Arms so tired. Legs so tired.

Hold out a little longer. Cannot. Cannot do it. No more energy. No more fight. No more life. Give up and die.

Nothing.

Blackness.

Forever the blackness of night.

"Sir, do you hear me?"

It is the captain's voice. Michel opens his eyes and looks at a sea of yellow torchlight.

"Sir, are you okay? You nearly drowned there, you know."

Michel tries to take in air, but his throat stings. Breathe anyway, Michel. Breathe anyway.

"You did what you were told and tied that rope around your waist. That's what saved you."

Michel looks up into the captain's eyes, not understanding.

Am I still in the water? Am I seeing a vision? Am I dead?

"Your rope got wrapped around one of our oars when we were out in the boat looking for you. It's as though the rope had a life of its own."

Michel realizes he is now safely back on board the ship.

"Here, take this bite of bread," a second man says. "You need something to take away that sting of the saltwater."

Michel takes the bread, but cannot chew it. It hangs up in his throat. He turns his head and spits it out.

"Someone fletch me some honey," the second man says to men beyond the yellow light.

Michel hears thunder. He flinches. It is just the footsteps on wooden planks. Footsteps of someone wanting to help.

"Would you like to try to sit up?" the second man asks. He scoots around behind Michel and pulls at his shoulders. The first man takes hold of Michel's arms to help him sit up the rest of the way.

"Are you angels?" Michel finally says in almost a whisper.

Laughter.

"Ha, ha. You're back with us," the captain says. "What a storm it was. But I've seen worse."

"Worse?" Michel echoes.

"Well, maybe not worse for you. Come. Sit up on this stool. The honey has arrived. Swallowing all that seawater is not pleasant."

The second man lifts a spoon of honey to Michel's lips. He takes it, then begins to slide down to the deck again.

"Grab him, someone!" It's the captain again. "Are we almost to shore? Cannot stay afloat much longer."

One of the sailors stops weakened Michel's slide just as he reaches the guard rail.

"Hang on, sir. We'll be getting you off the ship soon."

"Are we there?" Michel asks with his still-scratchy voice.

"Almost."

"Thank God for that. Now I can go back to draining the marshes."

"What marshes? It's all mountains and desert."

"My Eden. I have to restore my Eden."

"What Eden? What marsh? What are you talking about?"

"Haven't we arrived?" Michel asks.

"Well, we've almost arrived, but we didn't go anywhere. We're back where we started. The storm blew us in circles, and we're back at Hingol."

"Huh? No. No." Michel frees himself of the sailor and tries to stand.

"You're still too weak. I'll help you ashore. We're almost there."

"No. I don't want to go ashore," Michel says with his salt-injured voice. "I need Eden. I need to get to Eden."

The ship jerks, the timbers creak, the hull scrapes. Sailors jump overboard and grab a fist-size rope. They are joined by others onshore.

"Pull."

"Pull."

"Pull."

Michel gets on his knees, then grabs hold of the guard rail. For the first time, he sees the broken masts all askance on the deck. He sees the useless sails wet and trampled on. He sees sections of guard rail and the bridge torn away.

"Pull."

"Pull."

Then the final thud.

"Sir, come over here and climb into this basket. We'll have you on the beach shortly."

Michel looks up at the sailor and obeys.

Swinging. The basket swinging in nothingness. Like Michel's dream. Like that interrupting star.

Now onshore, he climbs out and sits in the sand.

"Sir, the dock where we started is a little way back up the shore," the captain says. "I have sent for some wagons to take the wounded passengers back in case they have friends or relatives there."

Michel says nothing. He follows instructions when told what to do. That is all. He cannot think. He cannot allow himself to think. He sits in the sand and looks around him at the chaos. Men running in all directions. The wounded moaning. The ship crippled and clinging to life.

Chaos.

Like his life. His marriage. His Eden.

He does not know how much time has passed, nor has he cared when another stranger approaches him.

"Sir, we have a wagon here now. Would you like to go back to the dock where the other ship are?"

"No," Michel mutters. "I don't want to go there. I don't want to go anywhere. Except to my Eden."

"Perhaps we can find a wagon going to Eden. Is it far?"

"A wagon cannot take me there. Nothing can take me there. Eden is under water."

"Did the storm get it too?"

"Yes, I guess you could call it that. Now leave me alone. I want to lie back and die."

The stranger shrugs and walks away.

Michel lies in the sand. He looks up at the sky and wishes he hadn't. The sun. So bright. Too bright. He cannot see it. Too bright to see—like God. Like Eden. Like his dream that no human has a right to.

Shouting.

Oxen lowing.

Men scrambling.

Voices out on the water.

"Okay, men. Attach the ropes from the ship to those oxen. Do the same to the boats out in the waterway. We've got to get this ship up to the docks so it can be repaired."

"Sir, you're going to have to move. You're in the way. Can I help you up to those rocks? You can lean on one of them."

Michel stands, leans on the stranger, and lets him take him to the rocks.

Now sitting. Now watching. What was strong and beautiful is now broken. Now dreaming.

He is with the other magi again. They are lying flat on the marble floor, and King Phraattes is beating them. Beating. Beating. Beating. Oh, how he hurts. Then the shouting. "Michel. Why did you do it? Michel. Michel."

He opens his eyes and sees Kumar, Dushatra, and old Yasib kneeling before him in the sand.

"You know you cannot go back," Yasib says. "None of us can until we find the meaning of the star. You know that, Michel. Why did you do it?"

"That star," Michel groans. "It ruined everything."

"Still, we must obey our king if we're ever going to be able to go home again."

Michel looks around. "Where are the others?"

"They're waiting for us up at the docks. Are you okay?"

"I almost drowned."

"Yes, when we were asking around for you, everyone was calling you the drowned man," Dushatra says. "Do you think you can handle going on a ship again?"

Michel squints at Yasib. "Why?"

"Remember our plans," Dushatra explains. "We did not find the meaning of the star among the ancient writings, the Buddhists or Hindus. So now we go to the great sacred library in Egypt to search among the sacred writings of their gods. Don't you remember?"

Michel stares at his friend.

"Come, friend," Kumar says, helping Michel up. "Our rented wagon is right here."

Michel lies down in the back of the wagon and closes his eyes. But he does not dream. He cannot dream. Not any more.

"So you found him," Syrian Borseen says. "Let's get on board. The captain is waiting for us."

"How did you buy my ticket?" Michel asks.

"We sold your camel along with ours," Kumar says. "Here is what you had left over plus a little more that we chipped in as a welcome-back-to-the-living gift."

"Thank you, friends," Michel says. "I think."

The eight magi walk up the gangplank and board their ship bound for Egypt.

They take their tents and baskets of supplies off their backs and set them together for one of them to guard. They hear bells, the scrape of chains raising the anchor, heavy footsteps on the deck, and orders from the bridge.

"Are you all right, Michel?" Katazuli asks once they are

out in the open Indus Sea.

"Yeah," Michel says with his scratchy voice.

"Here is some sage tea for that injured throat. I've mixed in some ginger to help you get your energy back."

Michel reaches up and takes the small cup. "Thank you, friend. We are lucky to have you."

"No, we are the ones who are lucky to have you."

"Why? They call me a dreamer and, well, I guess they laugh at my dream."

"Let them laugh. I'm a dreamer too. I want to restore the capital of my people—the Hittites—up in Anatolia. I was raised near the ruins. My father educated me with ancient writings he dug up from there and rescued."

Katazuli sits next to Michel. "We dreamers will stick together," he says.

The ship continues heading west on the Indus Sea. One day. Two days. Three. Four.

"The captain says we should arrive in four more days," Yasib says.

"Ah, it will be so good to be home again," Hophni says, stretching his arms heavenward.

"Home!" he shouts at the seagulls following the ship and its garbage.

The eight are leaning against the bridge, eating whatever they had brought with them.

"Whatever happened to Tus and Givv?" Michel asks, having mostly recovered from his near-drowning four days earlier.

"When you took their transportation with you..."

"Oh, that's right. They were riding my camel."

"Well, when you took your camel, they decided to return home. Some pilgrims were there from Turbot, and they doubled up on a ride to get them back out of the mountains and up the desert."

The next morning Demetrius is the first to wake up. He goes above board and looks out at the sea. He rushes back to his friends. "You should see the ocean. It is so beautiful. It is like glass," he calls down the hatch to the others. "I've never seen anything like it before. I think I'll write an ode to it."

"What are you talking about?" Michel says, standing and bumping his head on a rafter.

"Come, look for yourself."

Michel climbs up the ladder, followed by some of the others.

"See, fellows, isn't it beautiful?"

"Oh, no," Yasib says. "Oh, no."

15 ~ BECALMED

"What's wrong, Yasib? It's beautiful," Demetrius responds.

"It's beautiful, like a poisoned apple."

"Huh?"

"We have been becalmed."

"What's that?" Kumar asks, still staring at the glassy sea. "Oh, I think I know."

"Look up at the sails," Yasib tells Demetrius. "What are they doing?"

"Well, nothing. They're limp."

"Without wind, we are going nowhere," Dushatra says, having joined them. "We are stuck out in the middle of the sea and cannot go in any direction. There is absolutely no wind."

"When will I get home?" Hophni asks, though he knows there is no answer. "Maybe if I pray to the gods."

"We'd better call out to all the gods we know," Syrian Borseen says.

They sit in their usual spot below the bridge. They watch sailors wander around the deck with nothing to do but pick fights with one another.

"Okay, men," the captain announces. "Now is the time to make repairs, repaint, polish, mend, and all the other little things we usually let go. Get to work."

"How long is this going to last?" Michel asks.

"A day. Two. Maybe a week," Yasib replies.

One of the ship's officers approaches them.

"Gentlemen, you are wanted in the captain's cabin. Follow me."

"I wonder if we're going to be blamed for the becalming and thrown overboard," Katazuli whispers as they stand.

"That's what they did to Jonah, except their problem was a storm," Michel mutters back.

"Is that what happened to you last week?" Kumar says with a chuckle.

"This could be serious," Borseen says.

"Quiet!" the officer orders.

They climb to the bridge, then step through a hatch behind it. When they arrive, they line up at attention. The officer moves over next to the captain.

The captain is wearing a white kilt, sleeveless short white tunic tucked inside his kilt, and a gold band around his head. He puts his hands behind his back and walks from one end of the eight-man line to the other.

"Hmmm. You are a strange lot. All dressed different. Don't know what you're up to. That's about to change. Lieutenant Medi here is going to help me out."

Medi, dressed in a similar white kilt but with a bare chest, holds up a dagger and sneers.

The captain walks to the end of the magi line.

"Who are you?"

"I am Yasib. I am Xiongnu Mongol and sixty-five years old. I began serving as a magus for King Orodes of Parthia, and continued on when his son, Phraattes, became king."

"I see," the captain responds. "And were you in on that plot to kill ole Orodes?"

"No, sir. It did not make any difference to me who ruled."

The captain smiles. "Safe answer, old man. Safe answer. Does that knot of hair at the top of your head ever come undone and fall into your eyes?"

"When I was young and had thick hair, it did on occasion."

The captain moves to the next man.

"Now you must be Indus by nationality. I recognize that cloth wrapped around both legs and attached at your waist. Seems like it would be inconvenient whenever you have to, well, take it down temporarily," he says.

"I am Kumar, fifty years old, and yes, I was born in Hingol, not far from where we boarded your ship."

"And what is your occupation?"

"I am a magus, sir, for King Phraattes."

"I see you like to curry his favor by wearing the curled Parthian beard. Do you ever dye it blue? You Indus men are strange when it comes to your beard."

"When I was a young man, I did dye my beard. But I outgrew the desire."

The captain moves on to the next man.

"Are you a kinsman to this Kumar? You dress a lot like him. And your beard is the same."

"I am Dushatra, forty years old, and I was born in Kandahar on the other side of Indio-Parthia. So, no, we are not kinsmen, but we do both like to please our king."

"So, you are a magus, also?"

"Yes, sir."

"And who is this young man on the other side of you? He looks hardly old enough to shave."

"I am Borseen of Damascus and twenty-eight years old. True, I am the youngest, but I have a brilliant mind far in advance of any of my countrymen."

"So I suppose when King Phraattes heard about you, he grabbed you up to be one of his wise men also."

"Yes, sir. But I am not only superior with my mind. I am also a superior swordsman. My father was the greatest sword maker of his time. He taught me well before his unfortunate death in battle. I intend to lead an army someday."

The captain grins. "You just may do that someday, young man. And who is this interesting-looking man next to you? I must say that long kilt of yours doesn't show dirt like my white one always does."

"No, sir," Katazuli replies. "My kilts are of dark colors

and have more cloth in them. Otherwise, they are similar to Egyptian kilts as you call them. I am Katazuli, fifty years old, and a Hittite, from the city of Hattus, at one time the great capital city of my people."

"Where did you get that red hair?"

"My people intermarried with the Goths when they came down from the north country."

"So, what is your occupation? Oh, that's right. You are one of King Phraattes' magus."

"Yes, but I am also a physician."

"In that case, I want to talk to you in private about something. And next to you?"

"I am Demetrius, thirty-eight years old, and a Roman citizen by birth. I was schooled in all important languages and in the art of oration."

"Do you know Egyptian?"

"I recently learned it, sir."

"Next? I think you are a true Parthian. You wear the billowy pantaloons and sleeveless wrap-around vest. And that turban. I like your turban. But where is your curly beard? Don't you want extra favor of your king?"

"I am Michel, born thirty-five years ago in Uruk, proud city of the former Babylonian Empire and now part of the great Parthian Empire. But I am not a true Parthian by birth."

"What are you then?"

"I am Jewish. My ancestors were taken captive to Babylon six hundred years ago to help populate his cities, and as punishment for defying him."

"Yes, I have heard you Jews are a stubborn lot."

"My ancestor was Daniel, second only to the king during the reigns of Nebuchadnezzar, Darius, and Cyrus. When Cyrus allowed the Jews to return to Israel and build it up again, I and many others chose to stay where we were born."

"And finally, we come to my kinsman. How are you, young man?"

"I am fine, captain, sir. I am Hophni, born in the great

educational hub of Egypt, Edfu, thirty years ago, and I have been trained as a scribe. My father was Egyptian, and my mother is Kushite."

"I see. And does your mother live in Egypt or Ethiopia? That is what they call Kush now, isn't it?"

"It seems to go by many names, sir. Yes, she lives in Meroe of Ethiopia and serves the Candace as a lady in waiting."

"Lucky man, Hophni. I heard your Queen Amanish Aketo is a warrior queen."

"Yes, she is," Hophni says, adding with a wink, "and the Romans had better not try to break their treaty again."

"And loves her gold mines."

"That she does, sir."

The captain steps back.

"Well, now that I know all about you and how dangerous you could be to Egypt the Great, I need to know what to do with you.

"I have received reports that you are speaking a mysterious language among each other that no one recognizes. Could it be a language you have come up with to spy on Egypt?"

"Sir," Michel says, stepping forward.

"That is the language of our earliest ancestors. It is the language spoken four thousand years ago. We know the language so we can read ancient records."

"Why would you want to read ancient records?"

"Sir," Yasib says, also stepping forward. "We, as magi, need to be able to refer to the wisdom of ages long ago during the time of our ancestors."

"Why?"

"Sometimes, we face dangers that we do not understand and which our king demands to know how to handle."

"Name one."

Dushatra steps forward. "A star. Two months ago a star appeared in the western sky. It was very bright with a tail on it that reached to the earth. It stayed a while, then disappeared."

"Are you sure someone didn't just imagine seeing it?"

"I saw it myself," Dushatra says. "So did our King Phraattes. He demanded to know the meaning of the star."

"All we know thus far," Kumar continues, "is that it means a god was born. But its sudden disappearance is what is perplexing us and the king. The king needs to know if his kingdom is in danger from this disappearing god."

The captain puts a hand up to his clean-shaven chin. "I see. So, you researched the most ancient writings of mankind."

"Yes, sir," Kumar continues. "We did not find the answer there, so we have been to the desert and mountains of Makran. Now we are going to Edfu and Alexandria in your country in hopes of finding the meaning of the star."

The captain turns to his officer. "A single star can turn an entire kingdom upside down? Maybe Egypt should invade Parthia now while it is busy being afraid of a star."

He laughs. The officer laughs, though his eyes reflect that he sees no reason for laughter.

Silence.

The captain stares at the eight men before him. He turns his back to them, looks out a window with a view of the hawk figurehead.

He walks over to his berth and picks up a dagger. He takes it back to the line of magi and plays with it.

The men wait. Wondering if their quest for the star will only lead them to their death.

"What do you think?" the captain asks his officer.

"About what, sir?"

"These men who speak that strange spy language. Were they telling the truth?"

Yasib steps forward. "Sir, take me as your prisoner. Execute me if you think that will be enough to appease whichever god is causing the cessation of all wind."

"No, sir," Michel says, stepping forward. "Take me."

"No, sir," Kumar and Dushatra say, stepping forward in unison.

With that, all eight step forward.

"Take us all," Katazuli says. "We shall die together."

The captain stares a while longer.

"Well, my name is Horus, I was born in Aswan. And I welcome you to my table."

The officer does not smile. "Go on now and order enough food for ten of us to feast the rest of the day while the gods decide what to do with our ship," the captain tells him. "Leave."

He looks back at the eight magi, still standing at attention before him. "Come on. Do any of you sing? I love to sing. I have a lyre over in the corner. Hophni, you and I are going to have to teach them some good Egyptians songs."

The eight still stand at attention.

"Looks like I'm going to have to separate you. You sit over there, you over there, you over here, just spread out and sit. I command you."

The rest of the day is spent in song and conversation as the captain tries to get the sweltering heat and his becalmed ship temporarily off his mind.

The following day the situation is the same. And the day after. The magi are given permission to teach whatever language they want to the sailors, and the sailors are given permission to let the magi throw spears over the side and see what kind of fish they can snag.

Five days after it had left them stranded, a gentle breeze comes up, surges into a full wind, and they proceed on from there to the Red Sea.

"Friends," Hophni says as they enter the sea between the desert nomads of the Arabian peninsula and Egypt, "I would like to make a special request."

"What are you up to, Hophni?" Demetrius says.

"We are going to have to pass Kush on our way to Egypt. I would like to suggest that we stop in Kush, examine the records of our gods and the gods of other tribes south of us in the jungles of the Moors and Nubians."

"He has a point there," Dushatra responds. "Didn't he say his mother was a lady in waiting for the Candace? She would make their ancient writings available to us. Perhaps we will find the meaning of the star there, then be able to go home."

"Why not?" Borseen says.

"I'm in favor of it," Michel says.

A day later, the ship docks at Adulus. It is a small port city but serves the kingdoms of the interior sufficiently.

"The first thing we are going to need," Hophni says after they leave the docks, "is transportation. We cannot just walk in. Well, we could, but there are snakes and wild rhinos and lions and other creatures we do not want to face in our finiteness."

"What did you have in mind?" Michel asks.

"I would like to suggest either elephants or camels. We are on the edge of forests to our south and desert to our north."

"As much as I would like to try riding an elephant and watch people gawk at us up in Alexandria, I suppose we should settle for camels," Demetrius says.

"If you are all agreed, I know a camel trader just on the other side of the city."

Hophni leads the way, and the others stand aside while he negotiates with the trader. After a while, he returns to his friends.

"Bad news."

"What? What's wrong?"

"He does not have eight camels. With all the tents and supplies we have to carry with us, we each need our own camel."

"Now what?"

"He has four elephants."

"What?" Borseen declares.

"Never," Demetrius says.

"Now wait a minute," Yasib says. "I rode an elephant in my youth up in Xiongnu Mongolia."

"Dushatra and I have ridden elephants many times in Indus."

"Well, that makes four of us who are experienced. You

inexperienced ones can ride behind us." He turns to the trader. "We will take the four elephants." He turns to the other magi. "Okay, find a riding partner, split the cost, and pay the man."

The trader looks at the strange group of travelers, grins, and brings out four elephants one at a time.

"First, I need to explain to you novices how it is done in case your experienced partner is incapacitated and you need to take over. Also, you need to know when and how to approach an elephant, and when and how not to. Everyone, take the reins of your elephant and come over to this field with me."

The seven men follow Hophni, some with dread, some with anticipation, all with curiosity.

"First of all, if he is flapping his ears and swaying his trunk and tail, he is happy. However, if his whole body is swaying, he is upset; do not get close to him then. Remember, he is much bigger than you.

"Now to make the elephant kneel, reach up and push down with your fist behind one of his ears. Then step on his bent knee, hang on to his ear, and swing your other leg over. Do it quickly because he may not kneel for you very long.

"You must ride on the elephant's neck. It is stronger than his back. Put your supplies on his back; they don't weigh as much as you do.

"You tell him what to do with your feet behind his ears. To tell him to walk forward, press your toes behind his ears. To turn right or left, press your toes behind his right or left ear. That's all you need to know to start."

"Uh, how far is it to—what city did you say—Meroe?"

"These elephants will walk about as fast as a camel does. But they don't hold up as long as camels do. So, we could make it there in two days with camels, but four days with the elephants.

"They eat a lot of food. I mean a lot of it," Hophni continues to explain. "So, the rest of the time, they will be eating. And they love to bathe, so you can spoil them when we stop and wash them down. If you can get them to kneel in the river, you can splash the water up on them with your hands. You'll have a friend for life.

"So, now are you men ready?"

Michel climbs on behind Yasib. Borseen climbs on behind Kumar. Katazuli limbs on behind Dushatra. Demetrius climbs on behind Hophni.

The road to the interior is well worn and low-hanging branches cut off. Sometimes they travel through the bush, sometimes through meadows.

The elephants rock and sway as they walk and the men get used to the rhythm.

"Wait," Hophni calls out, raising his hand. "There are men on camels approaching us. They're in a hurry. Signal for your animals to move over to the right as far as they can."

When the camels draw near, Hophni sees they are royal camels and holds out his hand for one of them to stop.

"What's wrong?" he yells as they slow down to pass him.

"There was an assassination attempt on Candace."

16 ~ WARRIOR QUEEN

"Oh, no. My mother is in danger," Hophni says, turning to the other magi behind him. "We cannot hurry these elephants, and there is nowhere along here for me to get a camel or horse. Pray to your gods for my mother and the Candace," he shouts. "Pray to your gods."

"You are very concerned about your mother," Michel tells Hophni when they stop for the afternoon heat and ensuing night.

"When my mother was alive, I worried about her all the time," Michel continues. "She was sickly. Finally died of typhoid. My father was gone all the time, so if anything got done, I had to do it. I knew no one else would. I guess I feel that way about a lot of things still."

"You were close to your mother?" Hophni asks.

"Yes. So I understand your worry. I keep praying for your mother to the one true God, Jehovah. What is her name?"

"Saba."

"And your queen?"

"Candace Amanish Aketo. You have become a good friend, Michel."

Late on the third day, they see ahead of them a long row of pyramids.

"We will stop here and go on to the palace in the morning when we are fresh," Hophni says.

"I heard the Egyptians have pyramids but did not

know the Ethiopians did," Michel says.

"Yes, our queen is very advanced. She has overseen the building of many of them."

"What is that over there?"

"It is a temple to the sun god, Amun Ra. But we will be passing them to get to the palace as soon as possible. Stay on the watch for people who look suspicious," he tells everyone.

"We're strangers here," Yasib says. "We wouldn't know what is suspicious and what is not."

The next morning, the magi draw near to a large structure with a wall around it and many guards.

"Sir, my colleagues and I wish entrance into the palace," Hophni says.

"Not with those elephants."

"Where is your trader in camels and elephants?"

Hophni is given directions to a corral south of the palace.

"I paid the trader in Adulus for one week. He said you are his partner. Here is my proof of our payment."

The trader looks over the clay tablet and hands five bronze coins to each of them since they did not keep their elephants a week.

With that, the magi put their supplies on their backs and walk to the palace.

"Once again, we request entry," Hophni tells the guards.

"Not with those packs. You could be slipping in a dagger. You will be required to put them in this room in the wall. You may have them back when you leave—that is, if I let you in. Now, who are you?"

"I am Hophni, son of Saba, lady in waiting to Her Majesty Candace Amanish Aketo."

"Wait here."

The magi wait standing up so they do not soil their fresh clothes. Finally, they hear the wide gate into the palace open.

"Son," the woman says, rushing toward Hophni, her

arms opened. Hophni easily picks up his mother and swings her around.

Saba is petite with black hair plaited into six braids and caught together in the back with a single gold ring. She wears a green wrap that goes to her knees and is tucked together under her arms. She wears a necklace of green, white, and red beads in several strands close to her neck. She is barefoot but wears similar beads around her ankles.

Hophni sets her down, and they hold each other at arm's length.

"You have been eating well," she laughs.

"But, Mother, should you be out here in the open like this? The assassins may go after you to get to the Candace."

"Poo, poo. We're in no more danger than you."

"But those palace guards that passed us on the road?"

"They get excited like that. The run will do them good." Saba says. She turns to the guards. "This is my son, who is a magus for the great King Phraattes of the Parthian kingdom. These are his friends. You must let them in."

"Mother, these are not just my friends. We are all magi and are on a mission for the king."

"Did you hear that?" she says to the guards. "Unless you want the wrath of our Candace on you, you will let them in immediately."

"Yes, ma'am. But we will be watching them."

The magi leave their supplies in the guard room and enter the palace grounds. As they do, an arrow flies over Michel's head. In quick succession, arrows fly over the heads of the other magi. All but Hophni's.

They run for cover and try to hide behind gold-covered columns, decorated with silver and opal.

"Hah! You cowards!"

It is a woman's voice and coming from a balcony overlooking the courtyard.

Hophni calls out to his friends. "It's the queen. Bow. Bow."

Immediately Hophni drops to the alabaster-tiled floor, and the others come out from hiding and bow completely prostrate also.

"My lady, my Candace," Saba call up to the woman on the balcony. "My son is here on behalf of Phraattes, great king of Parthia. Hophni is one of the king's magus. His companions are magi also. Their king considered your greatness and sent eight of his best to approach your throne."

The woman on the balcony grunts and disappears.

"She has gone to her throne room," Saba tells the others. "She is waiting for you there."

"Is she planning to execute us when we arrive?" Demetrius asks.

"No, no. Oh, the arrows? She just wanted to remind you of who is in charge."

"No wonder they call her the warrior queen," Dushatra says.

The men follow Saba up a grand staircase to the second floor. The steps are embellished with a lion on each side. Each lion is carved from a giant elephant tusk.

When they arrive at the throne room, Saba bows completely prostrate, and the magi follow her example.

"You may rise," the queen finally says after making them wait longer than monarchs normally make their subjects wait.

Saba calls out. "May I approach, Your Majesty?"

"Yes, yes," the deep voice responds.

"As I said, these are King Phraattes' ambassadors."

"Well, come closer, so I don't have to yell at you," the queen calls out to the magi. They eye the bent bow propped up on one side of her gold-and-copper throne, and spear on the other side.

The Candace is tall and ample. Her exquisite black skin is highlighted by her wide headband of gold with two emerald-eyed cobras of deified monarchy rising up above her forehead.

Her hair is long and greased so that it comes out from her head like wings of eagles.

Her face is square, her lips and cheeks full. Her eyes

are slanted slightly, giving her the look of a goddess, though she is blind in one eye. Everyone assumes it was earned in battle, but no one speaks of it.

She holds out an ivory, garnet-tipped scepter, which is matched by her ivory, gold, and garnet necklace and heavy armbands. She wears a long wraparound of many colors and thongs of reed with straps embellished with pearls.

"Your Majesty," Hophni says, clasping his hands in front of him in humility. "We bring greetings to you from His Majesty, Phraattes, King of Parthia, and defier of Rome."

The queen chuckles. "Yes, I have heard about that. He doesn't let those Roman rats run all over his kingdom. Me neither."

"Yes, Your Majesty. We have heard about your prowess and keen military mind in making Rome back down from taking over our glorious kingdom. It only makes me proud to be one of your loyal subjects."

"Okay. Okay. Enough of flattering me. Now, what do you want?"

"From you, oh my Candace, we want nothing. Just being in your presence gives us joy."

"Well, in that case, you have enjoyed my presence. Now I have other things to do. Goodbye."

The Candace begins to rise.

"Uh, Your Majesty."

"Well, say it."

"Your sacred writings of the gods."

"What about them?"

"Our mission is to search the world to find the meaning of a star that appeared two months ago, lasted but a few moments then disappeared. The king believes it means a god was born. He does not know if the god died immediately or went somewhere else to plan the downfall of the Parthian Kingdom."

The Candace leans back in her throne, folds her arms, and raises one hand for her chin to lean on. She peers at Hophni with her one good eye.

"Three months ago, you say?"

"Yes, Your Majesty."

"I do believe I saw that very same star. Hmmm. I wonder if it had anything to do with my kingdom and not his."

"That could be the case," Hophni says.

The Candace stands and speaks to the guard standing behind her throne, though does not look at him. "Escort these gentlemen to our archives." Looking back at Hophni, she adds, "Do I have your vow that you will let me know what your findings are?"

"You have our word, Your Majesty. And thank you."

The magi bow prostrate to the floor, and Hophni's mother follows the queen out of the throne room.

When they hear the door close, they raise their heads far enough they know it is safe. They stand and see the guard in front of the throne.

"The sacred writings are not here."

"Not here?" Hophni echoes.

"They are down at Naqa. Meet me in front of the palace tomorrow at dawn. I will have camels for you. We will arrive at Naqa by tomorrow night."

The magi return to the public courtyard of the palace and find seats. Hophni sees a maid and requests that she notify his mother where they are.

They spend a happy evening in a large room for overnight guests. Saba is allowed in the room with all men and enjoys telling stories about her son when he was young.

The following morning, they are met by a young man who identifies himself as Nata Kamani, the crown prince.

"I have been wanting to go down there," he tells the magi. "I will be crowned king in four or five years. Perhaps I will build a temple to myself down there."

They head south to Naqa. It comes into sight just as the sun turns red. They are not allowed to sleep in any of the temples. However, there is an open-air kiosk near the temple to Apedemak.

At dawn, they go to the temple to Apedemak. The prince is already there, worshiping. They remain quiet until he is through.

"This lion-headed god is our god of war," he tells them, turning toward the exit. "My mother has led us to victory numerous times against marauding nomads from across the Red Sea as well as invading tribes from the south. But, of course, her greatest achievement has been keeping Rome away from our borders. Rome respects Ethiopia. Well, I must be on my way back to the palace."

The magi walk around the sacred ground to check out who the various temples are dedicated to.

"Okay," Hophni finally says. "Let's divide up. Michel, you take the temples to Apedemak and Serapis. Yasib, you take the temples to Mut and Khonsu. Kumar, you take the temples to the Kushite Pharaohs.

"Dushatra, you take the temples to Shu and Tefnut. Borseen, the temples to Geh and Nut. Katazuli, you take Osiris and Seth. Demetrius, you and I will take the temple to Amun Ra.

"If any of you finds reference to a star, come tell the rest of us."

"You are going to do what?" the high priest shouts before the group of intruders breaks up. "Never!"

"We have permission of both the crown prince and the Candace," Hophni says. "If you do not comply, you will face stern consequences."

The two men stare at each other.

"You will pay for this," the high priest shouts, shaking his fist at Hophni.

The rest of the day and two more days are spent going through every sacred writing of every god in the complex, looking for any references to a star.

With each request, the priests of each temple grow angrier.

On the third day, Michel makes his report. "Nutt is goddess of the sky and is associated with many stars. Hophni, I believe we should investigate Nutt further."

"Anyone else find references to a special star?" he asks. No one responds. "Then, we will investigate the goddess Nutt further."

"No! You have desecrated our temples," the high priest says, intercepting them.

"You must not be remembering the directive your queen gave you," Hophni warns.

"She did not give you permission to do this."

Borseen steps forward. He pulls out his dagger. "You will cooperate, or else."

The high priest backs away, gritting his teeth.

The magi sort through every writing they can find. Some of the writings are on clay tablets. Some on papyrus and others on parchment. They divide them up.

The priest to Nutt sometimes walks around behind them, reading over their shoulders. The longer they look, the angrier he grows.

"You are not cleansing yourselves," the priest declares periodically to each magus. "Stop. Stop this," the priest shouts at them, following one magi and then the other.

Dushatra is the first to speak up. "This says Nutt is not a single star. Actually, she is not any star. She wears the stars. She hovers over the earth at night covered with stars."

"Anything else?" Hophni asks.

"She was never born as a star," Yasib begins. "She..."

"Look!" Michel says, pointing toward the front entrance.

The magi rise at their tables and stare as all the priests of the sacred compound march toward them, sacred spears in their hands.

"You will not depose me," the priest of Nutt shouts. "You will not announce another star goddess and dethrone the majestic Nutt."

"That is not our intention. It never was," Hophni says.

"We are through with our research," Michel says, his stomach turning inside out.

Demetrius steps forward, his arms stretched upward.

"Oh, stars of heaven," he sings. "Behold your goddess. She pines for you. She yearns for you. She is your protectress, your mother, your goddess."

"Stop that!" the high priest shouts. "Stop singing. She's not your goddess. She is ours. You defile her even with your song."

"Your holiness," one of the other priests says. "Let them go."

"Yes. The sooner they go, the sooner we can get back to normal."

"No! Never!"

"Your holiness, they have not harmed anything."

"They harmed our gods. They harmed their good name."

"No, they didn't."

"They're statues. They looked upon them as though they deserved to. They don't. They never will."

"What can we do to make it up to you?" Michel asks.

"Yes, anything," Kumar says.

"No! They must be punished. They are our enemies. Tie them to the stakes," the high priest demands.

"But the Candace," one of the other priests says.

"She is only in power because we allow her to be. Now obey me, or you will be there with them."

"Yes, your holiness."

The high priest steps aside while the other priests touch the point of their spear to one of the magus. One by one, they force them out to the center of the compound around which the temples are built.

Michel is tied to the first post. Then Yasib. Then Dushatra. Then Kumar and Hophni and Katazuli and Demetrius and Borseen.

Michel looks up into the heavens. "God! Jehovah God! Forgive me. I have let you down!"

"Be quiet," Dushatra mutters. "Die like a man."

Now for the wood. Wood from the forests nearby. Dry wood. Wood that burns hot and strong and well.

"Forgive me, Jehovah God," Michel resumes. "I left the most important thing in the world—your Eden—to go chasing after that star. Forgive me. Forgive me…"

One by one, the wood is piled at the base of each stake.

Michel: The Fourth Wise Man

"Now, the torches. Light the torches."

17 ~ DOOMED

Each priest goes to his temple to light a torch from the sacrificial fires of his Ethiopian deity. One by one, they come back out to the center of the compound where the eight blasphemers await their fiery doom.

"No! Wait! I have money," Demetrius calls out.

"We have gold mines in our country. We don't need your money."

One by one, the wood is set fire at the feet of each of the magi.

"Someone! Anyone!" Borseen shouts. "Anyone out there? Hiders in the forest? Help! Help us! We didn't do anything wrong. We love all the gods."

"Peace," the high priest pronounces. "Or I will have your tongue cut out."

The others remain quiet, trying to maintain their dignity even amidst their terrible torture.

"Mighty Jehovah," Michel prays in a whisper, "I tried. I tried to bring your Eden back to glory so you could walk with us again." Tears of remorse and repentance come to his eyes.

The flame grows and draws closer to his feet.

"If only that star hadn't interrupted everything…"

"What was that?" the high priest calls out. "That loud boom?"

The priests and condemned all look around.

The flames lap at their toes.

Michel: The Fourth Wise Man

A flash through the trees.

A gust of wind, swirling, swirling, swirling.

Another boom. Another crash.

Rain.

Invading rain that pours down on the compound as though from a great waterfall in the sky.

"No! It cannot be! Tefnut, what are you doing? Why are you overruling your daughter, Nutt? Tefnut. Do not do this? Why are you angry at us?"

The priests walk in circles looking up at the sky as their leader pronounces a prayer to the rain goddess, then run for cover.

Michel looks up into the blackened sky, his face now wet from new tears.

"Jehovah God," he whispers. "It is you. I worship you. I am so unworthy."

The next thing Michel knows, he is shouting through the noise of the downpour.

"Ha, ha! He did it! Jehovah God answered my prayer."

"Hold still," someone says, standing behind him.

"He is the Creator of us all and saved us," Michel shouts. "He is the only true God!"

"I said, be still." It is Yasib.

"How did you get loose?" Michel shouts as another thunderclap bursts overhead.

"I was on the end, and one of the priests sneaked over and cut my rope," Yasib shouts back.

Michel now joins Yasib in helping the other six break loose from their death stake.

He looks around, soaked to his bones. "Our camels. Where are they?"

Kumar shouts through the rain, "Over here. Over here."

The men rush through the mud to the corral at the far end of the sacred compound. Kumar holds the gate open for them.

Without harnesses and reins on the camels, each man orders his animal to kneel, climbs on, and directs it into the forest the way they had come. Yasib is in the front, Kumar in the rear.

The rain eases. Kumar shouts to the others. "Stop up ahead in that meadow!"

"No! We cannot stop," Borseen shouts back.

"I let all their animals out. They have no transportation."

The men slow their camels, stop, and dismount.

"Is everyone okay?" Michel asks.

"I'm going home," Demetrius says. "I did not volunteer to come to be burned to death."

"You didn't volunteer," Hittite Katazuli says, slapping his friend on the back. "You were recruited."

"Besides, after Edfu and Alexandria, we will be going to Rome next. Then you'll be home," Dushatra says.

"Not forever, but for a while, you'll be home," Syrian Borseen says, grinning.

"Well, let's get going," Hophni says. "We'll go back to the palace, report what we found about the star…"

"…and report the traitorous priests…" Demetrius adds while a distant thunder rumbles.

"Yes. Then we need to be on our way."

Late that afternoon, when rays of welcomed sun peak through the clouds, the magi arrive back at the palace.

The guards let them in, and they are immediately escorted to the throne room. They stand in the corridor until the queen arrives.

"Oh, great queen," Hophni says. "We will always be grateful that you allowed us to look through the sacred books of the leading gods of Ethiopia. We did not find a star god as such."

"I am sorry to hear that," Candace Amanish Aketo replies. "But remember your other promise."

"Yes, Your Majesty. When we do find the meaning of the star—and we are confident it will happen—we will send word to you."

"I trust my priests treated you with respect and dignity."

Michel: The Fourth Wise Man

Silence.

"You are not answering me. Is something wrong?"

"They, well, they, uh, well, our toes got singed just before the rains came."

The Candace stands. "They did what?" she roars. "Guards!" she shouts.

One of the guards standing at the door to the throne room steps forward.

"Your Majesty?"

"Get my camel ready and alert the garrison. Those priests will not live to see another sunrise."

She turns to the magi. "It is dark. But I think you need to leave now. My personal bodyguards will escort you to the Nile and put you on a boat going north into Egypt. You should be safe there."

The magi bow to the floor as the queen leaves out her private door.

Saba lingers behind and rushes to her son.

"Be careful," she says, leaning her head on his big chest.

She looks up at him. "May the gods bring you back to me soon. I will talk to the Candace. She will hire you as one of her scribes. This work as a magus is too dangerous. We will be together again."

"Yes, Mother. Oh, and I am learning about the God who sent the rain. Michel told me about him. I will tell you about him when I come back home."

They hear the hooves of galloping camels down below. Saba leads the magi out of the throne room and down to the palace outer courtyard where the Candace's bodyguards are waiting for them, their camels now saddled.

The guards deliver the magi to the river port on the Nile soon after midnight.

"I have ordered the pilot of that boat over there to leave now and not wait for other passengers in the morning," the captain of the guard tells Hophni. "Oh, and here is some money the Candace ordered that I give you. Good luck now. And may the gods be with you."

The magi take their packs off their camels and climb onto the riverboat.

It is made of strong reeds, much in the same shape as the ship they had taken there from Indo-Parthia. It is six man-lengths long and three man-lengths wide. It has a canopy in the middle that is two man-lengths square. The sails are unfurled to take advantage of the night wind and are red.

"There may be enough room for all of you to sleep under the canopy with the mosquito netting," the captain tells Hophni, whom he gathers by his white kilt is Egyptian.

"When did you change out of your Ethiopian wraparound into the white Egyptian kilt?" Michel asks.

"Just now," Hophni replies with a grin. "It always pays to blend in."

Grateful for the canopy, the magi pick a spot and lie down under it and the mosquito netting.

"Hey, get away from him," they hear.

Michel and the others open their eyes. It is still dark. They shift around to find out if enemy priests are attacking their boat.

"Move out of the way," the captain shouts at Borseen.

Borseen falls backward into the boat. Four crewmen continue beating something with their oars.

"I said, move out of the way," the captain repeats.

Borseen crawls toward the canopy, then sits up.

The crewmen continue beating something in the water.

Then it is over.

"Stand up, you fool," the captain says, hovering over Borseen. Borseen does as he is told.

"I should have let them have you," the captain barks at his passenger. What were you thinking?"

"My toes were hurting."

"Your what?"

Michel stands. "Sir, his toes really were burned. That's why the Candace's soldiers arranged for our escape. Some rebel priests tied us up to stakes and..."

"I don't care if his whole leg was burned. You do not dangle any part of your body over the side of this boat. You know we have crocodiles in the Nile. You know that!"

"Yes, sir," Borseen replies, looking down at the deck rather than into the eyes of the livid captain.

"Do you realize, because of your foolishness, the crocodiles will now come closer to other boats on the river looking for food?"

"I am sorry, sir. What can I do to make it up to you?"

"When we arrive at Edfu, you will replace the oars that were chewed up in the attack."

"Yes, sir."

"And you will take an oar right now and rotate between the crewmen who rescued you, taking their place and letting them rest. Now!"

Borseen moves toward the oarsman and takes his seat, an oar in his hand.

"The rest of you may as well go back to sleep."

"I cannot sleep now," Michel says. "It could have been any one of us."

Michel steps over to another crewman, takes his oar from him, seats himself, and begins rowing. The others follow Michel's example.

The sky turns light gray, then yellow, and finally gold. The captain makes his way back to the magi.

"Ha, ha! This is great! You fellows sure have a lot of energy in you. We should be in Edfu by tomorrow noon—a day and a half instead of the normal two days."

The magi and other oarsmen grin in celebration while not missing the cadence.

"You are welcome to ride in my boat any time you want," the captain says. "All except him," he says, glaring at Borseen.

The magi spend their day under the canopy's shade, discussing their findings at the temples in Ethiopia. That night they each grab an oar from one of the crewmen.

"No need for that," the captain says upon realizing what they plan to do. "Boats do not normally travel on the

Nile at night. Too many snakes and crocodiles. It's not worth it. Unless, of course, a queen pays you triple to take the chances."

They sleep peacefully through the night with the sound of water swishing and rocking the boat now tied up to a pier.

The next day, they plan their research strategy. When the sun is high in the sky, they look at the west shore of the Nile ahead of them and see it—Edfu.

"Amazing!" Katazuli says.

"I've never seen anything like it," Borseen says.

"One of the greatest libraries of the world is here," Dushatra says."

"I cannot wait," Michel says.

The magi disembark, putting their tents and other supplies on their backs.

"Well, we need to find an inn first," Yasib says.

They walk down the walkway along the river and find a suitable inn. They deposit their traveling gear and return to the temple.

They walk through the high gate of the wall surrounding the complex. Once inside, they see over to the left the sacred lake for ceremonial washings. They start down the avenue leading to the pylon. The avenue is lined with sphinxes.

They reach the pylon with portrayals of the god Horus in bright colors on every portion of the great gateway. It reaches with majesty thirty man-lengths toward the sky. Temple guards stand on each side.

"What is your business?" one of the guards asks.

"We come from Phraattes, King of Parthia," Hophni begins. "We are his ambassadors searching for the key to great wisdom which we believe your temple to Horus houses."

"You are not allowed in here. You are not believers."

"Sir, we do not wish to disturb your sanctuary to the great god Horus, or even enter your dedicated halls. We simply want to go into your library and search through your books of wisdom," Hophni continues.

"Wait here."

The guard opens a door and whispers something to someone, then closes it back. Everyone waits. Moments later, the door opens again.

"You may enter," the guard says. "But you must be accompanied by one of our priests. He is waiting for you."

The eight magi enter and are met by a priest wearing a long robe and cone-shaped turban.

They walk through a courtyard that is ten man-lengths long. Great columns are on each side, all depicting scenes from the escapades of Horus, god of the sky.

They arrive at a building with no door. Inside are columns that are even greater than the ones in the courtyard. It is dark inside.

They know that, beyond this hall is another, then an offering hall, and in the far back is the hallowed sanctuary of Horus with his statue in it. But that is all they know.

There are stone tables near the entrance to the first dark hall. The priest turns and faces them.

"Now, specifically, tell me your business."

"Two months ago," Hophni begins, "our king saw a great star appear in the western sky."

"I, too, saw it," Dushatra says.

"And I," Michel says. "We know it is true."

"The birth of a god," the priest says. "It must have been the birth of a god. Do you know which god? Tell me just where in the sky it is."

"It is no longer there," Michel continues. "It appeared, grew large, lingered, then disappeared."

"It what? Do you mean the god was born and then died?"

"That we do not know," Yasib says. "Perhaps the god went somewhere else for a while. King Phraattes believes the god may have gone over to the side of his enemies."

"If it was a star, it could affect almost any nation. Even Egypt."

"That is true," Kumar says.

"We need more information for our king. And possibly also for your pharaoh. That is why we come to you," Hophni says. "We wish permission to search your sacred writings for any reference to a star god."

"Our library is just inside this Hall of Consecration. You are not allowed to enter this hall. However, because the star could affect Egypt as well as Parthia, it seems we should cooperate with you. However, I will need to speak with our high priest. Come back tomorrow, and I will have your answer for you. If permission is given, you may read at these tables normally used by worshipers to place sacrifices on."

"And your name, sir?" Hophni asks.

"Soter. Priest Soter."

The magi turn around and head back to the other side of the outer wall of the compound.

"It's just as well," Borseen says. "It will be dark soon."

"We can rise early in the morning and be there as soon as they open the gate," Demetrius says.

"Look at the children playing," Hophni says. "My mother keeps asking me when I am going to marry and have children."

Michel remains quiet, remembering Meira and what might have been in their brief marriage.

"Uh, oh. Their ball landed in the reeds. Wait while I fetch it for them," Hophni says.

He rushes to the edge of the water and reaches down to retrieve the toy.

"Ouchhh," he cries out, standing back up with a jerk.

"What's wrong?" Yasib says, rushing over to his friend.

In that moment, he sees the snake hanging from Hophni's hand. He grabs hold of its head, forcing its fanged jaws open, and flings it into the river.

"Hurry, we've got to get you to the inn," Dushatra says.

Katazuli goes to one side of Hophni and Michel to the other.

"Hold that hand down," Katazuli says. "Don't let the poison spread into any more parts of his body."

They get halfway to the inn when Hophni vomits and

goes into convulsions.

LIBRARY OF HORUS IN EDFU

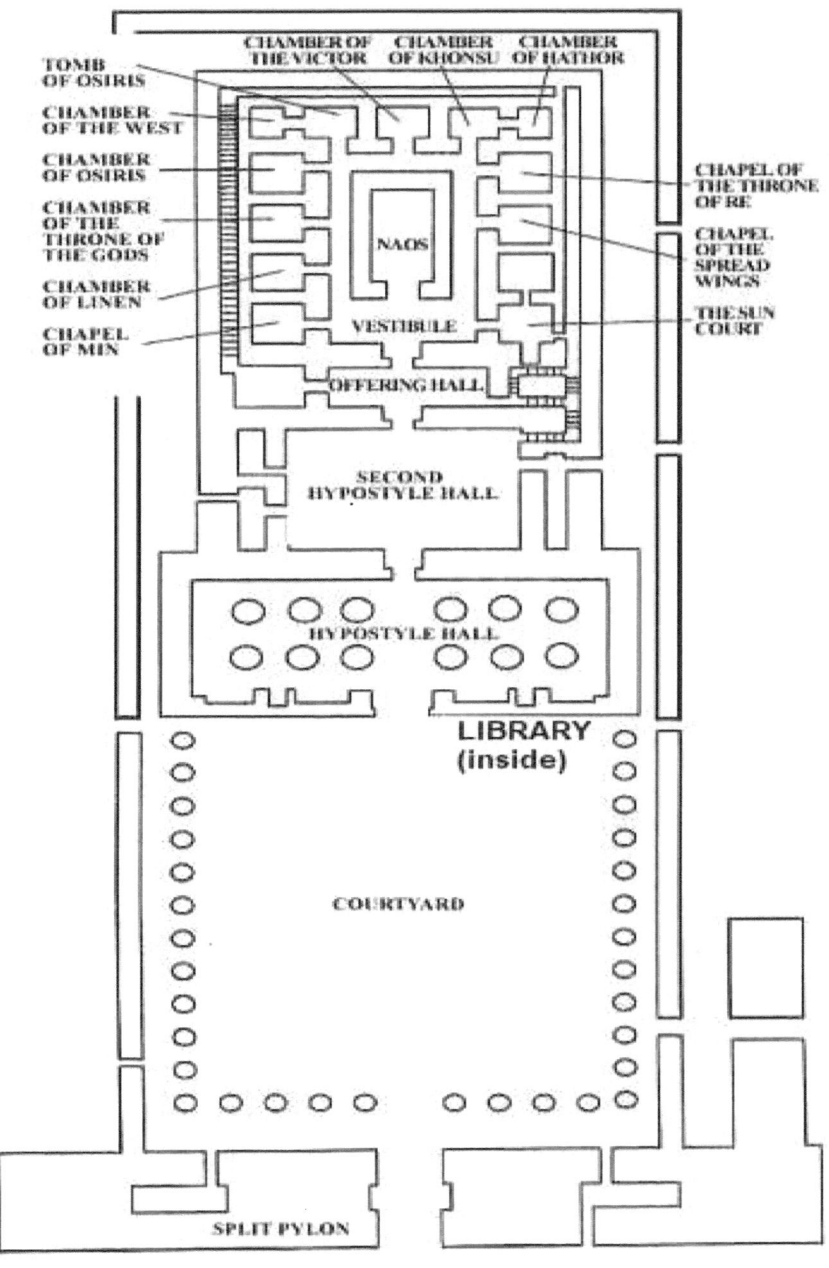

18 ~ CONFUSION

*T*hey lower Hophni to the ground as gently as they can. The other magi gather around him in a protective circle so that passers-by cannot see their friend in his weakness.

The convulsions stop. Tall, muscular Hittite Katazuli picks up his injured friend and carries him the rest of the way to the inn.

He lays Hophni on the bed and looks at his hand, where the snake had bitten him. He looks through his leather pouch, but cannot find what he is looking for. He empties the entire contents of the pouch onto a pallet on the floor.

"There it is. I knew I had some." He opens a small pouch with leaves of the ophior-hiza mungos plant and hands a small cup to Demetrius. "Will you ask the innkeeper if he has any water sitting out in the sun? If so, fill this cup with it, pour these leaves in, and stir it."

Demetrius disappears with the leaves and cup.

Katazuli looks closer at Hophni's hand. "It has started swelling."

Demetrius returns with the warm water, and leaves stirred in.

Katazuli takes a second pouch. "I forgot I had this gentian. It is good for poisonous bites also." He adds that to the tea.

"Hophni," he says. "Hophni, can you hear me?"

Hophni opens his eyes. "Oh, where am I?" he asks,

looking around.

"You are back at the inn," Katazuli says. "You were bitten by a snake."

"But it was a small snake, not full-grown I don't think," Yasib says, standing out of the way with the other magi.

"I need you to drink this tea. It is good for poisonous bites. When you're done drinking it, I will put some aloe oil on the bite to ease your pain. Do you feel much pain?"

"I feel a little, but it isn't unbearable."

When Hophni finishes drinking the tea, he puts his head back down and closes his eyes.

"What's wrong?" Demetrius asks. "Why did he close his eyes? Is he dead?"

"Stop that, Demetrius," Katazuli says. "He is just resting. Here, go get another cup of warm water so I can prepare more of the mixture for when he wakes up during the night."

"I'll take a turn sitting up with him," Michel says. "When you get sleepy, just wake me up. I don't require as much sleep as some people do."

The night is spent with Katazuli, Michel, and Yasib, taking turns watching Hophni.

Morning comes. Everyone speaks in soft tones as they prepare to return to the temple.

"What about Hophni?" Borseen asks just after everyone indicates they are ready to go.

"What do you mean, what about Hophni?"

"Huh?"

"You're not going without me," Hophni says, sitting up in bed.

"Hophni! What are you doing? You were snake-bitten," Demetrius says. "You're supposed to be sick."

"Well, I'm not anymore. I'm just fine. You said it was a young snake, didn't you?"

Hophni stands and reals a moment.

"Uh-oh. Give me a moment to make the room stop spinning, and I'll be all set to go."

Katazuli watches his patient. "Are you okay?"

"Yes. I'm fine now."

"It must have been the vomiting. You must have vomited out the snake's venom. We don't know much about how to cure a snake bite, but your body must have known. Here you are back with us," Katazuli says with a grin.

"Where are my clothes?"

"Right where you left everything yesterday," Dushatra says.

"Wait for me. As soon as I put on a clean kilt, I'll be ready to go. Don't leave without me."

With the entire group of men now in good spirits, they leave the inn and walk toward the temple to Horus, god of the sky. When they arrive, Hophni once again takes over, this being the homeland of his father and where he had grown up.

"We were here yesterday," he tells the guard at the gate. "Priest Soter told us he would meet us here."

The guard disappears a few moments. While he is gone, the other men grin at Hophni.

"You are one hearty human, friend," Kumar says with a grin. "You are your old self again."

The guard comes back. "You may enter."

The magi go through the door into the temple complex and see Soter waiting for them at the other end of the courtyard.

When they arrive, they see piles of clay tablets.

"I obtained permission from our high priest for you to investigate our sacred writings. This is what we will do. First, I will bring out to you the writings of Horus' priests that are the oldest. When you are through with them, I will bring out newer writings on papyrus and parchment. Is that agreeable?"

"That is more than agreeable," Yasib says with a large grin.

"Everyone, take a tablet and see if it refers to a star, especially a newborn star."

"Hophni, you are amazing," Michel says. "You are back

to being your old self already. I'm proud of you."

The magi settle down to reading. By mid-afternoon, they have finished reading the clay tablets. Hophni asks a young priest passing by if he could find Soter for them.

"How have you done today?" Soter asks moments later.

"We have finished reading the tablets," Hophni says. "Tomorrow, we would like to read your sacred scrolls as passed down by your god Horus."

The following day, they are as successful as the day before. Although still in a good mood over Hophni's amazing recovery, they are discouraged over not finding any mention of a special star.

"Yes, he is your sky god, but he is not a star," Michel explains.

"Don't worry, friends," Soter says, smiling. "You are not through."

"We're not?" Michel asks.

"Besides the inner sanctuary to Horus, we have smaller chapels in the wings to other gods—Osiris, Khonsi, Hathor, and Min. You can probably complete the readings of one god a day."

Four days later, in the early evening, the magi send for Soter.

"We have read all your sacred writings," Hophni reports. "We are sorry to say we have found no mention of a star god, a new star, a newborn god, or anything like that."

"We have other gods, you know," Soter says. "We have gods of the sky, the sun, and the moon."

"They are not star gods, sir," Yasib says.

"Well, the only other thing I can suggest is that you go to the sacred library in Alexandria. It is even larger than ours."

"That is our plan," Hophni says.

The following morning, the eight magi leave the inn and walk down to the docks where they find a large reed boat taking passengers up the Nile to Alexandria.

On the boat, they talk with each other, walk around

Michel: The Fourth Wise Man

to get some exercise and talk with other passengers.

"Michel, can I talk to you?" Hophni says.

"Of course. What's on your mind?"

"I never thought I'd say this, but I am very frustrated over the gods I have believed in all my life."

"I can see why," Michel says. "They don't make sense. An ancient tablet says one thing, a scroll written centuries later says something else."

"They're always changing their mind," Hophni says. "Gods have someone as a wife, then that goddess is his mother, then his sister. Michel, do you think they are real?"

"Do you want an honest answer?"

"That's why I asked you."

"No, they are not real. A statue cannot talk or hear or walk. What god would rely on humans to move them around and even put clothes on them?"

"They act like spoiled overgrown humans," Hophni says. "They fight with each other half the time. We pray to them just so they won't include us in their fights and destroy us."

"The one true God loves everyone and tells us what is right and wrong. Wrong he calls sin. Sin is anything that ultimately hurts humans."

"How can he love us all?"

"God is a Spirit and is everywhere."

"Like what the Hindus and Buddhists believe?"

"Their spirit gods have no personality. They are just the essence of the universe. The true God, Jehovah, can love and respond to our prayers and guide us."

"I think I like your Jehovah."

"Well, he loves you."

"He does?"

The boat arrives in Alexandria when the sun is red in the west.

When they disembark, they realize they are at the foot of Aspendia Street lined with columns on both sides.

"If we walk straight up this street, we should run into the library," Hophni says.

"Let's find a room at an inn along here," Michel says, "so we can be there first thing in the morning."

"Did you know this is the largest city in the world—well, other than Rome?" Hophni says.

The traffic is heavy. Chariots, carts, horses, oxen, camels, people on foot.

"Watch out!" Michel says too late. "Hophni, are you okay?"

"Sure," he says, picking himself up off the road."

"Your mouth is bleeding," Michel says.

Hophni wipes the blood away with his hand. "Oh, it's nothing. Now there should be an inn right up here."

"I see it," Borseen says.

The magi check in, eat, and settle down for the night.

The next morning they continue walking on Aspendia. They pass temples on both sides of the street, then come to the city agora. Marble benches are scattered around on it where people can gather and watch the seagulls over the Great Sea on whose shore the city has been built. On their left is a fortress.

"I see it—the library," Dushatra says.

"That's the library?" Kumar says.

"It looks more like a city," Katazuli says. "What are all those buildings?"

They start up the grand staircase into the complex. Statues of a sitting pharaoh are on each side. Columns line the terrace. They go through another set of gates. Now a large courtyard.

"Are those meeting rooms or something on each side?" Demetrius asks. No one has an answer.

They continue to walk. Now another set of steps with a terrace at the top, and still another set of steps. Now at the highest point of the library complex, they enter a building with high columns on each side. They walk to the nearest clerk.

"Sir, we're..."

"You don't have to tell me. Some of you are from the east and some from the north. You are strangers and need directions."

"Yes, sir."

"Are you here to learn mathematics, medicine, zoology, agriculture? What are you looking for?"

"You have all that?" Yasib asks.

"We are the largest library in the world. We copy and translate writings from every language and every nation. Every ship that comes into our harbor is required to hand over their books. They are copied by our scribes, we keep the original and give a copy to the captain of the ship. So, I ask again what you are interested in?"

"We want to read through the sacred writings of the Egyptian gods," Hophni says, touching his bloody lip to check for swelling.

"Well, if you will go to that room right over there, someone will tell you which rooms have the writings you need."

"Are any of them on clay tablets?" Katazuli asks.

"No. We have tens of thousands of writings here, but they are all on papyrus. If you want to look ancient tablets, you'll have to go to the temples of the gods where they originated."

"We have already been to the largest library in the southern part of Egypt," Michel says. "Well, it will be much easier reading papyrus."

The men walk to the room where the writings are of Egyptian gods. They are directed to a larger room.

"Amazing," Michel says. "Absolutely amazing."

The room is lined with cubicles holding papyrus scrolls from floor to ceiling. Tall ladders are used to reach the ones higher up. People wearing clothes from all over the world sit at tables or wander around reading as they walk.

"Well, let's get started," Hophni says, still in charge. Someone said these smaller rooms each hold the writings of a different god or at least family of gods."

The magi divide up. Each one goes to a different room. They read the rest of the day. And the next. And the next.

On the morning of the fourth day before leaving the

inn, Michel makes an announcement. "Before we go back to the library, we need to make a decision.

"We have inspected the writings of every sky god we could find. Most of the sky gods are gods of darkness, the netherworld, the moon. But no star god."

"I see no reason to go back. Instead, since there is a large Jewish section to the city, I suggest now is the time to examine the Jewish sacred writings."

"I would like that," Hophni says.

"What about the rest of you?"

The magi look at each other and back at Michel.

"Well, while we're here, we may as well," Demetrius says.

Instead of walking straight up to the waterfront, they turn right. They go past several more temples, the palace, a gymnasium, and public gardens. Now out of the heavy traffic of the city, they turn left and walk toward the seashore.

"I see signs written in Hebrew," Michel says. "The Jewish Quarter is to our right a little farther."

They walk two more blocks and see a large synagogue fashioned after the typical Egyptian temple, but obviously a synagogue.

"At last. We will find the explanation of the star, we can all go home, and I can get back to work on more important things," he says as they draw closer to the synagogue.

"Are you never going to give up on that crazy scheme?" Kumar says with a grin. "The land is all under water."

"It won't be when I get through with it. I cannot wait to return home and resume this work. You know my ancestor was Daniel, and..."

"Yes, we know," Dushatra says. "How many times have you reminded us of that?"

"Wait here," Michel says.

Michel walks up to the portico of the synagogue and knocks. A man with a beard and long tunic opens the door.

Michel speaks to him in Aramaic. "Do you have copies of all our prophets' writings?" he asks.

"Yes, we do, but they are not here. We have more than one synagogue. The one that has them is down this street five more blocks."

"I'm getting tired," Yasib says. "Let's go back to the public garden and rest before we go down to the other synagogue."

"Sometimes I forget your arthritis," Michel says. "All those steps at the library complex must have taken their toll on your joints."

The magi walk back a little way to the public garden and sit with Yasib.

"Okay, friends, go ahead and rest while I go exploring. I want to see what kind of ships are docked out there," Borseen says.

"I'd like to look among the herbs planted in this garden," Katazuli says. "I wonder what kind of aloe vera plants they have here."

The others sit and chat or close their eyes for a morning nap.

"Hey, what is Borseen running for?" Demetrius asks.

Borseen shouts at them. "I've been bitten. Help me. I don't want to die."

Hophni jumps up and runs to his friend.

"Where were you bitten?"

"My leg. It wrapped itself around my ankle, then bit me in the calf."

"Sit down, and I will take care of you," Hophni says.

"What about Katazuli?" Borseen asks.

"I'll go look for him," Dushatra says.

"We cannot wait for Katazuli. You need help now," Hophni says.

Borseen sits on a park bench, and Hophni sits on the ground. He puts his mouth on Borseen's leg, sucks at the wound where the snake had bitten him and spits out the venom. He does it three more times.

"What are you doing, Hophni?" Katazuli shouts, running up to them.

"I'm sucking the poison out. You weren't here to treat

him yet, and I was worried."

"No! You cannot do that. You have a cut lip."

"But I already did, and am sure I saved Borseen's life. I..."

Hophni gasps for breath. He tries to suck in air, but cannot. He collapses and begins to bleed from his mouth, his nose, his eyes. He stares at Katazuli, who by now is kneeling next to him.

"Hophni?"

"Hophni?"

The struggling stops.

No one says anything. They stare at Hophni and know.

Katazuli looks up at them.

"Hophni is dead."

Michel: The Fourth Wise Man

LIBRARY AT ALEXANDRIA, EGYPT
(Suggested Since it fell into the Mediterranean Sea
In a 4th Century AD earthquake)

19 ~ MOURNING

"Let's take him over to this synagogue," Michel finally says. "A couple days ago, he told me he had decided to become a Jew. We will give him a Jewish funeral."

Big Katazuli picks up Hophni and carries him up the street to the synagogue.

Michel knocks on the same door he had an hour earlier. The same rabbi answers it.

"Sir, something terrible has happened. One of our group has suddenly died. May we come in and have his funeral here?"

"No, you may not," the rabbi replies.

Michel jerks his head back. "But why?"

"The Sabbath is in two days, and if I touch a dead body, I will be unclean for seven days. I cannot allow you to have a funeral here."

"But, you do not have to touch Hophni."

"Doesn't matter. It won't work. Not here. Try some other synagogue."

The rabbi slams the door closed.

Michel looks over at Katazuli, then the other five.

"I am so sorry. I do not know what he is afraid of, but it is something more than touching a dead body.

He looks up into the sky, then back to his friends. "An hour ago, we were talking to Hophni; now, he is just a lifeless body."

The seven magi walk back to the public garden and sit on the same bench where their Hophni had been talking with them such a short while ago.

They sit in silence, Katazuli holding Hophni on his lap.

"I grew up by the sea," Demetrius says. "Why don't I go over to the market and purchase a sheet. We can wrap him in it, have our own funeral here in the garden, then walk across the hepistadium to Pharos island and the deeper water, and drop him in there?"

"The rest of us can walk along the shore and pick up enough rocks he will stay down," Borseen says. "So, be sure to purchase some rope also."

Katazuli sets Hophni on the ground, and the others pick up heavy concrete benches to put in place around him for privacy.

An hour later, Demetrius is back. They stand in a circle front of their benches.

"I think he was the most innocent and honest of any of us," Yasib begins.

"How he loved life," Kumar says. "And people."

"His mother was very proud of him," Dushatra says.

"He died saving me," Borseen says. "I don't know what to say. How will I ever shed this feeling of guilt?"

"It wasn't your fault," Yasib says. "He wanted to save you, and no one was going to talk him out of it. He died a hero."

Michel sings a dirge. One written by David for his best friend. He sings it soft. He sings it sad. He sings it for their Hophni.

> *I am distressed for you, my brother Hophni.*
> *You have been very pleasant to me.*
> *Your love to me was more wonderful*
> *Than the love of women.*
> *How have the mighty fallen.*

Silence.

"We will miss you mightily, friend," Yasib says.

Demetrius kneels on one side of Hophni, Katazuli on the other side. Moments later, their friend is enshrouded and ready for his burial.

Demetrius and Katazuli lead the procession to the waterfront, across the causeway, and to the island. The men who had picked up rocks along the way tie them onto what is left of their Hophni.

"Farewell, friend," Michel says for them all.

Then Hophni is gone. They watch the water a while, the ripples becoming smaller and smaller, then turn back to the harbor.

"We may as well find a ship and leave. There is nothing more for us here," Dushatra says.

"What about researching the Jewish sacred writings?" Michel says, his eyes darting around, seeking acceptance.

"No," Dushatra says. "Now is not the time. Circumstances are not right. Maybe later. We need to go on to Athens now."

The magi walk in different directions around the harbor to find a ship for them

"Hey there. Is that you? Well, isn't this a coincidence?"

Michel turns. "Tefnak?"

"Yes, it is me. This is my home port. What are you doing in Alexandria?"

"King Phraattes has exiled us until we find the meaning of a star he is afraid of."

"Oh. I see. Kings are like that, aren't they? What happened to your Kingdom of Eden project?" He adds with a grin.

"Interrupted for something not nearly as important."

"I assume you have been searching for the meaning of your star at the library here."

"Yes, and a lot of other places. We're headed to Athens next. Might you be going that way?"

"You are in luck, my friend. My ship is headed for Athens in three weeks. That should give you enough time to search through all the books we have at our world-renowned library here."

"Oh, we cannot wait that long. We need to go now."

"Well, good luck."

"Michel! Michel!" It is Borseen. "We're in luck. I found us a ship. I told them there were seven of us, and we were on a mission for King Phraattes and were in a hurry."

"When does it leave?"

"As soon as we can retrieve our supplies back at the inn and go on board. The captain said he would hold it for us because he is honored to have ambassadors of the great King Phraattes on his ship."

Within the hour, the seven magi board the *Skandali*. Bells ring, chains pull up the anchor, sails are unfurled, and sailors rush around the deck doing their jobs.

"At first, he said we would have to stow our traveling supplies below," Borseen explains. "But, when I explained we did not bring along any servants to guard them, he said we could keep them with us on the main deck. He even suggested we take a spot near the bridge. That way, he can keep close watch on us."

"He said all that?" Demetrius says with a large grin. "It certainly pays to be in the king's service when traveling."

The magi set their packs down, lean on them, and return to their reverie.

"Hophni should have been here with us," Katazuli says.

"He was such a good man," Kumar says. "Why didn't the gods take one of us instead?"

"God has a plan for everyone," Michel says, knowing the words are hollow at a time like this.

"Ha. He sure loved to eat," Yasib says.

"Did you see the way he picked up his mother and swung her around?" Michel says. He pauses and stops smiling. "Did anyone think to write his mother?"

"I did," Kumar says. "She needs to know."

Later in the day, a man with a deep voice walks up to them.

"I trust your voyage will be a good one for you," the

man says. "My I introduce myself? I am Sextus, your captain."

Borseen rises and extends his hand to the captain. "Everything is as you said it would be. For that, King Phraattes extends his profoundest thanks."

"Oh, I think your king and I are going to get along quite well," Sextus says.

"About how long will it take to sail to Athens?" Dushatra asks.

"With a decent wind, about six days."

He leaves, and the magi return to conversing or napping or staring.

"The sooner we get there and solve the problem of the star," Michel says once again, "the sooner we can return home and take care of more important matters."

One day goes by. Two. Four. Five.

"Where are we?" Borseen says, looking up at the captain on the bridge.

"Pretty close to the island of Milos."

"There must be scores of islands near Greece. I never heard of that one."

"You will," Sextus says.

As each day has gone by, the crew has been watching them more.

"They must think we are pretty important," Borseen says.

"Well, we are important," Demetrius says. "We should be docking tomorrow. I'll be glad to be off the ship." With that, he strolls over to the railing behind some crates.

Silently, one of the crewmen grabs Demetrius, throws a small grain sack over his head, ties his hands behind his back, and forces him down into the hold.

"Hmmm. I haven't seen Demetrius in a while. I think I'll go look for him," Borseen says.

When he arrives at the railing behind the crates, a sack is thrown over his head, his hands are tied, and he is forced to join Demetrius.

One by one throughout the day, as the magi look for

their missing friends, they too disappear.

"Do we have them all?" they hear Captain Sextus ask.

"Aye, captain. We have them all."

"Good. We dock tonight."

"What's going on?" Michel asks.

"I think we got ourselves mixed up with pirates," Dushatra says. "I've been suspicious of them since the day we arrived on board."

"Why did you think that?"

"The name of the ship. *Skandali* is Greek for *hammer*. Didn't make sense. Merchant ships are named after people or places or merchandise."

They hear running of heavy footsteps on the deck above them.

"Douse the sails! Drop anchor! Stow the rigging!"

"What do you think they are going to do with us?"

"We're about to find out," Dushatra says.

They spend the rest of the night listening as cargo is unloaded and the crew congratulate each other.

"That shipment of silk we grabbed is going to bring us a lot of silver."

"Ha, ha, ha. What about the gold jewelry?"

"And what about those men down below?"

"They belong to the captain. That's all I know."

Morning comes, and the hatch is opened. Sailors jump down to where the magi are, untie their hands, and force them—still with sacks over their heads—to climb the ladder.

Their hands are retied. "Watch your step," they warn. "You're going down the gangplank. Don't fall in. Ha, ha, ha."

Once on shore, they are pushed into a wagon. At first, the road is smooth. Then it becomes rocky.

When the wagon stops, they are pushed through a doorway. The smell is like rusty iron mixed with urine and vomit and dead rats.

"Okay. I untied the hands of one of you. He can take the sacks off everyone's head so you can see the kind of hell you are now in," the gravelly voice says, "and even untie the hands of the rest of you. You're not going anywhere for a long, long time."

The door clangs shut.

Silence.

"Here, let me get those sacks off your heads." It is Yasib. "And those ropes. Don't know why they picked me with my twisted aching fingers."

Time loses meaning except for the little streak of light that comes in through a small window for ventilation at the top of their cell.

"You're in luck," their guard tells them one day. "King Phraattes has sent his answer."

"Answer to what?" Michel asks.

"Didn't you know? Captain Sextus has been holding you for ransom. If the king pays up, we let you loose. If he doesn't, we sell you as slaves. Either way, the captain gets his pay, and we get our cut. Ha, ha."

More time passes. Then the answer.

"Looks like your king doesn't think much of you. He refused to pay up. That's okay. We've got slave buyers docking all day. Tomorrow, we will sell you."

"Demetrius, you sure got us in a mess," Borseen shouts.

"Hey, you believed the captain was our friend as much as I did."

"I never did," Dushatra declares.

The following morning, the door clangs open, four crewmen stand outside with daggers in their hands. Seven crewmen enter the cell, tie the magi's hands behind their back, and throw the small grain sacks over their head as they had done before.

They are pushed into the wagon and taken over a rough road that eventually becomes a smooth road. They hear laughter. Then a voice. The voice of Sextus, captain, and pirate. They're force up on a platform.

"Here they are, gentlemen. They are fine specimens, and I expect you to show your appreciation with your purses. Ha, ha, ha."

The sound of whirling overhead—whirling arrows.

Michel: The Fourth Wise Man

"What? What's going on?" Sextus shouts. "We're being attacked."

The magi are left standing alone. They hear men scrambling, and shouts of, "Grab your sword."

"Hey, over here," Michel shouts to his friends. "Follow my voice. I'm off the platform. There is more safety down here."

Shouting now. Down at the waterfront. Shouting and clanging of swords and whirling of arrows and spears.

Then it all stops.

Silence.

Waiting.

Nothing.

Still nothing.

Then footsteps. Marching. Closer and closer.

"Well, Michel, my boy. You certainly have gotten yourself into a mess."

"Tefnak. Is that you?" Michel responds.

"It's me all right, and you will be spending the rest of your life, showing your gratitude. Men, untie them and get those dratted sacks off their heads."

Once freed, Michel approaches his savior.

"How did you know?"

"I didn't at first. But I began hearing talk of a slave sale on Milos. Milos is notorious for harboring pirates."

"It is?"

"I asked around and learned the sale was being held by Sextus, one of the most notorious pirates alive today. On top of that, I learned he had been docked in Alexandria three weeks earlier, about the time you were looking for a ship to Athens."

"What luck. Praise Jehovah," Michel says.

"Luck has nothing to do with it. I wanted to protect my investment."

"What investment? I paid you in full for Eden."

"Yes. But I have my reputation to protect."

"Doesn't make sense, but I'm glad you came. As you said, I will spend the rest of my life showing my gratitude."

The other magi join Michel and Captain Tefnak. They walk to the ship and board it.

"We don't have any money," Michel says. "They took everything."

"That's okay. I have connections in Athens. You can go to work for my friends and pay me for your passage."

Michel sighs. "I'm never going to get back to my Eden."

The ship *Shar'n Shihab II* docks that evening in Athens.

"Stay on board," Captain Tefnak says. I will bring my friends to you.

The next day, men of varying levels of affluence arrive.

Yasib is hired to translate documents of ships from China, bringing in the new highly-sought-after silk.

Kumar is hired to paint murals in a new house.

Dushatra is hired to teach Buddhist beliefs at a school of philosophy.

Katazuli is hired to take care of an ailing senator.

Borseen is hired to show the local sword makers new techniques used by his famous father.

Demetrius is hired to teach oratory.

Michel is hired as a tutor for a legate's children.

Each evening, they return to the ship to hand their pay for that day to Captain Tefnak, and to sleep.

"You did not take us far enough to charge us much for fare," Michel says. "When are we going to finish paying you?"

"Oh, you finished last week."

LIBRARY OF ARISTOTLE IN ATHENS

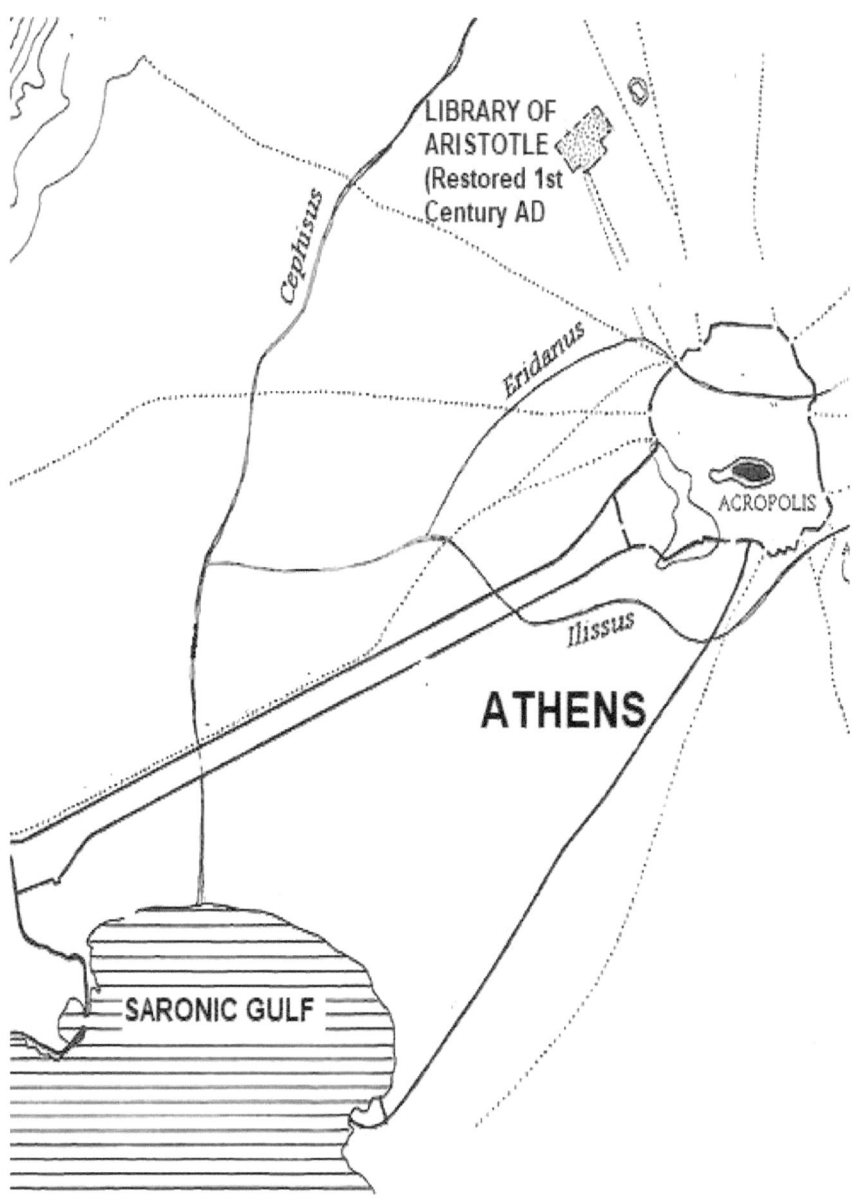

20 ~ HOPES

"What?" Dushatra says. "You are no better than that pirate."

"Didn't you say you planned to go on to Rome after Athens?"

"Well, yes, but..."

"I have a friend whose ship's home port is Rome. He said he would save room for you, but you had to pay him now. He doesn't trust holding space for passengers. Some back out at the last minute, and he ends up with unpaid space on his ship. So I've been paying your passage."

"You should have told us," Borseen says.

"I suppose so. But it was more fun like this. I didn't think you would consent to stay on my ship at night without paying me, and I don't want you to pay me. Am I right?"

"Well, I guess you are right," Michel says. "You've already done too much for us."

"Your passage to Rome should be paid for by the end of next week. It's a long way over there, you know. It will take at least six days." He turns to leave then turns back.

"By the way, once your passage is paid for, I want you to promise to stay on this ship while you're working at the Athens library. Agreed? If not, I kick you off right now," he says with a wink.

"You are a hard man to keep our dignity around," Michel says.

At the end of the following week, the men quit their

jobs.

"Are we ready to head over to the library this morning?" Michel asks.

"I am enjoying this autumn air," Katazuli says. "How long have we been at this, anyway?"

"The star appeared in May. It is now October."

They go onto the dock and head north on Panathenaic Way. They pass a temple to Ares and altar of the twelve gods on their left. Once past the agora, they walk out through the Diocharous Gate. They see ahead of them Lykavettos. They walk to where the Iridanos and Illissos Rivers come near each other and see a temple to Hercules Pagratis and Lykeios Apollo.

To their right in a grove of trees dedicated to Apollo is a large triangle building. They go inside. The largest part of the building is a gymnasium. The rest of the building is rooms for students and a larger room full of books.

"I thought it would be larger than this," Michel says.

A clerk at a table sees they are strangers, calls them over and tells them what topics are in which part of the library.

"We want the section regarding your gods, especially any star gods," Michel says.

That section would be in the room right over there," the librarian says. "But I can save you some time. We have eight gods of night time, but the one you want to investigate is Asteria. She is the goddess of nocturnal oracles and falling stars."

"Yes, yes," Dushatra says. "That is who we want."

"Her oracles are on the shelf left of the doorway."

The magi grin and follow Dushatra to the designated room.

They look through the rows of scroll cubicles with both papyrus and parchment, and divide up. They read the rest of the day.

"Nothing here," Kumar finally says. She is goddess of falling stars, but no one says who or what the stars are."

"She is goddess of oracles, but her oracles are

delivered in dreams, not in writing that can be proven," Katazuli says.

"I was really hopeful we had discovered the meaning of Phraattes' star," Yasib says.

"And we could return home and back to whatever we were doing," Michel adds.

"Like growing an underwater garden," Yasib says with a wink.

"Make fun of me all you want," Michel says, "but it will happen, and God will once again walk on earth."

"Well," Demetrius says, standing and stretching his arms. "Looks like I will be home in Rome this time next week. I have friends there I am anxious to see."

The magi make their way back out of the library, shoulders drooping and not speaking.

They stop by the ship of Tefnak's friend.

"You are just in time. I will be leaving here in two days," their new captain says.

They bid goodbye to Captain Tefnak, and two days later board the new ship.

The winds are only favorable part of the time. It takes them eight days to arrive at the port of Ostia, serving Rome.

"At least we did not encounter pirates this time," Michel says.

The ship docks at the mouth of the Tiber River.

"We are in my home territory now," Demetrius reminds everyone. "I know exactly where the library is."

"And where is that?" Michel asks.

"On Palatine Hill. It is part of Apollo's temple. Not only that, but it is attached or nearly attached to Augustus Caesar's home. Apollo is Caesar's patron god."

"Sounds like it will be hard for us to gain entry then," Michel says. "There will be a lot more security than the other temples we have visited, although I do not see how it could be any worse."

"You must remember I was schooled in that temple. I have met Augustus himself upon many occasions."

Michel and the others smile but do not respond.

"Follow me," Demetrius says, gathering up his parcel with a few clothes in it along with two blank parchment scrolls.

"At the first market we come to, I need to buy a new tunic and toga. And a wreath for my hair."

"Why a wreath?" Dushatra asks. "That's for winners of events or dignitaries, and you are neither."

"Since when are the personal advisors to the king of all Parthia not dignitaries? Now, follow me."

He leads the group of seven magi to the side where the gangplank is.

"Wait, you cannot go ashore yet," the first officer tells them.

"Why not?" Demetrius asks. It is not really a question.

"Royalty."

"Augustus? His wife, Livius?"

"No, Parthian royalty."

"Huh?"

"Ther Musa, Queen of Parthia, just arrived ahead of you."

Demetrius' eyes sparkle. His grin widens. "Then you must let us off so we may join her."

"Why?"

"We are the personal advisors of King Phraattes himself. We see Musa—we call her Musa, not Ther Musa—often. Beautiful blond hair and green eyes. Did you know she is Nordic?"

"No, I did not know that, nor do I care. And you are not leaving the ship until she and her entourage are well on their way."

"I will report you to the captain, and you will regret it," Demetrius declares.

"Come on, Demetrius," Michel says. "We will probably see her later. Don't cause problems."

Demetrius turns. The captain is standing behind him.

"I demand to leave the ship and join my queen."

"She may be your queen, but you are her subject, and you are not leaving until my first officer tells you that you can. Now go sit over there out of the way."

Michel touches Demetrius' arm. "Come on over here. It won't hurt. Yasib and the others saved us a place."

Demetrius refuses to sit. He paces for an hour while the other magi watch him with some amusement.

"You may leave now," the officer says, taking the chain down, blocking the gangplank.

The magi and other passengers disembark. Down at the dock, Demetrius looks around. "It is too far for us to walk—fifteen *milles*."

They look around for a solution to their problem. "We could travel there by boat like they do in Egypt," Michel suggests.

"Look. There is a *carruca* with enough seats for eight people, including the driver."

The magi each give a bronze coin to the driver and climb up into the carriage.

The ride gives them a chance to enjoy the villas and vineyards and lemon trees along the way. They stop briefly at a market where Demetrius buys a new suit of clothes.

They arrive in Rome and follow the Tiber until it divides and forms Tiber Island. "Over on the right is Palatine Hill," Demetrius explains. "Driver, let us off in front of the temple."

The driver proceeds up the hill but is blocked by Roman guards.

"Sorry, sir," the guard says. "You cannot come to the temple today. Royalty from Parthia."

"Sir, I am Demetrius of Rome. I am also advisor to King Phraattes himself. These are my colleagues. You will let us through."

"Excuse me, sir. I did not mean to offend. I will check for you."

Demetrius smiles. "That will be fine."

The guard gives a message to a soldier on a horse. The soldier goes up to the top of the hill. Decorative trees and columns along the roadblock the view.

As they wait, Demetrius fidgets with his ruby ring. He

turns to the driver of their carriage. "We will be getting out here. You are no longer needed."

"Are you sure?" Michel asks.

"I am sure. Trust me."

The magi climb out of their carriage and sit on marble benches placed between columns.

An hour later, the soldier reappears and says something to the guard out of their hearing. The guard approaches them, and Demetrius stands. "Well?"

"You have been given permission to enter. At the top of the hill, you will see Caesar's..."

"I know the way, sir. I have been here many times. Good day, sir."

Demetrius turns and motions for the other magi to follow him.

"Here is the temple to Apollo and its library. Perhaps we can visit it tomorrow. But, for now, I believe we have been invited to dinner."

They stand before the front gate to the palace.

"Are you sure this is the palace?" Michel asks.

"Yes. We have a Caesar who wants the people to identify with him, not like Phraattes who, well, likes to show off."

A gatekeeper opens the modest gate for them. They enter a courtyard and are led to a high arched door. It is opened for the seven magi.

"Did he build this house himself?"

"No, he bought it already built," Demetrius explains. "He liked it and didn't see any reason to build one just like it."

They are led down a wide corridor with colorful murals frescoed into the walls on each side. The floor is simple marble tile.

"Well, look who has traveled from the farthest reaches of the world to welcome me to Rome."

It is the voice of Ther Musa.

She is dressed in a long garnet tunic with blue robe accented with the billowy sleeves of the Parthians. Coming out from her crown is a long sash which is curled large on the back of her blond hair and drapes almost to the floor. She wears gold on each finger, gold earrings, and a multi-stranded necklace with gold coins dangling from each strand.

"My queen," Demetrius says, bending at the knee. The other magi do the same.

"You all may rise. Now, what are you doing here? Spying on me, you handsome demon?" she says with her lyrical voice.

"Yes, Your Majesty," Demetrius replies with a glint in his eye. "Spying on the beauty of your form, your eyes, your hair, your lips."

The queen laughs. "Well, follow me, everyone. We will be dining soon. They have brought out eight more dining couches for all of you."

Demetrius stops. It takes the queen a moment to realize they are not with her. She stops and turns around. "What is wrong?"

"There are only seven of us now. We lost Hophni."

"Hophni, that dear sweet boy," she says. "Well, no mind. We shall eat without him."

They enter the dining hall and are greeted by Caesar himself. The magi bow completely prostrate to the floor.

"I love the way the Orientals pay homage," he says. "You may rise. I am sorry my wife cannot be here. She is busy with some project or another. Do be seated. They are ready to serve our food."

The dining hall is large and opulent in the modest Roman style, though not living up to what Parthians consider opulent.

The evening is spent with entertaining talk, food, and harp players, sometimes joined by flutists.

That night Demetrius takes them to a guest house of the Apollo temple. "We will not have far to go in the morning when we begin our research," he explains.

As soon as they are alone, Kumar announces, "I heard she was originally a slave brought here after the

Germanicans lost a battle to Augustus."

"I heard that too," Dushatra says.

"You are right," Demetrius says. "She was raised to be a lady in waiting. But, when Parthia kept defying Rome, Augustus decided to give her to Phraattes, I think as a way of tormenting him. Beautiful, but a she-cat under it all."

"Well, we had better be careful what we say here," Michel says. "These walls could have places for peering eyes."

"I agree," Katazuli says.

The next morning, the magi walk over to the library of Apollo. It is made of white marble with columns across the front. Once inside, they see ahead of them the apse with the grand statue of Apollo. To their left and right are halls with domed ceilings and ending in their own apse. Their walls are lined with cubicles stuffed with thousands of both papyrus and parchment scrolls.

They see an attendant at a table and approach him.

"Kind sir," Demetrius begins, "could you tell us where the oracles of Apollo might be found?"

"They are in the hall to your left."

"Do you have sacred writings of any other gods?" Michel asks.

"If you mean gods of the night, yes, we do. They will be in the hall to your right in the back corner."

For two days, the magi search through the sacred writings of Apollo and the gods of the night.

"Well, I have found several gods and goddesses of the night—gods of dreams, ghosts, death, the moon, nocturnal thunder—everything but of stars." It is Michel.

"You may as well join us in reading Apollo's oracles tomorrow," Borseen says. "By the way, where is Demetrius?"

"He keeps disappearing," Kumar says.

"I have seen him slip back in here several times, pretending he hadn't been anywhere," Yasib says.

The following day they return to the library.

"If we do not find anything about a star god, especially a newborn one, I say we move on."

"We agree with you, Michel," Dushatra says.

They study through the scrolls a while.

"I am getting a little dizzy," Michel says. I did not eat much on the ship. Maybe it's catching up with me. Please excuse me while I go outside onto the portico a few moments."

The others grunt in approval, and he leaves. Once out on the portico, he decides to walk through a small grove of trees dedicated to Apollo. He stops and sits at one of the benches placed under a tree.

"Do you really think we can get by with it?" Demetrius says in a loud whisper.

"Of course we can. He is old, and it is time someone else becomes king of Parthia," a feminine voice replies.

"But he's your husband."

"What is so different from what he himself did? He killed his own father and all his brothers so he could be king."

"But how?"

Michel can imagine the queen looking up at Demetrius with a coy expression.

"An accident. A wheel could come off his chariot. The saddle strap of his camel could snap. He could drown in his swimming pool."

"What about poison?"

"Brilliant, Demetrius. Now, we need to figure out when to do it."

"And when I should make my announcement as king of Parthia," Demetrius adds.

"You don't need to do that, silly. I will marry you. Since I'm queen, that will automatically make..."

Michel stands and rushes back into the temple library. He walks over to his bench, picks up the scroll he had been reading, but does not see the words.

"What's wrong, Michel?" Yasib asks. "You're just staring at the table. Do you need Katazuli to give you something for nausea?"

Michel stands. "Tell the librarian we are returning to

our room. Hurry!"

Katheryn Maddox Haddad

APOLLO'S LIBRARY IN ROME

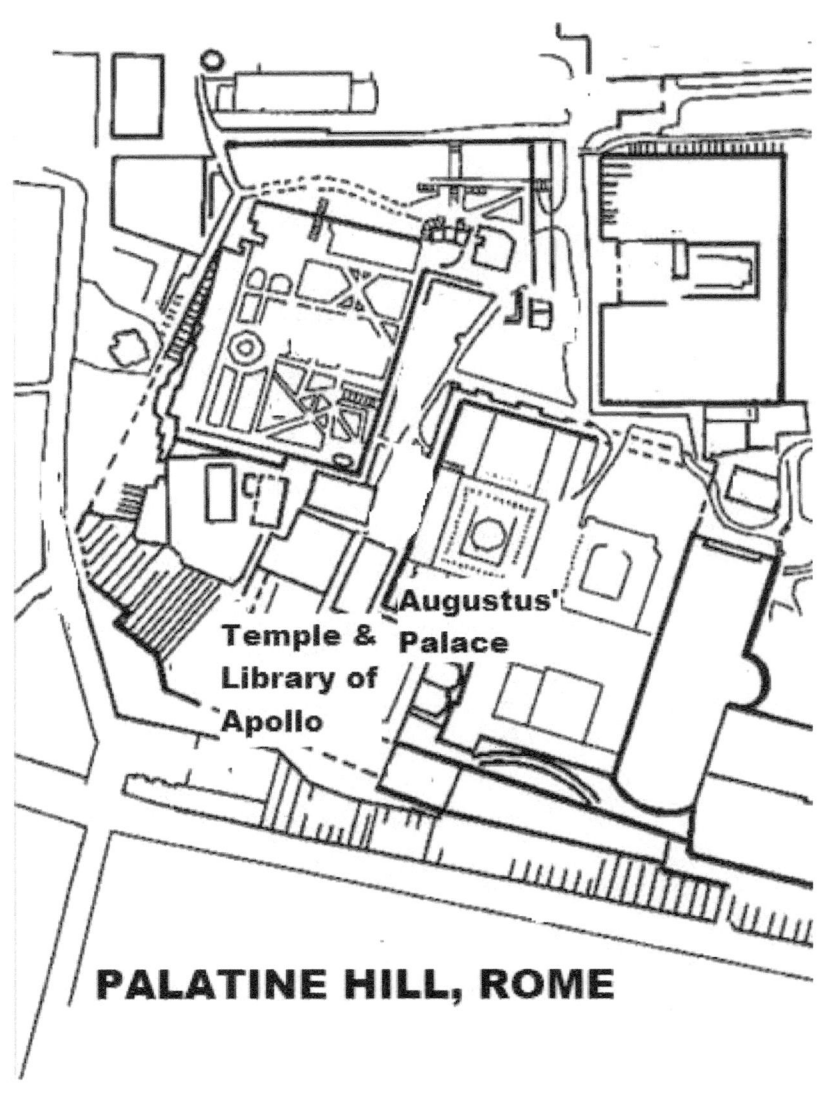

21 ~ BETRAYAL

"Demetrius, a traitor?" Kumar says.

"I knew it!" Dushatra says.

"There was always something different about him," Yasib says. "But I wasn't sure what."

"I suspected it," Borseen says.

"I didn't," Katazuli says.

"He will be here in a few moments. The librarian will tell him where we went," Michel says. "We have to decide what we're going to do."

"I know what I'm going to do," Borseen says, pulling his dagger out of his belongings.

They hear footsteps outside their door. Demetrius enters and sees what is in Borseen's hand. He stares at each magi, frowns, then shifts his expression.

"Ha, ha, ha. Are we going hunting for our dinner? I am pretty good with the bow."

No one smiles. They stand still and stare at Demetrius.

His expression changes back to confusion. "What's going on?"

Still, no one speaks.

"Well, if you're going to be that way, I am going to walk over to the market and buy something to eat."

Still nothing.

"What?" Demetrius jumps back. He looks into each face.

"What is this?" he asks, trying to form a grin that will

not quite form. "Oh. Did one of you hear us talking out in the garden?"

Demetrius turns his back on them, pushes his hands through his curly black hair, then turns back around, this time smiling.

"It was just a joke. You know how Musa is. She is never serious. She lives in a world of make-believe. That's why she has a lion on a leash that she walks around the palace with. She pretends it is a kitten. You know how she is."

"Yes, we know what our queen is like. But we did not expect it of you, Demetrius," Michel says. "What has happened to you?"

"Nothing has happened to me."

Borseen raises the dagger over his head and lunges at Demetrius. Katazuli, both taller and heavier, reaches up and grabs Borseen's wrist.

"Don't do it, Borseen."

"Why? And give him a chance that he does not plan to give our king?"

"He is cruel and overbearing," Demetrius declares. "He imprisons people who say a single cross word to him, he executes people he is jealous of, he exiles people he doesn't trust. Look what he did to you, Michel. And you, Kumar, Dushatra and Yasib. You can never go back unless you have proof what that star meant. Cannot be done. No one can prove the meaning of what stars do and don't do."

"Demetrius, we cannot take the place of the gods and determine who sits on Parthia's throne," Yasib says.

"We are his advisors, not his executioners," Kumar says.

"You are a disgrace to all of us," Dushatra says.

Demetrius backs up against the door. His eyes are wide. "But he's a mad man."

"It is not our place," Michel says.

"Let me at him," Borseen says. "It should have been him who died, not Hophni."

"No! Don't let him get me!"

"You coward," Dushatra says.

"I've got money."

"No, you don't," Kumar says.

"You cannot bribe us," Yasib says.

"I've got more money than you can imagine. You can have it all."

"All of nothing," Dushatra says.

"You have your choice," Michel finally says. "I think the others will agree. You either continue on with us, and we turn you in to the king when we return home where you will be executed, or you stay here under the protection of Caesar if he happens to want to protect you. Those are your only two choices. If you choose not to continue with us, you will leave our presence immediately," Michel continues.

Demetrius steps toward his belongings.

"I said immediately. You will take nothing with you."

Demetrius stares into the faces of his friends.

"I was only trying to..."

"Go. Before we change our mind. Go."

Demetrius opens the door and walks away.

The remaining six magi stand where they are.

Katazuli shakes his head and sits on his bed. "I don't understand it. I just don't understand it."

"I do," Dushatra says.

"You should have let me at him," Borseen says.

"Well, we may as well see what he had hidden in his belongings," Kumar says.

Kumar looks through the large leather pouch. He throws clothes onto the floor. Then it is empty. "Nothing suspicious."

"Wait. What's this?" Yasib says.

He hands it to Michel. "It is in the queen's handwriting. It just says, "In the garden."

"Well, are we through here?" Yasib asks. "I think we are."

"I think so too," Michel says. "And I don't see any reason to linger. Let's go back to the port now. Maybe we can find a ship ready to leave in the morning. Maybe the ship captain will let us go ahead and board tonight. If not, we can always go to an inn."

The six remaining magi gather up their belongings and walk out the door, leaving Demetrius' things on the floor.

"I think we need to go over to Anatolia and see what we can find at the library in Pergamum," Michel says. "Is that agreeable with you, Katazuli?"

"Indeed, it is. It will be good being among my own people again. But, do you think we can find a ship going all the way over there? It's a long way? Probably an eight- to ten-day voyage."

The following day they take a boat back down the Tiber to Ostia. They find passage on board the *Collis* headed back to Athens. The winds are contrary, and it takes eight days.

They are quieter than usual. No singing like they used to do when they first started out on their quest. No joking and laughter and speculating. Just wandering around the ship watching the endless water and wondering. Wondering about many things with no answers.

"We were lucky to find a ship this late in the season," Yasib says. "Most ships have harbored for the winter."

"What a waste of time this has been," Michel says, leaning on a railing and watching the coastline go by. "The workers I hired probably are done diverting the water into a canal and the ground dry enough to start planting."

"Your chance will come," Yasib says. "Be patient. You're still young. You have plenty of time to chase after your dream."

"It's not me I'm worried about, Yasib. I'm worried about people in the world who do not believe in the one true God. You're one of them, Yasib. You believe in a god with no personality that is the essence of the universe. I want to convince you. I want to convince the one true God to walk on earth again as he did with our first parents, Adam and Eve."

Michel looks at Yasib without saying anything more. Yasib puts his hand on Michel's shoulder. "As I said, your dream will come true someday. Don't be in such a hurry for it. When your God is ready, he will make it happen."

At the end of eight days, the ship docks in Athens. The captain informs the passengers they must all disembark. He will go no farther until next spring.

"What are we going to do?" Katazuli asks.

"Well, we could stay here and go over to Mount Olympus and climb it," Kumar says.

"And interview the gods themselves while we're up there," Borseen says. "Brilliant! Why didn't I think of that?"

"I don't think Kumar was serious," Dushatra says.

"Why don't we check all the ships in port?" Yasib says. "If there is one willing to take the two-day trip across the Aegean to Anatolia, we go. If not, we stay here and climb Mount Olympus. Well, you young men climb it."

The six divide up and make their way down the docks. The harbor is full. Some ships do not have anyone on them at all anymore. Some have a guard on them. One by one, they work their way down. None of them have gangplanks out. There is no use even calling up to them. A few have some men on board preparing them for the winter stay.

"I found one. I found one!" It is Katazuli. "It is going to leave today," he shouts as he runs down the dock. Since so few people are on the docks now because of the winter inactivity, he is easy to spot.

The magi catch up and follow him on board the ship.

"I must be crazy doing this," the captain says. "But I need to get over there for the winter. The ship is full. Everyone rushing to get there just like me. You'll have to find a place to sleep. And let's hope I didn't let too many passengers on board."

The captain signals his crew who pulls in the gangplank.

"Weigh anchor! Hoist the sails! Cast off!"

The ship works its way eastward between the numerous islands off the Grecian coast. Then it is open water.

The six magi wander around the decks. They, along with the crew and many of the passengers, stare up into the sky.

"Fair so far," everyone says. "Nothing to worry about."

"What was that?"

A gust of wind bears down and rushes across the deck. Another gust. And another.

"Hold on," the captain shouts. "Unfurl those sails. Drop anchor. Everyone not on my crew, below deck. We're in for it!"

The magi climb below to the berth deck with the other passengers. They sit on the boards to wait it out. And pray.

The wind hits with a roar. They can hear waves slamming into the ship. It rolls one way. Then the opposite. Back and forth. On one side, then on the other.

They know the captain will be heading the ship into the wind and that the ship will be rammed down into each trough before rising and going nearly straight up to the top of the next wave.

Still, the wind. Roaring. Whistling.

Passengers hang on to posts and try not to let their bodies go sliding across the deck until they are stopped hard by the hull.

Screaming now. Of passengers afraid to die. Of passengers afraid to live. Of passengers afraid of fear.

Now the ship is straight up, and passengers fall to the stern. Then straight down, and passengers slide unmercifully in the direction of the bow.

Back and forth. Trying not to vomit. Trying to hold it down. Trying not to think of the nightmare they are living through.

Regretting. Regretting their decisions to leave the safety of the harbor. Regretting calling other ship captains cowards for staying behind. Regretting trusting the wind to not do what it always does every autumn.

Roaring. Crashing. Whistling. Things clanging on the deck overhead. Things clanging on the hulls. Clanging and clapping and battering.

Back on its side. Then its other side. Hoping the ship will be able to right itself and not capsize.

One hour. Two. Sailors now coming below deck. Sailors giving up. Sailors who always know what to do now do not know.

More hours. Daylight gone. Nighttime taking over. Night like ink. Night like inside the jaws of the earth. Night like that nothingness between bleak stars in their somewhere.

The captain does the unthinkable. He gives up, and he, too, comes down to safety. An unsure safety. A safety that cannot be predicted or guaranteed or made possible.

No one steering the ship anymore. No one now in charge. Except the wind. The wind and the waves take over. The wind and waves control it all. The wind and waves with no mercy, no heart, no soul.

A crash overhead. A hard crash. Another mast has snapped in two and plunged to the deck.

A day and a night. Two days. Still the storm. The unrelenting storm that does not know the word stop. The unbiased storm that does not care who or what it destroys. The mindless roaring of the monster.

Rolling and slamming. Pitching one way and another.

Smells. Awful smells. Smells of vomit and urine and sweat. Smells of fear and sickness and death.

Humans but not human. At the mercy of the inhuman. At the mercy of what comprehends no mercy.

Three days.

Then the thump. The awful thump. The thump of the ship scraping on the bottom of something. Looking around for possible holes in the hull. Hoping to find it in time. But in time for what?

The bilge of the ship now straining. The boards of the ship squealing and screaming and crying out in pain.

Then it is gone. As suddenly as it had come, the wind is gone. Silence. A dread silence. A silence that says reality must now be faced.

The captain stands, climbs a few steps up the ladder, and opens the hatch.

Blue sky. A sky that should not be blue anymore. A

betraying sky pretending to be a friend.

Officers follow the captain up. The sailors are next. Then the passengers. The brave passengers that want to know.

Michel joins them. He goes up the ladder, stands on the upper deck, and is stunned.

The front of the ship has hit rocks. The back of the ship is still free and being rocked back and forth by the vicious waves. He knows.

Michel shouts down the hatch.

"The captain is calling for abandon ship. Everyone. Come up while you can. Grab a board. Anything to float on. Abandon ship!"

The six magi stand together.

"Well, this is it," Michel says. "May we be reunited onshore."

With that, Michel puts a strong arm around old Yasib and his other arm around a wide board, and they jump into the drink.

Cold. Cold water. Down. Down under the water. Kick. Kick hard. Come back up. Back up to air and life. Kick. Struggle. Stay alive.

When Michel surfaces, he sees Yasib and swims over to him.

"Grab hold, Yasib. It is big enough for us both."

Yasib obeys.

Splashing all around them. Splashing of other passengers jumping overboard. Then the crew. All jumping into the abyss and hoping to get away from the ship before it takes its final plunge into the deep and an eternal grave.

Clinging, kicking, pawing, stretching, panting.

Michel and Yasib make it to the rocky shore. They grab hold of a boulder. It is wet. They cannot hang on. Their board takes them to another boulder. And another. Being slammed into a second death.

Then a beach. A beach with no boulders. A beach with small rocks and even sand. Michel and Yasib work their way to the beach.

Michel: The Fourth Wise Man

Their feet touch the floor of the sea. They push and struggle to reach final safety.

They lunge exhausted onto the sand and let the remnants of the waves lap hungrily at their feet.

More passengers join them. Passengers now whimpering and laughing both at the same time.

Michel manages to stand and help Yasib stand. They work their way farther from the shoreline, then collapse again.

Collapse and wait. Wait for the verdict. What about the other four? What about Kumar and Dushatra? What about Katazuli and Borseen?

They close their eyes. When they open them, it is dark. They look up into a sky, mocking them. A sky full of twinkling, sparkling stars wanting to play. They close their eyes again, and it becomes morning.

"There you are," Kumar says. "Have you seen any of the others?"

Yasib sits up but does not move further.

Michel joins Kumar as they look up and down the beach among people clinging to life. People in clothes that have been torn and battered and dirtied, just like their spirits. But still clinging.

"Over here!" It is Dushatra, Katazuli, and Borseen.

"Where is Yasib? Did he make it?"

"He's over there," Michel says, pointing.

The five go back over to Yasib. They huddle together—cold, wet, but having survived. Once more together. Once more on a single quest. A quest to stay alive. A quest to survive until they find the meaning of the strange star.

ATHENA LIBRARY IN PERGAMUM

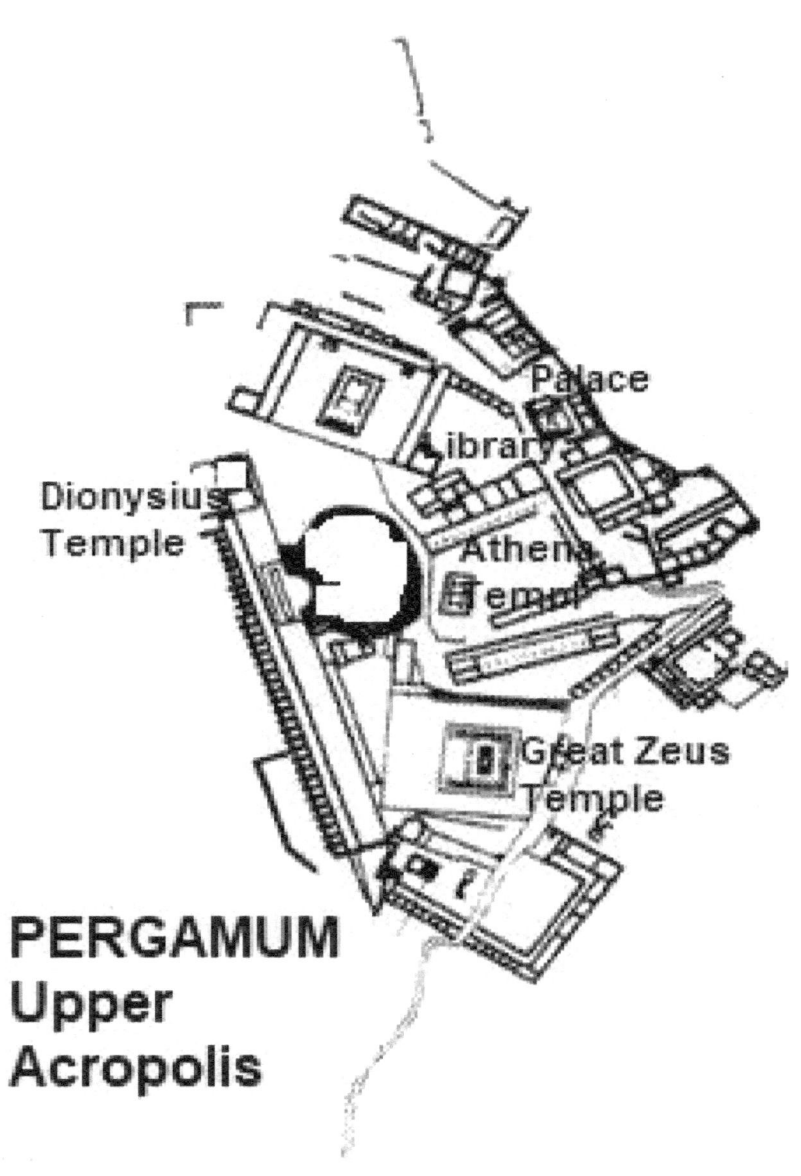

22 ~ TO HOPE AGAIN

"Now what?" Dushatra says. "We don't know where we are. We could be back in Greece."

"Let's hope not," Michel says. "Look over there. A man on horseback."

Michel stands and waves with both arms to get the rider's attention. The rider sees him.

"Where are we?" he asks.

"You're on the coast of Anatolia near the harbor of Salamis. If you walk the way I came, then turn east when you arrive at the inlet, you will go into the city. There are people there with food for you. And warm blankets. I'm sorry I cannot do more for you."

"Thank you, sir. God bless you."

"Which god?" he asks, then rides on.

The rider turns back. "By the way, if you want to go farther inland, just follow the Kaikos River."

The six magi work their way toward the city, shivering and cold against the lingering late autumn wind.

Yasib lags behind. Katazuli puts the old man on his back.

"I don't think I have ever been so cold in my life," Kumar says. "Give me the hot, steamy weather of Indo-Parthia any day."

They arrive at the harbor. Townspeople from Smyrna rush to them with blankets and direct them over to a large campfire.

"Sit over there. Someone will bring you some hot soup. We have set up some large tents. Go in there to sleep tonight out of the wind."

"I don't know if we have been blessed or cursed," Borseen says as they sip on the warmth of the soup.

"I guess both," Michel says.

Morning comes. They are awakened by voices outside the tent.

"Come grab a bite of bread," someone tells them. "Then, see those wagons over there? As soon as they are full, you will be taken into the city."

Within another hour, they are in Smyrna.

"We have lost everything, including our money," Michel says. "I am going to look for work."

"Wait," Kumar says. "I still have my money belt, and think I have enough for us to buy some decent clothes."

"Thank you, Kumar. That is generous of you. Then I'm going job hunting," Michel says. "Too bad Hophni is no longer with us; he was good at making papyrus. Well, I can do tutoring."

"I can hire on with a blacksmith," Borseen says.

"I will look for an apothecary that needs an assistant," Katazuli says.

"I can tutor," Dushatra says.

"I'm going to look for a contractor; I can paint a mural for someone," Kumar says.

"And you, Yasib," Michel says, "will find us an inn and talk them into letting you stay in a room before paying for it so you can rest. Just show them your crooked finger joints, and limp a little, and that should convince them."

"I don't need to pretend I am limping," Yasib says. "I am still very tired. When you look for me, I will be at the closest inn to the waterfront that I can find."

Every day, the magi head out to work while Yasib rests and goes for short walks and gives philosophical advice to anyone who wants to listen to him while he rebuilds his strength.

"I think we have enough money now to keep us going

until we return home," Michel says a month later.

"If we return home," Dushatra adds. "Remember, we're still exiled, and if we return without a provable explanation of the star, we will be food for the lions."

"We could have had the answer long ago if you had listened to me. The answer is in the Jewish writings. I know it is."

"Not that again," Kumar says. 'Your religion is too narrow-minded. One God? Ridiculous. One God cannot take care of everything."

It takes them three days to walk northeast to Pergamum.

"It is so good to be home," Katazuli says over and over as they walk.

"Were you born around here?"

"No, I was born in a village near Hattusa, farther east of here. That was the where our Hittite king was. The city was abandoned a century ago and has crumbled."

They walk farther, each thinking of his own birth home.

"My father used to go over to the old ruins and look around for our ancestors' books. He accumulated quite a few tablets. Built-up a sizeable library of them."

"Well, maybe we should go see his library instead of the one at Pergamum," Dushatra says.

"He died a few years ago. Beforehand, he donated his tablets to the library here in Pergamum. This is the place we should go."

Evening the second day, they arrive at the city.

"The Temple and School of Asklepius is here," Katazuli says. "I'd like to find an inn nearby. Asklepius is the god of healing. This is the most famous healing temple in the world. I studied here some when I was younger. I would like to study here again someday."

"Seems to me you should be one of their teachers," Michel says.

"I would have to be one of their priests to teach. Well, I do look forward to visiting it."

"You're the boss," Borseen says. "This is your territory."

"But tomorrow morning, we must first go up that hill to the library. That is why we have come."

The next day they walk up one of the hills behind the city. The road is paved with flat stones and has grand columns on each side.

"What is that temple on the left?" Yasib asks.

"That is the magnificent temple to Serapis, who the Egyptians call Isis. We cannot see inside the grounds, but it has a pool for ablutions. On each side of the temple, itself are two grand towers that the priests live in."

They continue to climb.

"What is that over on the hill way over there on the right?" Borseen asks.

"That is the amazing temple to Zeus. It can be seen from far away."

"Are we going much farther up this hill?" Yasib asks. "My bones hurt."

"We're almost there, friend," Katazuli says. "Remind me to give you something for your pain when we get back to the inn."

"What's that temple straight ahead?" Michel asks.

"That's the temple to Dionysius," Katazuli explains. "All the kings of this city claim to be descended from him."

"I certainly would not want him as my ancestor—a god with absolutely no morals. Take my ancestor: He was Daniel, a great prophet of the one true and moral God."

"Yeah, yeah, we know," Dushatra says.

"Let's walk around it," Katazuli says. "As you can see, it is next to this amphitheater. That's because he is the god of the theater and a lot of other things you and I don't approve of."

They walk around to the entrance of the theater and see on their right a temple to Athena.

"Don't pay any attention to that temple over there. Straight ahead is the library. Let's go in here."

"Sirs, are you here for the banquet?" a clerk asks once

they are inside.

"No, we are here to do some research," Katazuli explains.

"Well, you came in the wrong entrance. But I can take you to the other end. Let's go out to the portico so we can bypass all those classrooms and reading rooms."

They walk out onto the portico with grand columns all the way across the library complex.

"How wide is this?" Dushatra asks.

"About thirty-five man-lengths. Here we are. Just walk through that door. "

The magi turn left and enter the library itself over an hour since starting up the hill. In each corner and in the middle of the room are statues of the kings of Pergamum. The ceiling is high, and there are cubicles for both papyrus and parchment scrolls all the way to the ceiling with ladders available. On the back wall, they see flat shelves. Upon inspection, they realize the shelves are full of ancient clay tablets.

"I'm sure some or most of these were donated by my father," Katazuli says.

"Along the longest walls are writings of my Hittite people. The other long wall is divided up between the writings of the Pamphylians, Gauls Cappadocians, and a few Scythians."

The rest of the day is spent reading the sacred writings of the gods of the native people of Anatolia. Sometimes the other magi notice Katazuli speaking at length with the head librarian. Sometimes the two go outside together, and the magi suspect they are going to the palace, which is almost attached to the library. But they do not pry.

They spend the first two weeks of November in the library. Each evening they compare their discoveries.

"The closest I have come to a star god is Ellel, god of the sky, and Istanu, god of the sun," Dushatra says.

"I have found Kaskuh god of the moon, and Teshub god of weather," Yasib says.

"I ran into Arinnita, goddess of the sky, and Arma,

another god of the moon," Borseen says.

"The main Phrygian gods—Cybele and Attis—have nothing to do with anything but procreating," Kumar says.

"I keep running into the old Greek gods that we already studied over in Athens," Michel says.

"I have run into the same problem," Katazuli says. "No gods that are stars. There are a lot of gods that are depicted by many stars in the night sky, but none that are stars themselves."

"So, what do we do now?" Borseen asks. "I say we go on over to Syria where I am from.

"Not so fast, Borseen," Michel says. "I think our guide has more investigating to do."

Michel looks over at Katazuli and smiles. He looks back at his friends with a small grin of his own. "Would it be okay with the rest of you if we spent a little time at the temple to Asklepius? People all over the world go there to be healed. I want to learn a few more things about healing, especially broken bones."

No one says anything.

"Of course, I do not really need to do this."

"Katazuli," Michel says, "we owe you a lot. You have doctored all of us at some time or another, either on this trip or back in Parthia. I think I speak for the others that we would be pleased to spend another week here in Pergamum for you."

Katazuli smiles. He pulls on his mixed red and gray beard and blinks back a tear.

"Thank you, friends."

The next morning Katazuli rises early to go over to the healing temple.

"You're not going without us," Michel says.

"At least we don't have to climb all the way up the hill now," Yasib says.

When they arrive, they go through a gate in the wall that surrounds the temple complex. Within the walls are columns that surround the main building.

Within the temple itself along the walls are statues of

great healers of the past, mostly Grecians, but some Anatolians. In the center is a gigantic statue of Asklepius with curly hair and beard, wearing a toga, and clinging to his staff with a snake curled around it.

Back out in the temple complex, they see a healing pool and rooms around it for the sick to rest and pray. An annex to the complex is an amphitheater with a smaller seating capacity than the one up on the acropolis at the top of the hill, which they assume to be for lectures on the art of faith and healing.

"May I help you?"

They turn and see a priest wearing a simple long white tunic and pointed conical headdress.

The other magi step back while Katazuli introduces himself. When they see him disappear with the priest, they slip back out and go down to the bottom of the small hill where the main market is.

"I'm going to buy a supply of parchments," Michel says. "The local people are telling me this is where the process of making parchment was developed. Then I am going to sit down and write some letters."

"Good idea," Dushatra and Kumar say.

"I'm going to take a walk up to the citadel on the other side of the palace," Borseen says. "I may learn something new about sword making."

"Well, I'm going to bed for a nap," Yasib says. "You men are wearing me out."

The week goes by. The men are packing their belongings.

"The great library in Antioch is next," Borseen announces. "At last, you are going to find the meaning of the star. I am sure of that. Syria has a long history, and our knowledge is beyond comprehension."

"Well, perhaps not that much," Yasib says, "but the books at Antioch are rare and worth investigating."

"Have we found a ship yet?" Dushatra asks.

"I made a trip back to Smyrna two days ago," Borseen announces, "and made arrangements for passage."

"I'm not going with you," Katazuli says. "I know discovering the meaning of the star has to be done, and it is important to King Phraattes. But what is here is important to all of humanity. There is so much about healing that I did not know before. I want to learn it. What I learned about fixing broken bones this week has shown me just how much I do not know. I'm sorry."

The magi stare at Katazuli a moment, not sure what to say. Michel says it for them.

"I cannot claim this comes as a surprise to us. You have been in a very special world these past three weeks, both at the library with writings of your people, and at the healing temple. It is a world you belong in. We have seen that."

"Thank you for understanding," Katazuli says. "And I promise, if I do run into any kind of star god, I will let you know immediately."

"I'm sure you will."

The next morning early when the remaining five magi prepare to leave, Katazuli puts on his heavy coat and walks out the door with them.

"You don't have to dress that warmly just to go down the street to the temple," Kumar says.

"I'm going with you."

"What?" Michel says. "I thought you were staying."

"What I meant to say is that I am walking with you out as far as the highway."

"Oh."

At the city gate, they say their goodbyes. Katazuli heads back into the city. The other magi turn west toward the coast to the Aegean Sea.

"Brrrr. It's cold here," Kumar says, pulling his coat around him tighter.

"I don't think I have ever been in a colder place," Dushatra says.

"I have," Yasib says. "You fellows don't even know the beginning of cold. Have you ever been in Xiongnu Mongolia in the winter?"

Michel: The Fourth Wise Man

"No, and I don't intend to," Kumar says.

"My father went there once," Borseen says. "Being the famous sword maker that he was, the army took him along to repair swords and replace those left behind in battle. He hated the weather there."

"Well, give me Parthia or Judea," Michel says. Neither of them is this cold."

"You forget our Parthian Zagros Mountains in Parthia," Yasib says.

As they draw closer to the coast, the stronger and colder the wind blows.

"It is close to December. Mother earth has died," Borseen says. "But I never shall die," he pronounces.

"You young people are all alike," Dushatra says. "You think you can conquer anything."

"I don't know about them, but I... What was that?"

The others look around.

"I don't hear anything but the wind," Kumar says.

"I don't see anything but barren fields, barren trees, and barren rocks," Michel says.

A man jumps down from the boulders along the highway onto Yasib, pinning him to the ground. Another man jumps down on Kumar. They keep coming until all the magi are under control of the bandits.

"Okay," the man apparently in charge announces. "Hand over your money belts."

"We cannot. They're under us," Dushatra mumbles.

"We're going to let you up enough to turn over and grab your money belts, but do not try anything that would make us mad."

Borseen's attacker eases up on him just enough for him to reach for his money belt. Instead, he reaches for his dagger, slashes his attacker's face, and jumps to his feet. He runs to the leader of the gang, grabs hold of his head enough to expose his throat and makes his demand.

"Let go of my friends, or your leader is a dead man."

The other robbers let go of their prey but run for Borseen. They push him to the ground, and one rolls with him, trying to get the dagger out of his hand. Another hits him over the head and knocks him out.

That done, the robbers turn their attention back to Yasib, Kumar, Dushatra, and Michel. Each is beaten in the head until he is unconscious. One man climbs back up one of the boulders along the road and jumps back down with a tree branch in his hand. He beats on the legs of the unconscious men.

Now it is quiet. The four magi lay completely still on the deserted highway. Dead.

LIBRARY AT ANTIOCH, SYRIA

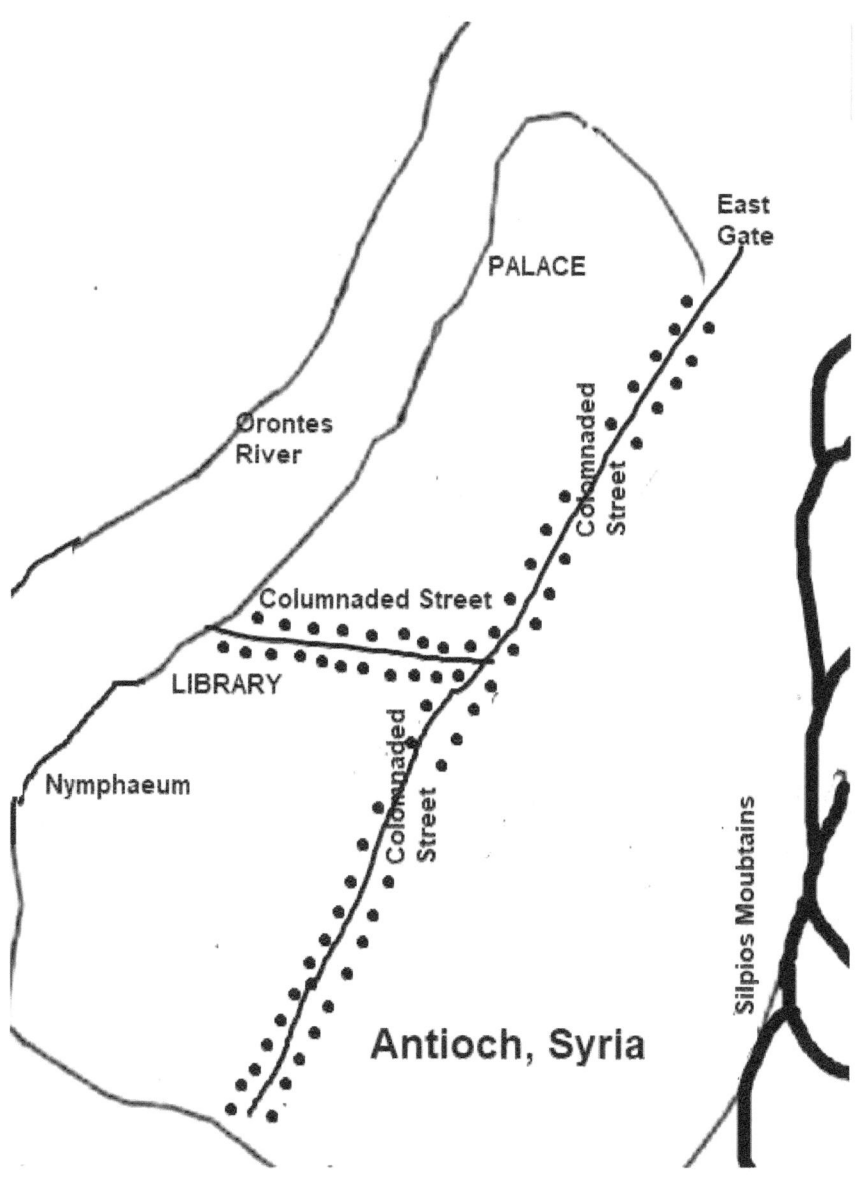

23 ~ RESURRECTION

Katazuli and his temple companion walk up the highway. "I hope I can catch up with them before the ship leaves. They're lucky the o-innkeeper was honest enough to report the money belt one of them left behind."

They go around a curve and stop in their tracks. Before they can blink, they take off running.

"No. No. No!" Katazuli shouts, his eyes filled with fear and dread and remorse over deserting his friends.

He comes to Yasib first and kneels by him. "Yasib, Yasib, do you hear me? Yasib? Please don't be dead, Yasib."

He moves over to Dushatra. Dushatra groans. "Where did they get you, friend?" Katazuli asks.

"Help, help the others," he groans.

Katazuli moves over to to the next victim. "Michel, Michel." He taps his cheeks and raises his eyelids with his fingers.

"Uhhh."

"Michel. You're alive, Who did this? Where are you injured?"

Katazuli looks over at his temple companion. "This one is alive too," the priest says. He next goes yo Yasib.

Katazuli looks back at Michel, who is now trying to sit up. "No, don't do that. Lie still. I need to check you. Where did they get you?"

"They beat us all in our legs," he moans, "I guess so we wouldn't follow them."

Michel: The Fourth Wise Man

Katazuli calls over to the temple priest. "Can you go back and bring a cart for my friends? I'll wait here with them."

The temple healer leaves. One by one Katazuli, tall and strong, picks up every magus and takes him to the side of the road. He gives each of them a drink from his water skin periodically and feels their forehead for evidence of fever.

Two hours later, Katazuli's temple companion returns with a wagon. They get the four injured magi into the wagon and take them to the temple of healing in Pergamum. He puts them all in the same room, and the high priest comes to look them over.

"The youngest one. What is his name?"

"Borseen. He's Syrian."

"He has one broken leg. The legs of the others are badly bruised, but not broken. Do you remember what I taught you about mending breaks?"

"Yes, sir. I hope so, sir."

In another hour, all four magi have been treated, and warm blankets placed over them. The big Hittite sits in a corner watching them.

"Katazuli? Katazuli?" It is Michel.

"Yes, friend. Do you hurt?"

"I'm okay," Michel moans. "I just wanted to thank you."

"Thank me? Why would you do that? I deserted you. I deserted all my friends. All I could think of is what I wanted instead of what you wanted. You all have needed me from the beginning of the trip. Why would I think you no longer needed me?"

"Don't think that way," Michel says in a loud whisper.

"I deserted my friends."

"No, you did not."

"This is my homeland. I could have protected you from my people."

"They didn't attack us because we looked like foreigners. They attacked us because we looked like travelers, and travelers always have money."

"I am so sorry, Michel. So sorry." He looks at his friend and realizes he has gone back to sleep.

The injured magi stay in the healing temple for three weeks.

"I'm ready to go," Borseen says. "I've learned how to manipulate these crutches well enough. I'm ready to get out of here. Syria awaits me."

"You cannot go yet," Katazuli says.

"Watch me. By morning I will be gone."

"We're going with you," Kumar says.

Morning comes, and the five magi put on heavy coats, ready to walk down the highway. Katazuli puts his on also.

"You don't have to walk us out to the highway," Michel tells him. "We will be okay. Stay in here where it is warm."

"I'm going with you," Katazuli says.

"It is not necessary," Michel repeats.

"It is necessary. I will never desert you again," Katazuli says. "I am going to continue searching for the star with you."

Michel stares at his friend. "Are you sure?"

The other four look up from their packing. "Are you sure?" they all ask, almost in unison.

"I am sure. I can come back here after we have completed our mission. Now, I have rented a wagon and two strong horses. Ships go nowhere in January and February. It's all arranged. They are waiting for us. Let's go."

The journey is a hard one. It takes them two weeks traveling on the highway along the southern shoreline of Anatolia. They cannot take the inland route which is much flatter because of the snow-covered Taurus mountains at the east end.

They work their way down to the province of southern Lydia, then east through the provinces of Lycia, Pamphylia, and Cilicia. Even then, they run into some snow as they skirt the southern coast of those provinces in the foothills of the mountains.

As they travel, the men gradually regain their strength. All but old Yasib. They are worried about him.

Periodically Kumar, Dushatra, and Michel climb out of the wagon and walk beside it to build up the strength in their legs. Borseen tries it with his crutch, but slows them down and is not allowed the exercise until they stop for the night.

On the other side of Tarsus, they finally turn south, enter Syria, and pick up the Orodes River. The weather here is considerably warmer.

At last, they arrive at Antioch. Although Mount Silpio on the far east side of the city is snow-capped, the lower city near the coast is pleasant.

Upon entering the city, they pass through the market. Then, on their right are baths, monuments, and the imperial palace, while on their left are houses of the affluent.

They cross over the Parmenias River, where the street is lined with columns on both sides. On their right is a park dedicated to water nymphs and a large reflecting pool.

On their left is a theater and amphitheater. The library is on the east side of the two structures.

Borseen works his way farther down the colonnaded street until it ends at the Cherubim Gate out of the city. He looks around and sees an inn.

"Men, we have arrived," he says after renting a large room for them.

Michel, Kumar, Katazuli, and Dushatra have no trouble walking into the inn. Yasib does.

"Tomorrow I am challenging you men to a race," Borseen declares. "Even with my crutches, I will beat all of you."

The other magi look at him, grin slightly, and keep walking toward the inn's front gate. Katazuli picks up Yasib and puts him on his back.

"If you are so tough, Borseen," Katazuli says, "why don't you grab Yasib's things and bring them in?"

After everyone gets settled, they go out to the market to buy something to eat and pick up any personal supplies they need.

Although Borseen had a square, curly beard like the

king, upon arriving in Greece, he had shaved it off. He also had changed from the Parthian billowy pants and shirts to tunics like Demetrius wore. At all times, he had carried his carved dagger. Today he also wears a sword.

The next morning, the magi prepare to leave but do not waken Yasib. When he wakes up anyway and sees what they are doing, he barks at them. "Oh, no, you don't. You are not going over there without me."

Once everyone is ready, they walk back up the colonnaded street to the cultural center of the city and enter the grand library.

The domed ceiling far above is embellished with tiles formed to create scenes of various gods. The building is round, and beneath the high ceiling are arches. Between the arches are columns with a statue of one of the gods in front of each.

Within the arches are the cubicles in which thousands of scrolls have been stored. Some scrolls are papyrus, and some are the more durable parchment.

There are four wings coming out from four sections of the library, all with tables and benches in them for the convenience of the researchers.

In the middle of the library is a giant column that stretches from the floor to the highest pinnacle of the domed ceiling. At eye level are painted instructions telling which types of writings are located in which parts of the library.

"Yes, that's the way we do things in Syria," Borseen says. "No having to find a librarian for instructions. So, I will be over at one of those tables while the rest of you pick out what we should be reading through."

The magi make their selections and settle down to read. Back and forth, they go to the cubicles putting back what they had just read and getting out more scrolls.

They continue their routine for two weeks. Then they have their usual meeting to share results and make final conclusions.

"Okay," Borseen says. "Did we find the meaning of the star or not?"

"I found Attarsamain, god of the morning star, but we all know that star is actually the planet Venus," Yasib says. "I also found Shamayim who is the god of the heavens, but he is not a star."

"I found Yarikh, god of the moon," Kumar reports. "I also found Siccuth and Chiun, but they are the planet Saturn. None of them are stars."

"I ran into the Queen of Heaven in several places," Dushatra says. "They are referred to as either Isis, Astarte, or Inanna, all mother goddesses. They definitely are not stars."

"I had pretty much the same results as you, Dushatra. I found Aglibol, a moon god," Katazuli says.

"Well, I found Baal, also called Hadad in some places, a sky god," Borseen says. None of them are star gods."

"Guess what, fellows?" Michel says. "I found Hual, a moon god, Nuha, a sun god, and Sin, a moon god. That means we still have not found the meaning of the star we saw."

The magi sit in silence. "You should be listening to me," Michel says. "The answer is going to be in the sacred writings of the Jews."

"Okay, Michel, you have told us many times, but you are always wrong," Kumar says.

"If you had listened to me in the first place, we would be back home doing our regular work, and I probably would have the Garden of Eden replanted and flourishing by now."

"It is almost February. The star appeared in May. I'm beginning to doubt we will ever find its meaning," Katazuli says.

"We have wasted nine months and lost Hophni. If you would only listen to me."

"No," Dushatra says. "It will never happen."

"Well, everyone," Borseen says. "It's time to go back to Parthia."

"You know that means our lives," Yasib says.

"Not my life. Or Katazuli's. He only threatened you, Dushatra, Kumar, and Michel."

"That's not fair to them," Katazuli says. "We cannot just go off and leave them, or take them back to Parthia to their execution."

"Okay. Okay," Borseen retorts. "We will think of something. We are all the king's wise men, his magi. We should be able to come up with some kind of logical explanation of the star."

"You seem to forget we must have proof," Michel says.

"Okay, this is what we can do," Borseen says. "We will sell the wagon and mules and buy five camels."

"We cannot sell them for the price of five camels," Kumar says.

"I've got a gold ring," Yasib says. I can sell that."

"No, Yasib," Michel says. "We cannot let you do it."

"Yes, you can. I got it when we were working up in Smyrna after the shipwreck. Someone said they liked the way I taught, and just gave it to me. It has no sentimental value to me. So tomorrow I will sell it. And that is final."

"We cannot let you," Kumar says.

"Who is oldest? The discussion is closed."

"Okay, so we will buy our camels," Borseen says. "Then we go straight across the desert to Mari. We should be able to make it in two days."

"Mari? That is an abandoned city," Michel says.

"But it still has the palace, the armory, some old temples and what is left of the world-famous library it used to have. My father and I used to visit there. He used to say Mari would rise again, and Syria would become a world power then. More powerful than Parthia or Rome either one."

"Borseen, you don't make sense," Dushatra says.

"My point is that the library is still there, and I am convinced many of the ancient clay tablets are still there waiting for us to rediscover them. They, my friends, will have the answer. They will give the meaning of the star."

Silence.

"You know I am right," he adds.

"Well, it's on our way back to Ctesiphon," Katazuli says.

"It wouldn't hurt to at least look," Kumar says.

"Then it is settled," Borseen says. "Tomorrow, we buy our camels and leave immediately for Mari."

Michel and Yasib say nothing.

For the next two days, the magi rely on their camels to get them across the desert. They had had enough money left to purchase a goat-hair tent large enough for all six of them to sleep in comfortably.

Late on the second day, they arrive at the abandoned city.

"Let's just spend the night in our tent," Katazuli says. "We cannot tell anything in the dark, and the sun is almost completely down."

The next morning, they look around.

"Good thing we didn't go any farther last night," Kumar says. "The Euphrates River is right ahead of us. We'll have to cross it to get to what is left of Mari."

After picking up their tent and supplies and crossing the shallow river, they tie their camels up by a deserted building.

"Are you sure you and your father used to come here?" Michel asks.

"You're questioning my integrity?" Borseen challenges back.

The city is round with two sets of walls, much of which have crumbled. Within the outer walls, they see evidence of small homes and markets. There are a couple of small temples.

They find a collapsed section of the stronger and thicker inner wall and go through it. Inside the more secure section of the city they see the deserted palace. They also see two buildings, which were obviously temples to some great god. Statues within them have long ago fallen and broken apart.

They walk through several other buildings, which they determine must have been treasury buildings or guest buildings for visiting ambassadors or prominent citizens of the Mari kingdom.

They see one building that is long with columns all the way across the front.

"That reminds me of the library in Athens," Yasib says."

"Well, let's go in and see what is left of it," Borseen says.

They walk in and see collapsed shelves with pieces of tablets on the tiled floor.

"I don't know," Dushatra says. "Can we put enough of these back together we can read them?"

"Let's go back out and see if we can find a well or cistern," Borseen says," so we can fuse them back together. "Surely the palace and all these government buildings had at least one well and probably several. Being this close to the river, they would not have had to dig down very far to hit drinkable water."

They go back outside and scatter in different directions within the inner complex.

"I don't see one in this direction," Kumar calls out.

"The street I went down doesn't seem to have one either," Katazuli responds.

"Look harder, everyone," Borseen says. "There has to be water. Then we can fuse the clay tablets back together. No telling what kind of mysteries we will discover. Then we'll be famous, and King Phraattes will let everyone back in and restore your position as his advisors. He may even make us governors of some of his provinces."

Everyone looks for a well but Borseen. Borseen stays in the doorway of one of the buildings leaning on his crutch.

"Keep looking, men," he calls out periodically.

Finally, everyone goes back to him. "There are no wells in this city—or what is left of it," Michel says.

"Guess what, men?" Borseen says. "I wasn't just standing here being lazy. I was looking too. And I found a well."

"Where?" Yasib asks.

"Right inside this building. It must have been a building where they made wine or something. Go on in and look."

The other five magi enter the building.

"It's dark in here," Dushatra says.

"Of course, it is. But your eyes will adjust. Do you see it now?"

"No, it's too dark.

"Well, it's over there in that corner to my left. See it over there?"

The magi wander over to the corner. They hear squeaking and a metallic slam. By the time they turn around and realize what has just happened, Borseen has secured the barred door with a new lock.

"Borseen, what's going on?" Michel yells.

There is no answer.

24 ~ TRAPPED

The men grab hold of the bars of the door and shake it. The hinges are in the wall too firmly. The lock is too secure.

"Borseen!"
"Borseen!"

Their voices echo around the room and out into a ghost city.

"Borseen!"

They think they hear sadistic laughter, but are not sure.

"He is out of his mind," Dushatra says.

"He will be severely punished," Kumar says.

"But first, we need to find a way to get out of here," Katazuli says.

"I think I see a splinter of light up in that corner," Yasib says.

"I'm tall. I'll check it out." Michel checks the suspicious vulnerable corner but sees nothing.

"Katazuli, would you kneel here so I can stand on your knee?"

Michel checks again. "I still don't see it."

"Now, what?" Kumar asks. "We've got to figure out a way to get out of here," repeating Katazuli.

"Maybe we can kick our way out," Katazuli says. "Ouch. That wall is more solid than some of the others we saw out here."

"Ha, ha! Maybe you should try your head."

"Dushatra, help us think of a way to get out of here," Michel says. "How about a tunnel?"

The men drop to their knees and dig with their fingers.

"The floor is solid over here," Yasib says.

"Is this tile or concrete, or what?" Kumar asks. "Hey, it is tile. Let's scratch between each one and work it out. Then we can start a tunnel. Anyone have anything sharp on you? A knife? Anything?"

"I have some surgical tools in my pouch here," Katazuli says. "I'll find a seam, dig around a tile, and you fellows can pry the tile loose."

For the rest of the afternoon, the men work on the first phase of their escape.

"I'm tired," Yasib says.

"Me too," Dushatra says. "Don't know if it is day or night, but I need some sleep."

Soon the scraping and scuffling stop, and the men fall into a restless sleep.

It is now morning, though the men do not know this. They begin anew to pull up the tiles in the floor of their cell. All morning they work at it.

"I think we've loosened enough tiles, we can begin digging our tunnel," Kumar says. "Katazuli, can you use your tools to loosen up the clay?"

They wait as Katazuli scratches at the floor. He scratches in one section, then another, and another."

"Why are you moving around?" Michel asks. "Stay in one place."

"I cannot. I cannot find a place where the soil is loose enough to dig into."

"Concrete. There was concrete under the tile," Yasib says.

"A tunnel is out," Kumar says. "Now what?"

"We've got to think of something. We weren't hired as the king's advisors because we had no minds," Dushatra says. "Think of something."

The outside door opens. It is daylight. "Getting

hungry?" Borseen says.

"Borseen! You rat!"

"You brash, unscrupulous, underhanded, young hornet!"

"Traitor."

"You ungrateful, egotistical, devious human scorpion!"

"Monster."

"Let us out of here or we'll..."

"You'll what? By the way, thank you for the compliments. So, how has your first night in my new kingdom been? Oh, I see you have been doing some digging. That's why I chose this building. I knew what you would try. Didn't work, did it?"

"Let us out of here, Borseen."

"Oh, I cannot do that. But, you never did answer my original question. Are you hungry?"

"Well, I..."

"Shut up, Kumar. Don't tell him anything."

"That's fine with me. Well, I have a lot of work to do getting Mari to rise again."

Borseen turns toward the outside door, stops, and looks back. "Oh, isn't that what you want to do with your—what did you call it—Garden of Eden, Michel?"

"They are nothing alike," Michel responds with a hiss.

With nothing more to say, Borseen closes the outside door and leaves them once more in darkness.

"What are we going to do?" Katazuli asks. "We've got to get out of here."

Silence. The men resume sitting on the floor that is now torn up with piles of tile and mortar.

"Yasib, you're pretty quiet. Are you still with us?" Michel asks.

"I'm over here, and I am as fine as the rest of you."

Silence again. The silence of wondering and trying to figure out how to become free of an unsuspected trap like that of a hungry spider and its web.

"What does Borseen want?"

Michel: The Fourth Wise Man

"What is he up to?"

"What does he want us to do for him?"

"Die."

A week passes. Borseen brings them a piece of flatbread every day and a skin of water.

"Divide it up among yourselves. And no being selfish."

Silence. Silence like being down in a well in the middle of a desert with the moon even out. The silence of nothingness. Only the muffled sound of a mouse chewing something somewhere in their cell.

"I guess he'll tell us eventually. Otherwise, he would have killed us outright."

"Maybe he wants us to starve to death."

"Maybe he wants to torture us so he can see us suffer first."

"Or beg him for mercy until we do his will."

"What is his will?"

"Borseen! Where are you? What do you want?"

The outside door opens. "You sure are noisy in here. I'm going to bed now. You should do the same. Sweet dreams."

The door slams closed again. Closed on freedom. Closed on hope. Closed on life.

Morning. They hear the honking and sputtering of camels. And voices. And clanging. More voices. Shuffling. Dragging. Slamming. Then the noise drifting away.

More nothingness.

More quiet. Except for a mouse chewing away at something.

An unmanly whimper sometimes.

The outside door opens. It is morning once again.

"You've been here over a week. Aren't you hungry yet? I would think you'd be doing a little begging by now."

"What do you want, Borseen?"

"What do I want? I want my kingdom. I want Mari to rise again with me as the emperor."

"That's impossible. This city has been dead a hundred years."

"And it's been way over a thousand years since it was great."

"Doesn't matter."

"Where are you going to get people to rule over?"

"Oh, I'll conquer a few small countries like Palestine to start with, then go bigger."

"With what?"

"Didn't I tell you? I've been building up a stockpile of swords, spears, and arrows for the past few years. Actually, when my father died, I got the idea because he left behind his own stockpile of swords he had made."

"And where do you think you're going to get soldiers to fight for you?"

"I have that covered too. I am going to give land grants to all my soldiers. For every year they fight for me, they get a parcel of land. You see, I have thought of everything."

"Everything but loyalty. No one will stay loyal to you."

"Yes, they will. They will love me for giving them a chance to be landowners."

"Landowners of a desert."

"The Euphrates is right here. That's all they will need. They will even name their sons after me."

"Never. It will never happen."

"I'm tired of talking to you. You have no imagination. Well, I guess that's why you're stuck in there, and I am the only one who is free. Goodbye."

The outside door closes again.

Back to sitting and thinking and listening to that lone mouse gnawing on whatever has its attention.

"Too bad his father is dead. Maybe he could talk sense into his son and get us out of here," Dushatra says.

"Were you fellows ever close to your father?" Yasib asks.

"I was," Katazuli says. "He loved books of all kinds, whether they were clay tablets or papyrus or parchment. He didn't care. Sometimes he would read to me. When he got older and blind, I would read to him. That was a good time in my life."

Silence.

"I was never close to my father," Dushatra finally says. "He was the *Sangharaja*, the supreme patriarch of Buddhists in Indo-Parthia when I was a child. He had no time for me. I became a monk for a while, but he still didn't pay much attention to me. I guess I wasn't important enough for him."

Silence. Except for the mouse and its incessant gnawing.

"How about you, Michel?" Kumar asks.

Michel sighs. "My father wasn't as famous as Borseen's or Dushatra's, but he was famous in his own way. He was a *cataphract*, a warrior with shining armor. His horse even had the armor on him. I guess he was a hero to a lot of people. He was also a devout Jew and tried to convince his fellow warriors to believe in the one true God with him. He was my hero for a while, but I finally gave up on him."

Michel takes a deep breath and sighs. "I remember one time he came back from war. The city of Uruk had erected a statue of him. They had a parade, and he dressed me up in full armor like his. I was thirteen at the time, but big for my age. He put me on a Nisean horse just like his—armor and all. We rode together through the city with him waving a scroll of the Jewish Torah, and the pagan people of the city cheering him."

The mouse chews and gnaws away.

"It was the most memorable day of my life. I'll never forget it. I would give anything to relive that day."

"What about you, Kumar?"

Kumar is asleep.

Another week passes.

The outside door rattles. "Good morning, everyone," Borseen declares, bursting in on their nothingness.

"Today, you are going to convert. You are going to turn from King Phraattes and become my personal advisors, my magi."

"Borseen, go jump in the Euphrates."

"Well, it's a little cold for that. It's still winter, you

know."

"You want us to advise you. That's our advice."

"Oh, you are going to advise me, all right. Or you will pay in ways you cannot imagine. Now, I need to know where to get my army. Cannot be a king and start invading without an army. Now I've been thinking. Not far from here is a school. They teach boys—young men actually—how to be scribes. They would be perfect. But, first, I need ideas on how to talk them into joining me. Anyone? Anyone at all?"

Silence.

"Okay. That's fine. I want all of you to put your hands through the bars. You get no bread for today until you do."

The magi comply. Borseen ties their hands to the bars. Kumar is on the end. He does not tie his hands.

"Okay, I am going to open your door. You are all tied to it, so cannot get loose. All but one of you. That one will come with me."

He opens the door and puts his dagger up to Kumar's throat. "You're it."

He grabs Kumar from behind and pushes him out the door.

Silence returns. Then the scream.

"Pray for him," Michel says.

"Help him hold out until we are ready," Yasib says.

"Ready for what?"

More screaming. Then silence. Then the outside door flung open. Borseen shoves Kumar into the room, unlocks the cell door, and pushes him in.

"I'm going to be nice now and untie your hands from the bars. But I will be back. Next time, one of you will be more cooperative."

The outside door slams shut.

"Kumar. What did he do to you?"

"He crushed my fingers one at a time. I don't know if I'll ever be able to write again."

The magi sit on the floor. And pray. In silence. Silence except for the mouse gnawing in its private little corner.

"We've got to hurry before he comes back," Yasib says.

Michel: The Fourth Wise Man

"Hurry to do what? There is nothing we can do."

"Yes, there is. I have been working with the tool Katazuli used to loosen the tiles. I have a place here in the wall large enough we can crawl out through it."

"You couldn't have. We have seen no daylight in here at all."

"I was careful to scrape out all but the last layer on the outside. Tonight, I will scrape out the rest of it, and we will escape."

"What if he has guards out there?" Dushatra asks.

"He has no guards out there," Kumar says. "He is completely alone. He sometimes calls out to his guards, but they are imaginary."

Yasib continues to work in his dark corner. "Okay, men, I have a small hole open to the outside. It is nearly dark. Be ready."

"Kumar, can you crawl with your hands in that condition?" Michel asks.

"No. You fellows go on without me."

"We will not leave you behind," Katazuli says. "The first one out will reach back and get you by your arms. One of us will push from behind. You're not staying behind to face that mad man."

Silence again. Then the gnawing again.

"It is dark," Yasib says.

The gnawing grows louder and more aggressive. "I'm through," Yasib finally says in a loud whisper. "Katazuli, you go first."

"No, you did all the work. You go first. We insist."

"Hurry," Dushatra says.

Yasib crawls out and looks around. "I don't see him," he whispers.

He reaches back and takes Kumar's arms. Finally, Kumar is out. Then Katazuli. And Dushatra. Lastly, Michel.

"Wait," Michel whispers. "What's that noise?"

The five magi lean against the building that has been their prison for two hellish weeks. Or has it been three?

Borseen comes into sight. He is singing. They see him

take a drink out of a wineskin. He continues on down the deserted street away from them. Still singing.

"Okay," Katazuli whispers. "Which way?"

"When he had me out, I noticed where the wall had crumbled just ahead of us," Kumar whispers.

"If we can get through that and the outer wall, we can orient ourselves," Dushatra whispers.

Yasib takes the lead. They follow him, stooping and praying that Borseen is as drunk as he is acting. Blind drunk.

By starlight, Yasib sees the break in the wall and leads the others through it.

"Over here," Dushatra whispers.

"The others follow him, zigzagging and finally crawling over a break in the outer wall."

"Where to now?"

"The north star is over there. Go southeast."

Into the night, the magi run for their freedom. Into the night, wondering if they have been baited to escape and are being followed. Into the night wondering if they will ever see another day.

Run, magi, run.

"I'm getting out of breath," Yasib says.

"We've had hardly anything to eat."

"Keep going."

Michel puts Yasib on his back. "We've got to go as far as we can while it is dark."

"Dushatra, are you okay?" Katazuli asks.

No answer.

"Dushatra? Where are you? Dushatra?"

25 ~ ESCAPE

"I'm right here," Kumar whispers. "Who's missing?

Katazuli runs back the way they had come, still stooped to avoid detection. He sees someone running toward him. He lies flat on the desert floor. The man has a wineskin in his hand.

The man passes. Katazuli follows him and plans his attack. The man calls out in a loud whisper. "Where are you?" It is Dushatra.

Katazuli smiles to himself and catches up with his friend. "I thought you were him waving your wineskin."

"I went back."

"Huh?"

"There you are," they hear Michel say. "Where have you two been?"

"I went back," Dushatra says. "I knew we'd need water, and I knew he kept water outside our door.

"All we need to do is follow the river," Kumar says.

"Too predictable," Yasib says. "We'll be too easy to find. We've got to go through the desert."

The men sit in the shadows resting, then go again.

No longer stooping. Running. Escaping a madman. Running to live another day.

"I cannot go farther," Kumar says.

"The sky is gray," Yasib says. "We need to stop. It's getting pretty rocky. Look for a good place for us to hide.

We'll continue on when it is dark again."

"Over here, men," Michel calls out to them. "This spot is surrounded by boulders. We should be safe here."

Soon they see a red glow in the east. Then the sun. It warms them.

"It must be early or mid-March by now. But I'm still cold."

"That's because you're so skinny, Michel," Dushatra says with a wink.

For the first time in a very long time, the five remaining magi smile.

When the sun is at the other end of the sky, Katazuli wakes up the men.

"I've been out scouting around for medicine for Kumar and found a stubborn acacia tree. It is not large, but is large enough for breakfast. Follow me."

The men follow their friend out of their hiding place and down an incline. At the bottom is the tree. They take turns breaking off one of its spindly branches and gnawing on it. Sometimes they pick at it with their fingernails until they can pull a string of pulp off. They wind it around their fingers and put the whole thing in their mouth. They chew and eventually swallow it, whether or not it is sufficiently crushed.

Dushatra hands around his water skin and each man takes a single draw.

Katazuli tears off the bottom part of his robe and wraps two strips around Kumar's hands.

"This won't make them heal, but it will protect them. I will look for something along the way for pain."

Now completely dark, the magi resume their escape. They follow the stars that are in the southeast.

"I wonder if that mysterious star in the west will ever appear again," Yasib asks, now able to walk on his own again.

"I wish I had never heard of that star. It ruined everything," Michel says.

"Well, maybe so," Dushatra says. "We have discovered

absolutely nothing that can provide a reasonable explanation of its appearance or meaning."

They walk the rest of the night in near silence.

Two nights later they drink the last of the Dushatra's water.

When daylight comes, they wander around the desert, looking for some sign of water but always keeping each other in sight.

"Fellows," Michel calls out. "I found a wadi."

The others join him, kneel, and dig with their hands.

"Let's hope it has rained around here recently, and there is still some water under this dry river bed," Michel says.

"Over here," Dushatra says. "There's water over here."

Dushatra fills his waterskin, then the others take turns lifting the remaining water to their lips.

They stop and sleep. When darkness arrives again, they begin their walk once more.

Four days. Five. A week. The elevation is higher. They sometimes find caves to sleep in. Sometimes back in the caves, there is water. They see small patches of grass. They follow animals to their hidden watering places. They drink and eat what the animals drink and eat.

More days of walking and escaping. The hills diminish. The rocks grow smaller. They see it ahead of them—the Tigris River. It will take two more days to get to it. They travel during the day now.

Now walking skeletons. Clothes torn and barely clinging to them. Cheeks sunken, lips split, face burned by the early springtime sun, feet and hands cracked, tongue swollen

The great advisors to a mighty king. Hanging on to life. Trodding slower and slower. One step at a time. And another. And another.

"Hey, what are you men doing?"

A man on a camel hails them. The five magi collapse onto the desert floor. They cannot go farther.

The man stops his camel, climbs off, and rushes to the

magi.

"Anu," Michel manages with a parched groan, "Anu...help us."

"I'm sorry. How do you know my name? Who are you?"

"Anu, it is...me, Michel."

"Master. What has happened to you?"

"Hurry," Michel says. "Get help...for us."

Anu hands Michel his waterskin. "I'll be back as fast as I can."

Anu climbs back onto his camel and puts it into a gallop.

"Okay, I'm ready," Michel hears Anu say.

"Anu, haven't you left yet?" Michel asks.

"I have been gone two hours, Master. I brought a wagon drawn by two strong mules that will take you to the city fast."

"Not the palace. We're supposed to be in exile. It's too dangerous for us there," Yasib whispers.

"My house," Dushatra says, his words slurred. "Take us to my house."

Anu helps the five men onto his wagon and takes off with them, the mules in a gallop.

The magi hear the splash of the Tigris River when they cross it. They hear camels and donkeys and horses honking and braying and neighing. They hear people shouting and threatening. The wagon barrels past them.

The wagon turns down Dushatra's street. "Open the gate!" Anu shouts. "Open the gate."

They arrive, the mules panting and soaked in lather. Anu pounds on Dushatra's gate.

"Open up! Open up!"

They hear the bar slide off its path and hinges creak. Dushatra's gatekeeper open it wide. "Master!"

Anu and Hamar help the men out of the wagon. Hamar calls out to the maid. "Hurry. Bring rugs and blankets."

The maid rushes out to the courtyard with two rugs. She lays them down and rushes to get more. The magi make their way into Dushatra's courtyard and lie down on the rugs.

"Here, Master," Hamar says. "I will take you to your bedroom."

"No. Out here," he whispers. "I need to be out here with the others."

Then the quiet. In a far distance, the magi hear the clopping of mules being led away. Then sleep.

For three days, the magi are tended to. Keya, Kumar's wife, comes every day to nurse her beloved. Yasib's manservant comes. Anu and Hamar take care of the other men.

Each day the men grow stronger and sit up longer.

"I need to go to the palace," Dushatra says at the beginning of the fourth day.

"No, Master."

"What do you mean, no?"

"The king is not there yet. He is still in Susa, the winter palace. We are having a cool spring."

"What month is it?" Dushatra asks.

"It is the beginning of April."

"I know you do not want to hear this," Michel says, his voice having recovered, "but we still have not investigated the Jewish sacred writings. This may be our chance before King Phraattes arrives here for the summer."

"Not that again," Dushatra says.

"Not that again," Kumar says.

"Let him speak," Yasib says. "Michel, do you have these writings in your possession? If so, it would only be a matter of you bringing them to us. We can read through them and be done in a few days. Then everyone will be happy."

"Everyone but the king," Kumar says. "The explanation of the star is not in there. The Jews only have one God. It is an impossibility."

"I do not have them," Michel says, not paying any attention to Dushatra.

"Then let's stop talking about them," Dushatra says.

"They are in Ecbatana," Michel says.

"What are they doing there?"

"My ancestor, Daniel, put them there. Nebuchadnezzar not only wanted the smart young men of every nation he captured to be some of his magi, but he wanted them to bring their books of wisdom. Daniel was one of those young men. Then Esther, the Jewish Queen of Parthia, wife of Artaxerxes, protected them."

"Why didn't you tell us this before?" Yasib asks.

"You never gave me a chance. I tried."

"I don't know who you all are talking about," Katazuli says. "But we need to investigate those holy writings."

"And you know for sure the meaning of the star is explained in them."

"While we were in Borseen's prison, I did a lot of remembering. I used to read Daniel's writings a lot when I was young. When I moved away from home and came here, they disappeared. I don't know if my father got them or what. But I do remember reading about stars, not only in Daniel's sacred writings but the writings of a couple other of our prophets."

"Then, we shall go to Ecbatana," Yasib pronounces.

"Are you sure you are strong enough, Master?" Anu asks Michel.

"I am sure."

"But, Kumar, you can no longer write. That beast destroyed your fingers," his wife, Keya says.

"I can read, my dear. I can still read."

Three days later, the five magi climb on camels experienced in going through desert mountains. Xiongnu Mongolian camels. Camels Yasib has arranged for them.

They do not want guides. The mission is too important. They have been through too much. They are told where the mountain passes are. They are told where the rivers and mountain springs are. They are told where the caves are that will give them the most protection from mountain lions and bears and the strong possibility of a late spring snowstorm.

Michel: The Fourth Wise Man

For three days, they trudge through the mountains on their sure-footed camels. Five camels carrying the five remaining magi on a mission to save their life. And possibly even the kingdoms of Parthia and Indus.

Each carries the supplies with him he needs. They do not carry tents. They rely on the caves they have been told about. They do not carry extra water. They rely on the mountain springs they have been told about. But they do carry extra heavy robes. Because of the strong mountain winds. And in case of snowstorm.

They are quiet. They have been through it all. For nearly a year, they have traversed the world in search for the meaning of the strange star in their western sky.

They have investigated kings and gods, oracles and prophecies, uprisings and downfalls. They have investigated two-thousand-year-old clay tablets and one-year-old parchment scrolls. They have talked to priests and paupers, kings and criminals, scholars and the illiterate. They have crossed rivers and oceans, deserts and marshes. They have run from animals and soldiers and barbarians. They have escaped fires, sandstorms, and crumbling castles.

And so they move on. Following the ever-fading memory of the star, the star they have thus far followed to all the wrong places.

At last, they descend the Alvand sub-range of the Zagros Mountains and see a city rise up out of the valley below, a city the size of Athens. A city in a circle surrounded by seven walls. It is Ecbatana.

The magi stop and pull out their most elegant silk robes and turbans. Upon donning them, they put tassels of gold and blue on the camels—the royal colors that will be recognized by all who see them.

In the middle of the city is the highest hill. On it is the palace and other royal buildings. Then a wall. Then more buildings and a wall. As the city works its way down into the valley, it adds more walls on higher inner hills.

The magi guide their camels down to the Lion Gate with two great lions on each side. They cross the moat. The guards on duty salute them, and they pass through.

As they go deeper and higher into the city, they go through another gate and another. At each gate, they are saluted.

Finally, the palace gate. The palace with bright silver tiles on the roof.

Once within the compound, they turn left and go to the tall round building, the old one holding the archives of Babylon, Media, Persia, and now Parthia and Indo-Parthia.

They dismount and hand the reins of their camels over to stable hands in blue uniforms. The double doors of cedar are held open for them by blue-uniformed doormen. The guards on each side salute them.

Once inside the building, they walk down a corridor tiled with silver. The columns on each side are covered with gold and decorated with silver and every imaginable precious stone. The walls and ceiling are covered with striking frescoes of conquerors, captives, crowns, and battles won.

They arrive at the other end of the corridor and enter the main archives room with scrolls along two walls and clay tablets along the far wall. There are halls of more scrolls leading off of the main room.

"Gentlemen, in these archives, are the books of the Law of the Jews, commonly called the Law of Moses," Michel says. "The Jews also have books of prophecy. We will read them all, just like we did the writings of the other religions, and look for any references to a star. Agreed?"

"It could take us another week to read through all those writings," Kumar says.

"But, if we are going to be able to go home, well, we have to do it," Dushatra says

"I will do whatever the rest of you do," Katazuli says.

They leave the grand archives building, reclaim their camels, and go out through the most interior gate of the city. Once in the second most secure section, they look for a royal guest house.

Michel enters and arranges for them to have the best suite of rooms in the guest house.

Michel: The Fourth Wise Man

The magi are quiet as they walk into their suite, followed by five servants carrying their belongings. A doorman greets them with a tray of fresh grapes, cheese, and wine.

Two more servants enter with large jars of heated water. For the next two hours, they are treated with baths and rubdowns with precious oils.

They do not speak of their discoveries.

"I think I am going for a walk," Dushatra says.

"The rooftop of this guest house has gardens that I would like to show Katazuli," Kumar says.

"There was an older gentleman sitting by a fountain when we first arrived," Yasib says. "I think I'll go out and see where he is from."

Michel asks the doorman to bring him a blank scroll.

He sits at a table and draws two long wavy lines. *That's the Euphrates, and that's the Tigris. Now, let me see. I should plant apple trees over here, grapevines over here, oh, and make wide paths.*

Michel looks over his drawing, smiles, and climbs into bed. Sometimes during the night, he hears a door open and close but goes right back to sleep. He dreams of his garden and God walking on earth again.

"Everyone up," he announces at daybreak.

An hour later, they are back at the archives building walking down the long ornate corridor.

Michel talks as they walk. "The Jewish sacred writings predicted the rise and fall of nations around the world," he says.

"That's impossible," Dushatra says.

"I will be showing you predictions of the rise and fall of nearly every civilized kingdom on earth."

"We don't want to see all that," Kumar says. "We want to know about our kingdom and that star."

"You will get your wish," Michel says as he leads them to the section of the archives dealing with his ancestor, Daniel.

"Are you suggesting the star we saw might mean the

end of our kingdom just like King Phraattes dreaded?" Dushatra glares at Michel. "I knew we shouldn't have come."

Dushatra turns to leave.

Michel: The Fourth Wise Man

ECBATANA WITH ITS SEVEN WALLS

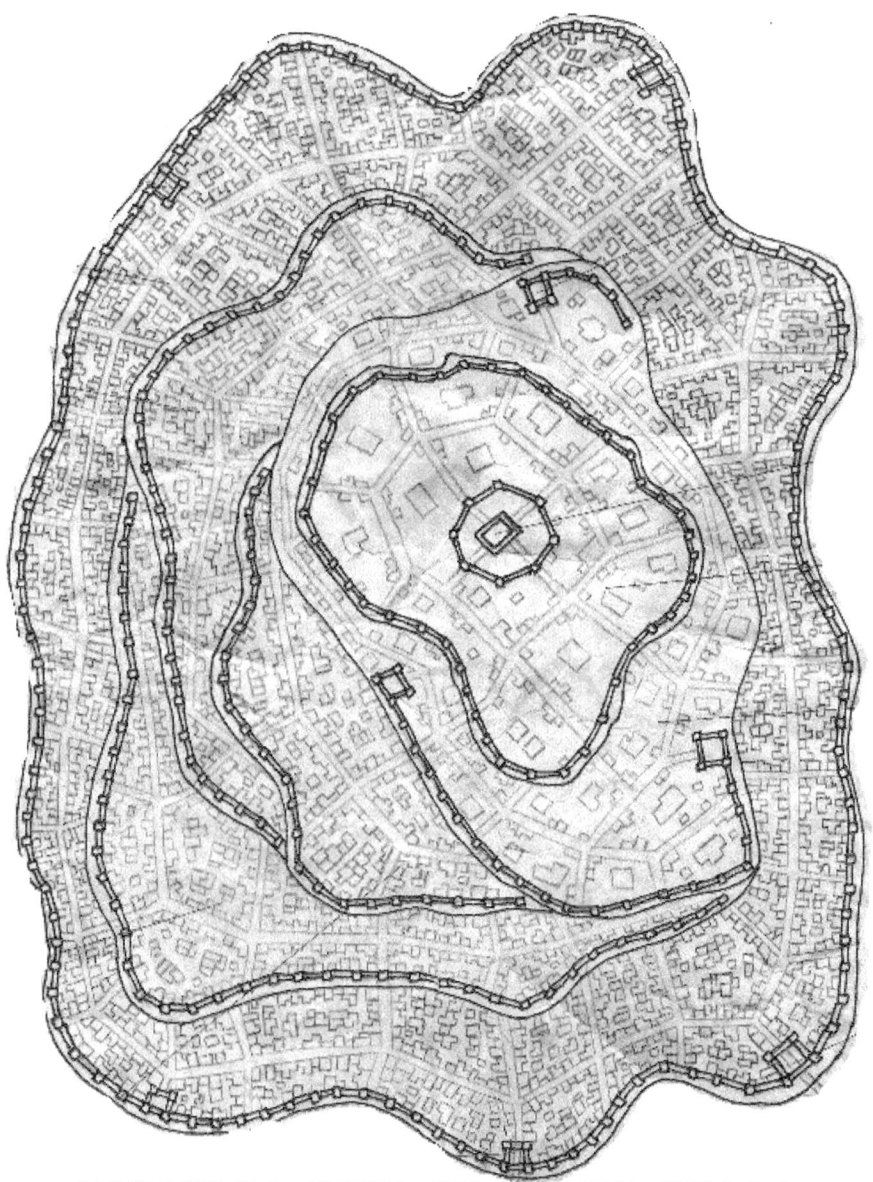

ECBATANA WITH ITS SEVEN WALLS

26 ~ THE IMPOSSIBLE

"Come on back, Dushatra," Michel says. "Remember all the time we waiting for you down in Indo-Parthia?"

"You cannot know what is going to happen to Parthia or Rome or any other kingdom," Dushatra says, walking back up to Michel.

"No one can predict the future that successfully," Yasib objects, pausing to stare at an Egyptian sitting nearby and thinking about Hophni.

"But the Jewish prophets already have." Michel leads them toward one of the side halls, talking as he goes.

"What do you mean?" Katazuli asks.

"The Jewish sacred writings predicted the downfall of numerous kingdoms, including Egypt long before they actually occurred. As you are well aware, all the kingdoms on the east coast of the Great Sea long ago fell under the power of Babylon, then the Medes and Persians, then the Greeks and finally now the Romans.

"One prophet actually predicted that the Jews taken exile to Babylon would be freed—the exact year," Michel continues proudly: "The seventieth year of their captivity. Furthermore, another prophet predicted the exact name of the emperor who would free them—over a century before he was born—Cyrus."

"Excuse me, sirs," a man dressed in a colorful Ethiopian wraparound says. "Do you happen to know where the archives are with dealings of the Nubians?"

"No," Katazuli says, grateful for the interruption. "You need to ask a librarian."

Michel continues looking for the scrolls he needs.

"As is widely known to historians, one of our country's magi government leaders six hundred years ago was Daniel, a descendant of Jewish royalty and my ancestor. He was greatly respected and held in high esteem by our emperor."

"There he goes again," Kumar says, "bragging about his ancestor."

Michel pays no attention to him. "Daniel himself wrote a book which he left behind in our archives. Oh, here we are. If you will be seated, gentlemen, I will find it and read the portion that predicted the unknowable centuries before it occurred."

The other magi find a table and wait.

Kumar gets up and looks at the titles of the scrolls on the shelves nearby, searching to see something that might be helpful.

Katazuli stares as the silver on the columns and wonders if the metal originated in Parthia or Anatolia.

Dushatra walks over to a nearby table and sits alone.

Yasib stays seated, puts his chin down on his chest, and falls asleep.

"Here it is," Michel finally says, rushing back to them. "Are you ready? Come back here, everyone. Are you ready?"

They wander back to the table, and Yasib wakes up.

"During the time of King Nebuchadnezzar six hundred years ago, Daniel predicted the rise and fall of the Babylonians, the Medes and Persians, and the Grecians. The fourth kingdom he predicted would crush everything in its way. That fourth kingdom, gentlemen, is the Roman empire of our own time."

"No. It cannot be done. No one could know the future that far ahead," Kumar objects.

"Now listen to this, and I quote," Michel continues undaunted.

During the time of the last kings, Jehovah, the only God, will establish a kingdom that will never end... It will destroy every other kingdom, but it will never end.

"Never end?"

"Did Nebuchadnezzar believe it?" Dushatra responds.

"The king made Daniel ruler over the province of Babylon with daily access to the royal court."

Michel reaches for another scroll, a continuation of Daniel's writings. "Furthermore, he gave the exact year the predicted one would be anointed as high priest and king of the kingdom."

The others stare at Michel in astonishment.

"No," Dushatra declares. "I do not want to hear any more. What you are reading has to be a hoax."

Michel goes on. "Since Jewish priests do not serve until they are thirty years old, if the priest king was born with the star last year, he would begin ruling exactly 29 years from now."

The other magi look at each other with doubt and anger in their eyes.

"I'm leaving," Kumar says.

"No, you're not," Yasib says. "He gave us our chance. He has put up with us for nearly a year. It is his turn now."

"Then prove it. Show us where he predicted the exact year." Dushatra leans back in his chair, eyes narrowed.

In anticipation of their request, Michel has just now scrolled to the passage.

"Here it is, gentlemen. It's been in our archives six hundred years. No one had anything to gain by changing it. This is what it says:

Pay attention: From the time the king orders Jerusalem rebuilt until the Anointed One, the priest and king comes, it will be seven 'sevens' and sixty-two 'sevens.'

"So, 7 x 7 = 49. And 62 x 7 = 434. Adding these together, you have 483 years," Michel concludes.

"So, what? That doesn't prove anything," Kumar says.

"Our Jewish book of Ezra, a copy of which is right here in these archives, says that King Artaxerxes ordered Ezra to return to Jerusalem to begin rebuilding the city during his seventh year. Artaxerxes gave this order 453 years ago as of last year when the star appeared. If this priest king begins to reign when he is age 30, that will make it exactly 483 years."

Michel says no more.

Silence.

Yasib, Dushatra, Katazuli, and Kumar look at each other, then stare at Michel.

Still, the silence.

Dushatra is angry. He rushes to the entry corridor. They hear the outside door to the archives building slam shut.

Kumar stands, walks to the corridor, and puts his hands on his head. He leans against one wall and slides down, then puts his head on his knees.

Katazuli wanders back into the dark aisle where Michel had found the strange scroll and sits on the floor.

Yasib stays where he is, but stares at the scroll. He begins reading it for himself. He does not take his eyes off it. He scrolls back and forth over what Michel had just read to them.

"There are no mistakes in it," Michel says. "Daniel would not have allowed his writing to be distorted."

Michel takes a seat at the now deserted table and continues to wait.

The stool next to Michel scrapes along the floor. Kumar is back. He is not saying anything, but he is back. Katazuli too.

If this solves all our problems with the star, Jehovah, I can get back to what really is important—the Garden of Eden.

They hear footsteps coming from the corridor. Dushatra cannot keep from making some noise when he walks. It echoes.

By now Yasib has seated himself back at the table.

Dushatra appears. He runs his fingers through his

hair. His eyes are bloodshot.

"I didn't know," he whispers. "I didn't know."

Yasib speaks first. "Well, uh, gentlemen, uh, perhaps we need to investigate the other writings of this Daniel. Did you say he had other writings, Michel?"

"No," Katazuli says. "This is too much to absorb all in one day. I'm going back to the guest house."

"Good idea," Kumar says. "I'm going with you."

Dushatra looks at Yasib, and Yasib shrugs his shoulders. They follow Katazuli and Kumar out.

Michel stands where he is.

What did I say wrong?

Carefully, he rolls Daniel's scroll back up, returns it to its proper cubicle, and follows the other magi to the guest house.

They eat. They go for walks. They joke about funny things that had happened on their trip around the world. They talk of everything but the prophecies.

"Do any of you have questions?" Michel finally says.

Yasib catches his attention and shakes his head.

Michel heeds the warning and says no more. Instead, he goes up onto the roof of the guest house and enjoys the breeze off the mountains nearby.

By the time he returns to their suite, everyone is asleep. He falls asleep and dreams a star is talking to him.

The next morning, Michel tries again. "Are we ready to search for a reference to a star?"

The magi put on coats to go over to the archives in the coolness of the early spring morning.

They walk back up the same corridor and choose the same table they had gathered around the previous days.

"Okay, Michel," Yasib says. "We are ready to search through your Jewish holy writings for mention of a star."

Dushatra clears his throat as he pulls out his stool and seat himself. "Indeed," he says so softly, the others have trouble hearing him. "That is what should be done."

Kumar mutters. "You won't find any mention of a star. But we must examine it so no one can say we didn't investigate everything and so you'll shut up."

Michel finds four more copies of Daniel's writings. "Luckily, the scribes back then made more than one copy of important documents."

He gives one copy to each of them. Each finds another table where he can spread out his work, seats himself and reads.

Michel looks up from his own reading now and then. *Are we close to the answer for King Phraattes?*

They read. For the next two hours they read.

"These are predictions of world powers that we know for a fact came true about Babylon, Persia, Greece and Rome," Dushatra says from his table. "This is impossible. But it's right here in certified copies of our ancient archives."

Kumar calls over from his table, this time with a grin. "This ancestor of yours, Michel, sure had nerve. He actually defied the great god of the Babylonians, Marduk."

Kumar scratches his head. "How did that Daniel manage to survive through four emperors in the royal courts?" The others shush him, and all go back to reading. Michel catches Kumar's eye and grins back.

"Okay, everyone," Yasib says from his table. "Turn to the section that talks about Daniel's dream. I just checked with the librarian, who gave me a copy of the zodiac chart. I thought there would be some significance of the lion, bear, and leopard among the stars. But it doesn't make sense."

"What about Daniel's dream of a ram and goat?" Katazuli asks from his table. "One of the horns of the goat throws some of the starry host out of the heavens and down to earth to be trampled."

They all put down their scroll and stare at Michel. He smiles. "I know what you are thinking," he says, "and you are right."

"You mean the ram represents the kings of Media and Persia, and the goat the king of Greece, Alexander the Great?" Kumar says. "Well, the ram could represent good, and the goat could represent evil."

Michel smiles as he watches each of them struggle,

their eyebrows together, their forehead wrinkled, their eyes focused only on their scroll.

"Okay, let's go back to the 483th year that Cyrus allowed the Jews to rebuild Jerusalem," Dushatra says. "Michel read it to us before. Maybe he read it wrong."

"No, he read it right," Kumar says. "From the time that edict was issued until the Anointed One, the Priest-King, is supposed to come and reign over the world is 483 years this year."

"That does it," Dushatra says. "I'm going back to our suite. That's too much for me. I have to do some thinking."

"Me too," Kumar says, joining him.

Yasib and Katazuli put their scrolls down and follow the other magi out.

Once again, Michel is left to pick up after his friends. He gathers up their scrolls and puts them back in their proper cubicle.

Then he, too, walks out of the archives room, down the corridor, and outside. But he does not go back to the guest house. He walks through the gate to the third section of the city. He asks around and is told there is a bazaar down the street two blocks. He walks to it, looks around, does not buy anything, and heads back to the guest house.

When he enters the suite of rooms, he is startled. Everyone is already in bed.

Is that a good sign or bad sign? He asks himself.

The next thing he knows, he is waking up. He sits up in bed and sees the other four magi already dressed.

"Where is everyone going so early?" he asks.

"Back to the archives," Yasib says. "We are determined to figure this thing out today. Do you plan to go with us or not?" Yasib asks with a grin.

The five magi walk over to the archives building.

"You know, there should have been eight of us doing this today," Michel says on the way.

"Who would have thought two of us would be traitors?" Katazuli says. "You just can never know for sure what is going on inside someone's thoughts."

They arrive at the archives and walk down the now-familiar corridor. They return to their respective tables and stare at Michel. He stares back.

"Okay," Kumar says. "He's not going to wait on us this time. We have to go get the scrolls ourselves."

The magi each pull out a copy of Daniel's writings and turn through it, trying to find where they had left off the day before.

Two hours later, Yasib calls out to the others. "It's toward the end," he says. He waits for the others. "Look for the word star. When they all indicate they have found the spot, he reads it aloud.

Hordes who lie buried in the earth will come back. Some will be delivered to live forever, others to die forever. Wise men will radiate like the heavens, and they who lead others to the right way will be like the stars!

Yasib rereads the passage. "Wise men? We magi are supposed to be the wise men that Daniel predicted?"

But, it warns not all the wise men will be accepted. "What must we do?" Yasib asks.

Over and over, they read the passage. "What must we do to be accepted?" Yasib mutters. "It says here we must lead others to the right. Lead others?"

They read on a little further. Dushatra stands so fast, his bench falls over and echoes across the room. "There it is," he calls out. "The Star! Each truly wise man will receive his own star. It is the wise who will shine like stars!"

When Kumar reads it, he rises from his stool, lifts his arms, and shouts, "Yes! We found it!"

By now, everyone in the library is staring at the magi. Some are shushing them. Some are laughing at them. The librarian is warning them.

Michel reads the entire passage aloud.

"No, this cannot be," Dushatra says, changing his mind. "We've been fooled before. We will not be fooled again. We've been fooled by references to a star in the Hindu writings, the Buddhist writings, the Zoroaster writings, and the others, but we won't again.

"Sorry, Michel," Kumar finally says, walking over to his colleague. "It's not enough. It doesn't prove anything."

"We're leaving," Dushatra says.

"Not again," Michel says. "You cannot keep walking out on this."

"We can, and we are," Kumar says.

"Give them time," Yasib says. "Give us all time, Michel. This is more than we imagined it would be. Much more. Give us time."

All the magi leave but Michel. He wanders around the archives. *I wonder if my Daniel walked on these floor tiles. I wonder if he saw the same silver columns I am looking at now. Daniel, when you left your writings in these archives, did you leave them for me to find?*

Daniel, can you hear my mind, my thoughts? Are you proud of me? My father never was. When we're through here, I will return to Eden. Will that make you proud too, Daniel? Is that what you would have done? Did you ever take a ride down to Eden? Did you walk around where the Garden was? Was it underwater yet?

Michel leaves the archives building and walks nowhere in particular for a while. Just before sundown, he returns to the guest house.

He participates in small talk. Then retires for the night.

The next morning, Michel watches his colleagues. Have they walked out of the archives for good? Have they rejected everything, even in the face of the facts?

"Well, are you coming with us?" Dushatra asks.

The five magi return to the archives. "What do you want us to read next?" Kumar asks.

Michel is uncertain. *Do they really want to know?* "Well, you need to read the rest of the Jewish holy writings," he says. "There are quite a few of them. Start with the first five; they are the beginning of the Jewish kingdom and the holy laws we obey, the Law of Moses."

"Then we had better get started," Yasib says.

They read the rest of the day in silence. But to no avail. Absolutely nothing.

Two more days.

Then Yasib spots it. With guarded excitement, he calls the others and reads it to them.

A star will come out of Israel's descendants. A crown will rise out of the kingdom.

'So, we have a reference to a star and it being a king. But we need more than this."

"Okay, it has possibilities," Kumar says. "But we must have more evidence."

"Tomorrow, we shall begin reading the Jewish prophets," Michel explains, daring to hope again.

27 ~ DISCOVERY

When the magi return to the archives the following day, Michel hands each of them the prophecies written by Isaiah.

He settles down to read, just like the others do. They read for an hour. Kumar sees it first. He calls the others.

"Listen to this, gentlemen." He clears his throat.

"'People in night darkness saw a great light, a light that has just appeared... For a baby has just been born, he will govern and be called...'"

Kumar stops reading. He looks at the others. They look back expectantly. He finishes the passage. In slow motion.

" '...He will be called God!' "

Once more, he pauses. The four magi stare at each other. Old Yasib's hands tremble. Dushatra pulls out a handkerchief and wipes his sweating brow.

"The star really was a god," Katazuli says, "and it was just born—a child-king."

There's more," Kumar announces.

His kingdom will never end.

Michel: The Fourth Wise Man

But, of course, he will have to take time to grow up."

They return to their reading. Michel tries to hide from himself a growing confusion over what Kumar had just read.

They read on until late afternoon. Dushatra shouts from his table. "I have found it!"

Others in the library call over to the magi to either be quiet or leave. Instead, the other four mark their reading places and rush to Dushatra's table to look over his shoulder.

"Did you find something, Dushatra?"

Without comment, he reads it to them.

The light will come to the whole world, and all kingdoms of the world will come see it!

"The light?" Yasib says. "The star?"

"It is not going to take over Parthia," Michel says. "This child-king will rule all kingdoms just as they are from David's eternal throne."

The five magi return to their respective tables and roll up their scrolls.

Michel approaches the archivist. "We are on an urgent mission for the king. It is imperative that we take with us the Jewish writing called Beginnings, a specific writing of Daniel, and a writing of a Jew named Isaiah."

"Uh, sir, I do not think I can let you take them with you."

Michel lowers his brow and stares at the young librarian. "As a direct descendant of Daniel, I am entitled to these documents. Now, do I have them, or do I notify the king that you have interfered with his business?"

"Uh, I guess it will be okay after all, you being related to Daniel."

Michel picks up one copy of each of the three scrolls and leaves the rest on the tables.

"Gentlemen," Michel says. "We have found the meaning of the star. The one who rules from David's eternal throne will be in Jerusalem."

"Our king will want to go to Jerusalem to honor their child-king," Dushatra says.

"Do you think he is back at Ctesiphon yet?" Katazuli asks.

"I would think so. If he is not, he will be soon," Dushatra says. "It is time to return."

Without hesitation, Yasib agrees. "It would be the prudent thing to do. Our King Phraattes will want to stay on good terms with this child-king."

"What about your Emperor Ai?" Kumar asks.

"Although I am Xiongnu Mongol Chinese, I do not claim that corrupt excuse of a man."

"My king will want to send an ambassador to the child-king," Dushatra says. "King Gondophares will want to be represented. I must leave at once. I will obtain gifts and letters from my king and meet you at Ctesiphon."

"Your hometown is closer to his palace than mine over on the Parthian Gulf," Kumar says. "Can you represent both of us when you go to Kandahar and Taxila?"

"Indeed, I shall," Dushatra says.

"Should we approach Augustus Caesar about this?" Michel asks. "I'm sure this child-king will be powerful enough to conquer Rome someday."

"That's up to King Phraattes."

"What about Anatolia, Katazuli? Or Scythia?" Kumar asks.

"I have been wondering about that. We'll be taking the northern route to Jerusalem through Haran," Kumar says. "Perhaps I'll check when we're there."

"So it is settled. We meet in Ctesiphon in a month." Dushatra smiles.

The magi return to the guest house. They gather up their belongings and go down to the stable. Their camels are brought out.

"Do you want one of us to go with you, Dushatra?" Kumar asks.

"No. Kandahar is not that far from here. I will be fine. You all go on back to Ctesiphon to put the king's mind at ease. I will see you in a month or less."

The remaining four magi head east and work their way once again across the Zagros Mountains.

"I'm kind of tired," Yasib tells the others as they let their camels find their own footing on the rocky trail. "I guess I never allowed myself to admit how tired I had become."

"I think you're right, Yasib," Michel says. "I haven't realized how tired I am either. Maybe we wouldn't allow ourselves to be until now."

"Well, our quest is almost over," Katazuli says.

"We started out with four, ended up with eight, and now there are five of us," Kumar says. "How I miss Hophni."

"It's been nearly a year since we saw that star," Kumar says.

A week later, they arrive back at Ctesiphon. They arrive at the great veranda and request entrance into the palace courtyard.

Michel is relieved it is all over. Now they can reassure the king, and he can go back to doing the more important—resurrecting Eden and preparing for God.

The two guards cross spears in front of them.

"You are under arrest."

"You're mistaken," Michel says. "Oh, you are new. You do not know who we are."

"We do know who you are. The king told you never to come back."

"We came back to clear our name," Kumar says.

"He told us that, if you came back, you were to be executed."

"No! You're wrong!" Michel says, sweat beading up on his brow and clinching the reins of his camel.

"If you do not climb down off those camels, we will be forced to execute you here and now."

"No! We will not," Katazuli says.

"Never!" Kumar and Michel say in unison.

The soldiers step forward, lowering their spears to attack position.

"Uh, kind sir," Yasib says. "I come with greetings from

Emperor Ai of the great Han Dynasty of China. I come bearing critical and vital information on his behalf that your great and mighty King Phraattes will be most pleased to receive. Now, sir, if he does not receive this information in time, there will be dour consequences to the Kingdom of Parthia and perhaps the entire world. Therefore, sir, if I were you, I would open these gates so that I and my entourage may enter expeditiously."

The soldier stares at Yasib, then at Kumar, Katazuli, and Michel. Michel puts his hand up to his mouth when he hears the soldier whisper to his companion, "Did you understand anything he said?" Thereupon, the soldiers part and let the magi into the courtyard of the palace.

"Your entourage, Yasib? Your entourage? I'm going to get you for this," Michel says.

"It worked, didn't it?"

They arrive at the stable and dismount.

"Welcome back," the stableman says. "Never thought I'd see you men again."

"Why is that?" Kumar asks.

"Oh, nothing. Just welcome back."

The four magi walk to the front doors to the palace. Guards in blue with gold conical helmets and shields salute them.

Their footsteps echo as they walk side by side up the long corridor embellished with gold, silver, precious stones, and frescoed paintings of the king and his assassinated father.

They pass the stairway on their right that goes to the roof, which is their observatory. They continue on to the throne room on their left.

Michel speaks to the guard at the closed doorway.

"We are here on urgent business to the king. We request an audience with him as soon as possible. Convey that message to him for us."

The guard salutes the magi and disappears through another door. They hear the conversation.

"Your Majesty, Kumar, Yasib, Katazuli, and Michel

wish an audience with you."

"Really? I never expected to see them again. Didn't I warn them never to come back unless they had an explanation of the star? How long ago was that? So they're back."

"Four of them are, Your Majesty."

"Lost some of them, huh? Good thinking. Do they expect to impress me this time? No one else has. Oh, well, nothing much else is going on today. May as well have an execution. Send them in."

The guard reappears and opens the door to the throne room.

Kumar, Yasib, Katazuli, and Michel walk toward their king with heads bowed, then bow completely to the floor at the throne.

"Rise, you fools," the king says. "So, you came back for your execution."

"Your Majesty," Michel says. "We have found the meaning of the star."

"Out! Guards! Come get them. Chopping off their heads will be too quick. Put them in a cell and get my wife's pet lion from her. Starve it a few days, then put it in the cell with these men. They do not deserve a quick death."

"Your Majesty," Yasib says. "What Michel is telling you is the truth."

"So, was it a new god?"

Michel does not reply.

"Yes, kind of Your Majesty," Katazuli says. "He should be around a year old now. We believe he will grow into a god."

"Is he going to destroy me?"

"On the contrary, Your Majesty," Kumar says. "He will exert heavenly powers and bless all kingdoms of the earth."

The king leans one elbow on the arm of his throne. "How do you know? Are you making this up? You magi have a bad habit of doing that. You don't think I know, but I do."

"We have brought the proof with us, Your Majesty," Michel says.

"In this ancient writing, it says the star will have a

scepter," Kumar says.

"In this ancient writing, it tells the exact year it will come," Katazuli says.

"And in this scroll, it says that wise men will alert all nations that the star has come," Yasib says.

"How do I know those writings really say that?"

"Here, Your Majesty. We present you with these ancient writings, opened to the sections we told you about. Read the prophecies for yourself."

The king takes the first scroll, rises, and walks over to a table where he lays it out.

The magi wait in silence.

"Amazing," he says. "Let me have the second one."

Michel hands them the writings of Daniel and goes through the explanation of the year the star will appear.

The king stares at the scroll and rolls it from one section to another.

"Let me see that last scroll," he says.

Once more, silence.

The king looks back and forth at the three scrolls. He compares. He mulls. He contemplates.

Silence.

"Amazing."

Silence.

He turns to the four magi. "Amazing. And you say when the star was born, a god was born?" He shakes his head and grins. "And to think, a god has been born in my lifetime. I've never seen a god before. I would like to see this god and pay homage to him," the king says, "but it is not possible."

"Would you like us to accompany you to Jerusalem?"

The king walks back to his throne. The magi follow him.

"Come closer," he says. "There is serious unrest in the palace," he says in almost a whisper. "They don't think I know about it, but I do. I have reliable spies. I will stay and protect my throne, and perhaps I can go visit this god later when I stabilize things here."

Michel: The Fourth Wise Man

He raises his voice to give his final decision.

"Therefore, since you are the ones who made the discovery, you shall go as my ambassadors."

"Your Majesty," Kumar hurries to explain, "Dushatra has returned to Indus to tell King Gondophares about this. We agreed to wait for him."

"Well, that's fine. I like to keep my underling kings happy. However, we will not pass this information on to Rome."

"Yes, Your Majesty."

"Speaking of keeping control of my kingdom, where are Hophni, Demetrius, and Borseen?"

"We are sorry to report that Hophni died in his homeland of snakebite," Yasib says.

"Well, what about the other two?"

"Uh, Borseen is holed up in what is left of Mari, accumulating swords, shields, and spears to begin his own empire."

"I shall deal with him. What about Demetrius?"

"We caught him in a plot to, uh..."

"Speak up, Yasib. What was he plotting?"

"Uh, sir, he was plotting to assassinate you."

"I have been suspecting him for a long time. I will send word to Caesar to have him brought back here for punishment. Is there any other bad news you need to tell me?"

"No, Your Majesty. That is all we know."

"Remind me, when you get back from Jerusalem, to reward you five."

"Yes, Your Majesty," Yasib replies. "Thank you."

"And, what should we take as gifts of friendship when we go to Jerusalem?" Michel asks.

"I will leave that up to you," the king says. "I understand you will have a few weeks before Dushatra returns to make your selection. He may be bringing something back from his king too.

"Yes, Your Majesty."

"Now, I don't want you traveling alone. There are too

many dangers out there, some of which you survived this past year. But I don't want to take any chances you will not arrive. Therefore, I want you to take twenty guards with you minimum—two *dathabams*. If you think you will need more, take them. I think you will need only one *dathapatis*. Take Arshad. He can easily handle two *dathabams*. "He has experience following maps. I will give him my maps to the lands to the north and down along the Great Sea."

The king grows quiet. They wait.

"Well, that will be all," he says. "I have some business to take care of around the palace."

Three weeks later, Dushatra returns. He contacts the other magi, asking them to meet in his home.

"We are glad you made it back," Michel says. "But we thought it would take longer."

"Gondophares is dead."

"Oh, no," Kumar says. "What condition is the kingdom down there in now?"

"Not good. His son has been trying to rule, but he does not have the influence over the people his father did. There is talk of deposing him and his cousin, Abdagases, taking over.

"I only got as far as Kandahar. I really did not want to get involved in the turmoil up at Taxila."

"So, you do not have any messages from your king for the new child-king," Katazuli says.

"None. I spent some time with my family in Kandahar, then headed back here. When will we be ready to go?"

"To Jerusalem? We can leave tomorrow. Everything has been arranged."

The following morning at dawn, exactly one year since the star had appeared, the camel caravan assembles in front of the palace of King Phraattes. There are twenty camels for the soldiers, one for their commander, five camels for the magi, five camels for servants, and ten camels for tents, food, water, cooking supplies, clothing, and the gifts for the child-king.

"Ah, it is a good morning to be traveling to see a child-

Michel: The Fourth Wise Man

king with his own star," Kumar says.

The forty-one camels travel north along the Tigris River.

Three hours after leaving, Michel's camel snortles, whinnies, and chews hard, shaking its head back and forth. An hour after that, he struggles to breathe and sits down in the road.

Michel climbs off and asks Yasib's servant, a herdsman, to see what can be done. The old man pries the camel's mouth open, then turns back to Michel.

"I had better check the other camels."

Captain Arshad orders everyone to have their camel kneel so they can be inspected.

Everyone waits while each camel is examined.

"I'm sorry, Captain, sir," the camel herder says, "But six of these camels have the pox. It is highly contagious. You must turn back. If you do not, they will be dying on the road. You must turn back. I'm sorry," the herder says.

Arshad instructs his first officer to sound the trumpet for retreat.

The caravan turns around in the road, the riders now leading their camels on foot.

More camels collapse on the road.

Arshad's officer sounds the trumpet again. He orders all the civilians to walk up the road back to the palace. Then they hear it. The swoosh of arrows.

The magi and others in the caravan turn and see all forty-one camels dead on the side of the road.

The travelers take what is most important to them off the backs of the camels, trusting that ox and wagons will be sent back for the rest.

They take one last look at the dead animals.

28 ~ FALSE BEGINNINGS

*B*ack in Ctesiphon, the magi return to their homes with their servants. They arrive after dark.

Michel stands outside in the street in front of his former estate with the stable he is now allowed to live in. He looks up into the sky.

"No! No!"

Anu stands by and says nothing.

Michel turns in circles in the street.

"Why? Not again. Now it's JerusalemAlways interruptions. Always something going wrong. Why?"

Michel sits and leans his back against the outer wall of his former estate, slides down, raises his knees, and puts his head down on them.

Michel breaks out in sobs.

"Master, it must have been for the best," Anu says, now sitting by him on the street.

"Whose best? Everything I do fails."

"No, Master. They have challenges, but you always stay with it until it does succeed. Look what you did for the king. You discovered the secret of the star."

Michel looks over at his servant and stares a moment. He pats his servant on the shoulder. "I did do that, didn't I?"

"Indeed, you did, and everyone is talking about it."

"Are they really?"Michel stands.

"They're going to have to find a new herd. All of the king's herds have probably been infected. We're going to have to wait while they find a herd that is not."

"Yes, Master."

"The wait will give me a chance to work on my plans for Eden."

He smiles and looks around. "I think I'll go over and have a talk with the king's gardener. I need to know what will grow best in our hot climate. What will grow best in the marshes? If the rivers change course and it becomes desert, what would grow best then?

Two weeks later, a soldier knocks on the stable door where Michel has his bed and a table.

"Sir, we have another herd of camels. A healthy herd."

"Where did you get them?"

"Over by the Caspian Sea where it is cold. Camels seem to be healthier where it is cold."

"I will be ready in the morning, then," Michel replies.

At dawn, the caravan of forty-one healthy camels leaves Ctesiphon, staying close to the Tigris River.

Ten soldiers in front plus their commander. The five magi. Five servants. Ten pack camels. The final ten soldiers.

People line up along the highway to watch the royal entourage go by and wave.

Six days later, the caravan reaches Samarra. The city is old and not well kept up. The citizens are old too. The young people have left. Some of the oldest buildings have crumbled, but not all.

The caravan stops outside the city, and the soldiers form a protective circle around the magi who are provided with fine rugs and cushions to sit on.

Their servants walk just inside the city to the bazaar. After a while, they return with baskets of fresh grapes, figs, pomegranates, and bread.

Three servants milk the camels while two set out a low cedar table with ornately carved legs and embedded with mother of pearl. They arrange the food on silver trays and pour the milk into fine blue lacquered pitchers.

As the magi eat, the soldiers put up a large goat-hair tent with partitions so each dignitary has his own room, and can also meet together in a larger room. Intricately woven rugs are placed on the ground.

"Well, we are finally on our way," Michel tells his four comrades. "There were a lot of times I had my doubts."

"Hophni should have been here with us," Katazuli says. "How I miss him."

"I will never understand what happened in the minds of Demetrius and Borseen," Yasib says.

"I can understand Borseen doing what he did; he was twenty-eight and thought he could do anything," Kumar says. "But Demetrius."

"He was bewitched by that blond former slave," Yasib says. "Michel, you are rather quiet."

"I'll bet he's not thinking about the star or the child-king," Kumar says with a wink.

Michel looks up at the others, stands, and excuses himself.

The next morning, the magi are awakened to the sound of a trumpet. They come out into the daylight to break their fast while the tents are taken down, supplies put away, and camels saddled. It is mid-morning by the time they leave Samarra.

The grand procession begins again.

"Do we know how long this trip is going to take us?" Kumar asks whoever can hear him.

"It is way over a thousand *milles* in the Roman measurements," Dushatra says. It will take us two months if everything goes smoothly. But, of course, we know it won't. So I'm guessing it will take us three months."

"That will be the end of summer or later," Kumar responds.

The barren mountains begin as foothills, but soon live up to their name. The up-and-down of hills and valleys as they progress along the Tigris River, which now winds itself along those valleys, sometimes far below the ancient highway the caravan travels.

When they move into a relatively flat valley close to the river, Captain Arshad orders the caravan to stop. Everyone goes through their assigned duties of setting up tents, then guarding them. Of pulling out and preparing food for both people and animals.

The next day at mid-morning, the caravan reassembles, and they resume traveling up and down the barren mountains.

"Oh, a city ahead. Perhaps we can find a good inn and stay in town tonight," Yasib says. "My old bones are aching."

"I doubt it, Dushatra," Katazuli says. "It looks like we're approaching a fort."

"If it is, it's an old fort," Kumar says.

Captain Arshad stops the caravan and rides back to the magi.

"Sirs, I am going to leave our soldiers down here by the river. "I will take you up the hill to Fortress Birtha. It is up to you whether you take your servants with you."

The magi decide to leave their servants with the soldiers. "Perhaps they will treat us to a good dinner at the fort tonight," Michel says with a large grin.

"When they go through the massive gates and enter the parade grounds of the fort, they are soon greeted by the commander.

"Welcome, my illustrious friends," he says. "I had no idea we were going to be hosting the very advisors to King Phraattes. We are honored."

Captain Arshad accepts the greeting on behalf of the magi.

"I want to share my table with you tonight," Commander Karani continues. "But first, I know you want to get the dust of the road off you. My stablemen will take your camels. Then you may follow my servant here up those stairs to private rooms for special guests. You will be treated with a hot bath. My stable hands will take your extra clothing and supplies on your camels up to you shortly. Then you may join me for venison, which was just caught this morning."

The evening is spent listening to the fort commander talk of his military exploits and Captain Arshad explaining to the magi just what the commander is talking about.

The next day after a lavish fastbreaking at the insistence of the commander, they remount their camels, ride out through the gate, and down to the river where they rejoin their servants and the soldiers.

"Did you hear what that Commander Karani said about fighting the Romans as a *cataphract*?" Michel says.

Who could miss it?

"He was no more a *cataphract* than Queen Musa is. My father was a *cataphract* hero. I should know."

"I didn't realize that," Katazuli says.

"It requires a strong horse to be a *cataphract*, and that horse he said had been loyal to him through numerous battles was too skinny and dainty to wear all that heavy armor, plus carry a warrior on his back also in armor head to foot."

"So your father was a war hero," Katazuli says. "You never talk about him."

"Well, he was never home. Always out fighting for whoever needed him, but mostly for old King Phraattes and King Orodes, his father. But, my mother and I got by fine without him. I took care of everything. I knew that, if I didn't take care of business, it wouldn't get done."

Late that afternoon, they stop in a valley near the river, sit outside on their rugs, eat leftovers given them by the commander of Birtha, and watch their servants play a rousing game of dice.

The next day, they continue north through the mountains. In mid-afternoon, they see ahead of them a great walled city.

"There it is. I would know it anywhere," Kumar says. "The great city of Ashur, the city of kings."

Captain Arshad leaves the soldiers and servants outside the walls to spend the night there. He leads the magi across the moat—which is actually the Tigris split to go around the city—and through the south gate of the old city.

"Would you like a tour before arranging for an inn?" he asks them.

"Lead on," Michel says. "I'll bet my ancestor, Abraham, stopped here on his way to his Promised Land."

"What's that?" Kumar asks.

"Oh, it's just an old Jewish thing. I'll explain it to you someday," Michel says.

They go through the residential area, then come to three ancient temples in the middle of the city—one to Sin and Shamash, the second to Nabu, and the third to Ishtar.

On the other side of those temples is an ancient palace that looks still lived in. To their left is another temple, this one to Anu and Hadad.

"Look at that ziggurat," Dushatra says. "Still standing after all these thousands of years."

"On the other side of the ziggurat is the great temple complex dedicated to the patron god of the city, Ashur," their captain explains.

"Let's go back and see the palace again," Yasib says.

"There is a newer palace on the other side of the temple to Anu and Hadad," Captain Arshad says.

"Well, let's go there, then," Michel says. "Does anyone know the name of King Phraattes' satrap here?"

"Parmys, I believe," their captain says.

"Do you know everything?" Yasib asks their leader, with delight sparkling in his eyes.

"I have been stationed many places around the kingdom," he replies, though he does not share the fact that the names of all satraps, sub-kings, mayors, governors, and procurators are listed on the maps given him by Phraattes. "Would you like to meet him? I'm sure he would like to meet you. It is not a daily occurrence that the advisors to the king come to a city."

"We would be honored to meet Satrap Parmys," Michel says.

The captain leads them to the front gate of the palace and introduces himself and his entourage to the guards. One of them disappears inside.

Shortly the front gate is opened and a man wearing red silk billowy pantaloons, with a purple wraparound vest, and gold turban stands facing them with open arms.

"Welcome, gentlemen," Parmys says. "Welcome to my humble home."

The magi smile and go into the expansive outer courtyard.

"My stable hands will take your camels and deliver your supplies to your rooms. This palace has been empty far too long. What a delight to be honored with you, the king's own magi. Why did someone not send me word ahead of time so I could be prepared for you?"

The men dismount from their camels without replying.

"Well, I may not have the most amazing meal you have ever eaten tonight, but I doubt you have seen such acrobats as I have at my disposal. Go with my servants to clean up, then be prepared to eat whatever I have and be astounded by my acrobats."

The evening lives up to the satrap's promises, and the magi retire for the night refreshed and in good spirits.

The next morning after a sumptuous breakfast of fresh grapes, fresh figs, fresh pomegranates, and fresh bread dipped in yogurt, the magi thank their host and leave the palace.

They exit the city out the west Tabira Gate and are met with the soldiers and servants.

"How did you know to meet us here?" Michel asks his servant, Anu.

"The captain sent word to us this morning, along with a large basket of fresh fruit."

The caravan now reassembled, Captain Arshad leads them back to the shore of the Tigris River and on north out of the Hamrin Mountains.

Late afternoon of the second day, they arrive at the mouth of the Upper Zeb tributary to the Tigris.

"This is far enough for today," the caravan leader announces.

"Uh, Captain Arshad, we would like to stop here at the bend in the river and send the soldiers and our servants on down a little way."

"Why?"

Michel grins with a glitter in his eyes but does not reply.

"Very well, sir."

The magi dismount.

"Leave our personal supplies here, Arshad," Michel continues. "You may lead our camels down to join the others."

"Will you be spending the night here?"

"No. When we are through with our business, we will join you."

"Yes, sir."

With that, the captain leaves, hanging on to the reins of five camels with no passengers on them.

When they are lone, Michel looks at the other four.

"Well, gentlemen, shall we?"

"Indeed."

"Let's do it."

"I'm going in first."

"I'll beat you."

Thereupon, five dignified advisors to a king jump in the water and go swimming.

All the following day, the servants and soldiers watch the magi with curiosity as they joke among each other.

That afternoon, they arrive at Newkkart, also called Hdatta. It is a busy market city full of flourishing artisans and merchants.

The magi take their servants with them and go from booth to booth, looking mostly at clothing.

"This trip is going to be hard on me," Michel tells Anu. "I'm going to need two more outfits, a new turban, and another pair of sandals."

That night the magi spend in a comfortable inn and allow their servants to stay with them to carry their purchases.

They get an early start the following morning. When the sun is high in the sky that afternoon, Michel sends word up to the captain to stop the caravan.

The captain takes his camel back to where the magi are. "Is there something wrong, sir?" Arshad asks.

"No, but we want to stop here while it is still daylight. This is a special place."

The captain looks west, then east of the river across the desert.

"There is nothing here, sir."

"Oh, but there is. This is where the great city of Nineveh, capital of the Assyrian Kingdom, was."

The captain looks again and shades his eyes with his hand. "I still don't see anything."

"Well, it's down there somewhere, and we intend to look for it."

The soldiers are given their orders and begin erecting the great tent for the magi, pulling out supplies and food, and organizing their guard positions and schedules for the night.

"Why is this city so important to you, Michel?" Dushatra asks as they walk on the east bank of the Tigris.

"Other than being one of the most magnificent and evil cities of any in the world, one of my people's prophets came here to warn them that the one true God, Jehovah, was going to punish them."

"Yes, I know they got pretty cruel," Dushatra says. "They skinned alive the generals of armies they captured. Even our King Phraattes does not do that."

"So, did the king skin your prophet alive?" Kumar asks.

"No, they actually repented and behaved themselves after that," Michel replies.

"Are you sure that's a true story?"

"Yes. The prophet's name was Jonah, and he left behind an authentic record of this. So, let's see if we can find any old foundations, perhaps of the city wall."

The magi spend the next two hours looking, decide they did indeed discover part of the ancient wall, then walk back to where the soldiers and their servants are waiting for them.

Michel: The Fourth Wise Man

The rugs and cushions are out, bowls of fruit are uncovered for consumption, and fires built around their temporary compound against the cool of the desert evening.

That night soon after retiring, the magi are awakened. It is Captain Arshad.

"Sirs, I need your advice."

Michel, Dushatra, and Katazuli are still awake and go out to Arshad.

"What's wrong?" they ask.

"Dohuk is where we should be going next. But, sir, I have lost the map to it. I do not know where the city is.

29 ~ LOST

"What are we going to do?" Captain Arshad asks. "I have never lost anything important in my life. I have always been well organized and always knew exactly what I was doing. I am more than embarrassed. You deserve better."

"Well, there is nothing we can do about it tonight," Michel says. "Go on back to your tent. We'll work on the problem tomorrow."

The men return to their pallets on the ornate rugs laid out for them.

Michel does not fall back asleep.

Not again, Jehovah God. Will we have to abort our trip again and return to Ctesiphon? We finally discovered the secret of the star, but is that all?

It has taken over my life. All I wanted to do is restore Eden, and you allow all these interruptions and interferences. Even the interruptions are being interrupted. What are we going to do?

Michel falls asleep and dreams he is being suspended from a ziggurat above the Garden of Eden, unable to go up or down. Meira is calling to him to come down. "Michel. Michel."

Someone shakes him. Michel opens his eyes. It is Anu.

"The others are up and calling for you. They seem to be upset about something."

Michel rouses himself and sits up. Anu has fresh

clothes out for him.

"Not those, Anu. No use getting them dusty too. I'll wear something that is already dusty."

When Michel spots the other magi outside his tent, they are on their way to Arshad's tent. He catches up with them.

"We're going to go help Arshad search for his map of Dohuk. If that doesn't work, we may have to return to Ctesiphon." It is Kumar.

They arrive at Arshad's tent.

"Okay, Arshad, bring all your maps out."

Arshad appears moments later at the flap of his tent with a large leather pouch. He opens it. "Here they are, sirs. But I have already looked through them a hundred times."

For the next hour, the magi look through the maps, passing them around to make sure everyone has had a chance to examine each one.

"We've looked at them all," Katazuli says. "What are we going to do?"

"Hand me the first one we looked at," Yasib says.

Arshad hands it to him. Yasib stares at it, stands, walks around with it, then bursts out laughing.

"Huh?"

Yasib walks back to the others.

"Your map has been updated. They don't call it Dohuk any more. They call it Beth Nuhadra."

"What are you talking about, Yasib?" Michel asks.

"People are beginning to call Dohuk by its new name: Beth Nuhadra."

The captain reaches over to take the scroll. "Are you sure, Yasib, sir?"

"Of course, I'm sure. I may be old, and my mind slowing down, but I'm not dead, and my mind isn't either. Look at the direction the river is going on your map. Now, look at the river itself over here. It's going the same direction. We're not lost, captain. We are right where we should be."

The captain stares a little longer at the map, looks at the magi with a large grin, and raises his arm in the air.

"We move out within the hour," he announces to his men.

On up the road. Out of the mountains and into a plain. It takes the rest of that day and all the next to arrive at Beth Nuhadra.

As always, the captain leaves the soldiers outside the city along with the servants.

When they enter, they see a crowd of people gathered around a large camel.

"What's going on over there?" Katazuli asks.

The magi dismount from their camels and go over to the crowd.

"What's all the excitement?" they asks.

"We were going to have our annual camel race, but the competitor to our prize camel tripped into a large gopher hole and broke his leg. Now the celebration is off."

"Oh, I wouldn't necessarily say that," Kumar says.

The stranger looks at Kumar. "What do you mean? Do you have a racing camel?"

"Well, I have a camel. I don't know how fast he can run, but I'd be willing to enter him in a race."

The stranger grins.

"I'd be willing to enter my camel," Dushatra says.

"Why not? The rest of us will too."

"I wonder if the others outside of the city would like to enter," Yasib says, anticipating some fun.

"Sir, go out the gate we just entered through, and ask that small army out there if they would like to be part of the race."

As the magi wait, they are given room by the crowd to walk up to their prize camel.

"A fine animal it looks like to me," Michel says.

"Yes, indeed. A fine animal."

The stranger returns to them. "They all said they would like to enter the race. But it is too late in the day."

"We will do it first thing in the morning. Then we'll rest until noon, and be on our way." Now show us to an inn."

"So, what shall the prize be?" the stranger asks.

Michel: The Fourth Wise Man

Michel turns around. "The glory. The prize will be the glory."

Indeed, the next morning at dawn, the race is held. Forty-one camels against the city's prize camel.

The boundaries and beginning and ending points are determined, and the race is on.

As predicted, the city's prize camel wins.

"We knew it would," Michel says. "But, well, we have been through some heavy things for the past year and thought this would refresh our spirits. Indeed, it did."

The camels are allowed to rest until noon. Then the caravan is assembled and the procession to find the child-king resumes.

The next night, they sit around a campfire. "We turn northwest now," the captain tells them. "Cities are going to be farther apart."

The following morning they prepare for a long two-day ride.

"I wonder how my people are celebrating," Michel muses as they ride their camels, swaying back and forth.

"Celebrating your newborn king?"

"Yes. I wonder how they are celebrating. We call him the Messiah—the anointed one. Our people anoint kings and high priests; we don't crown them. It's up to them to get a crown if they want to. It has always been our tradition to anoint them with special oil."

"Do you think we missed the anointing ceremony? The coronation?" Yasib asks.

"Probably. Unless they are going to wait until he is thirty—the legal age—to anoint him. But they will have a celebration of some kind for the one who will be sitting on David's eternal throne."

"At the palace? Or your temple? In just Jerusalem or in all the cities?"

"Probably all the cities will have some kind of celebration of their own. But, of course, there will be a main national celebration in Jerusalem. I sure hope we don't miss it."

"Yes. For your sake, anyway, I hope we don't miss it," Yasib says.

They ride the rest of the day in near silence.

That night they sit around a fire built for them by one of the soldiers.

"Is this Anatolia, or are we still in Parthia?" Kumar asks.

"This is Anatolia," Katazuli says. "My people, the Hittites, lived northwest of here."

"It must be exciting being this close to them."

"Yes, it is. I would love to just go for a little ride farther up there and visit with some of my people. I can speak the ancient Hittite language. The old Hittites will like that. The language is dying out."

The next morning, they continue on, following the Tigris River as it veers north and west.

Late that afternoon, they arrive in Nisibis.

"Well, we certainly look out of place here," Dushatra says.

"We certainly do," Kumar responds. "Here we are in our silk pantaloons and turbans, and all the men around here are dressed in short tunics with those wide leather belts and leather, well, helmets. They look like warrior helmets."

"Look. They're staring at us."

"Maybe they're staring at our camels. Not many camels up here."

"Maybe they're staring at both."

As usual, Captain Arshad leaves his soldiers and the servants outside the city while he leads the magi in to find a place to spend the night.

"Let's try that inn over there," Yasib says.

"Do they have a stable large enough to handle our camels?"

"They're so close to our border, surely they are used to men on camels coming through at least sometimes. Let's give it a try."

They dismount from their camels while Arshad goes inside to arrange a large room for them.

Michel: The Fourth Wise Man

He returns outside. "The innkeeper said they will have a room for you as soon as his servants clean it up. I told him who you were, and he said he would also send out for new sheets for the beds for you and bring vats in you can bathe in. So, there will be a short wait."

The magi enter and walk to the section of the inn serving food and drinks. They order their food.

Again, they watch people watching them.

Finally, Michel stands and walks over to the table of an older man watching them.

"I'll go first. I'll tell you what we are doing here. Then you can tell us what you are doing here."

The man smiles at Michel.

"It's a deal."

"Come join us, then," Michel says, matching the stranger's smile.

The magi make room for the stranger. They tell the man who they are and where they are going.

"Now, you," Michel says.

"Well, my name is Lelex," he begins. "My grandfather was from Greece. You may have heard of us. We are Spartans."

"Indeed, we have," Michel says. "You are famous warriors. I know because my father was—is—a famous warrior."

"Well, when we were taken over by the Romans, we lost some of our glory," the old Spartan says. "But not all of it. We still dress as our ancestors did in honor of them. I even have the shield my great, great grandfather carried in battle. Every soldier of honor returned home with his shield. He could return home without anything else, but never without his shield. His shield reflected his honor."

Captain Arshad looks up. "The innkeeper is signaling to us. I believe the room is ready."

The magi stand. They each shake hands and forearms with their new friend.

"Good luck to you, Lelex, and your honorable family," Michel says.

The others wish the old man well, then retire to their room for the rest of the evening while Captain Arshad stands duty outside their door.

It is not until the next morning that the magi realize what Arshad has done.

"We did not expect that."

"We are entering a land of people who may love us or hate us. I will guard you."

By mid-morning, they are on their way, still following the Tigris River. This time, the river turns straight west. They are away from the mountains now, and the weather grows as hot as it normally is this time of year down in Susa.

"I can certainly understand why King Phraattes has a summer palace," Katazuli says. "The one in Susa must be intolerable in the summer."

They ride on, ever west. Ever closer to the newborn king that isn't so newborn anymore.

"I wonder if he is walking yet."

"I don't know. He is just a few months past being a year old," Kumar says. "Perhaps. Some children do walk this early."

They grow quiet again. Swaying with their camels. Swaying and thinking and imagining.

"What will it be like being in the presence of a child-king brought into the world by a star?" Dushatra finally says. "How will he be different? If at all?"

"Will he be in the palace attended by a multitude of servants?" Kumar says. "Will he have angels attending him? Will he have wings? After all, he is a star child."

Yasib chuckles.

"What?" Michel says, smiling back.

"I wonder if he is talking yet."

The magi smile and go back to their imaginings.

The sun turns red and eases down to the horizon. The captain raises his hand, and everyone behind him stops. The soldiers go to work on the tents, the servants on supplies and food, and various comforts.

They eat and look up into the sky, wondering.

Michel: The Fourth Wise Man

"Will his star ever reappear?" Michel asks. "Or is it gone forever?"

"Was it just sent as an omen, a prophecy, a warning?" Dushatra asks.

"Star, where are you?" Kumar asks.

The next morning, they are back on their camels. It had taken three days to get to Nisibis. It will take four to get to Harran.

They notice Mount Siryar south of them and wish they were on the mountain with its coolness.

Michel thinks about his warrior father. *Oh, Father, why did you have to be a hero? Why couldn't you have stayed home and been my hero? You were never there for Mother and me. If anything ever got done for us, I am the one who had to do it. Why was that, Father? I didn't want you to be everyone else's hero. I wanted you to be mine.*

On the third day, they see ahead of them a strange city.

"This is Harran," Michel explains. "My ancestor, Abraham from Ur near where the Garden of Eden was—is—stayed here several years with his father. The city was named after my ancestor's brother, Harran. He was a great a mighty warrior. Well, my ancestor had his own army, so I guess that made him a warrior too. He had nearly four hundred of his own soldiers."

"I'll bet you have some interesting stories to tell about your Abraham," Yasib says.

"But, please don't tell them," Kumar says.

"You can tell them to me in private," Katazuli says.

"What are those strange buildings?" Dushatra asks Michel.

"I can tell you," Katazuli says. "You probably call them beehive houses. They are just houses made out of mud with sloped roofs like a helmet."

"Why sloped? It's doesn't snow here," Yasib says.

"Well, I don't know. I would say rain would fall off the roof better sloped, but it's pretty deserty here."

"I wonder if any of their inns are like that. I'd like to

stay in one," Katazuli says.

"Perhaps so. But I plan to look for their palace. That's where my ancestor's brother would have lived. And possibly my ancestor too. That's where I want to stay."

"You act like you're going to be here more than a day," Kumar says.

Michel stops his camel. "Could we? I'd like to stay here a week even if you don't mind. It will give that newborn king a chance to grow some more before we arrive. Who knows? Perhaps he will be walking and talking both by the time we arrive. Could we, men?"

"You carried me on your back when I wasn't strong enough to run from Borseen," Yasib says.

"You helped me give Hophni an honorable burial," Katazuli says.

"You led us to the holy writings that explained the meaning of the star," Kumar and Dushatra say.

"Yes, of course," Yasib says.

They arrive at the gate of the city, and Arshad leads them in.

"We're going to do things differently this time," Michel tells him. "Let the soldiers go on into the city if they want and find a place to stay for a few days. Just warn them not to get drunk and get us all removed from the city."

"We would like our servants to stay with us in our rooms," Kumar says.

"Yes, sirs," Arshad says. "Just let me know where you will be staying. I will arrange for two guards to stand at the door to your rooms at all times."

"You do not need to do that," Dushatra says.

"Yes, I do. These people look suspicious."

"A lot of them are related to the Hittites, just like Katazuli here," Michel says. "They are not dangerous."

"Still, that is my decision."

"Okay. If you insist," Kumar says.

"Besides, I have a bad feeling about this city or the cities around it. I keep feeling like something is going to go very wrong here. Are you sure you want to stay? I have a very bad feeling about being here. Very bad."

30 ~ THE PREMONITION

Rather than be in a single domed inn, the magi find a row of small domed houses that are available to rent just like one would a row of rooms in an inn.

As promised—and insisted upon—by Captain Arshad, two soldiers are assigned to stand outside the door of each magus. With this arrangement, ten soldiers are required at a time while the other ten rest or do whatever they desire in the city.

"I want to find the palace," Michel tells Yasib, their first full day in Harran. "Would you like to go with me? Anu is going to stay back and wash my clothes. They have gotten way too dusty on the road. Besides, they smell like a camel."

He laughs, and Yasib agrees. "However, you have to agree to not walk too fast or too far," he warns his younger companion.

"Well, promising to not walk too far, I cannot do," Michel says. "But I will walk slow. How's that?"

"That is a compromise I believe I can live with. To start."

They walk away from the residential part of the city and head toward the older sections with the permanent buildings.

"Did you know those dome houses are rebuilt year after year?" Michel says as they walk. "I've been told they can put one together in a day or less. Someone keeps watch for when the tax collector is going to be coming, and when

Michel: The Fourth Wise Man

they learn of the exact date, they take their houses apart, set them up like fences around their crops, and are taxed only for crops, but not houses. Then, after the tax collector leaves, they put their houses back together."

"Ha, ha! I wonder if that's true," Yasib says. "Seems like a lot of trouble to go to, so one does not have to pay taxes."

"Well, if the taxes are unreasonable."

"All taxes are unreasonable, my son. At least to the taxpayer. Aren't most of the people around here nomads? Wouldn't it make more sense that they take their houses apart when not here, so they don't crumble, then put them back together fresh and strong when they return?"

"Who knows?"

So, do you think your ancestor's palace was in the direction we're walking?"

"I do not know. They have a temple to Inanna, so-called god of the moon, here. If it is as elaborate as I have been told...oh, there it is."

"Whoever informed you about the elaborateness of this temple probably was not exaggerating. It is magnificent," Yasib says. "Would you like to go inside?"

"No. First, I doubt the priests would allow us to. Second, I do not believe the gods have to divide up running the universe among each other to avoid confusion or being worn out or having too much to do. I believe in only one God—the one who made the universe and everything in it. If he can make it, he can run it. Wouldn't you think so?"

"Michel, sometimes I get very angry at you. My Hindu training tells me you are wrong, wrong, wrong. But you do make sense sometimes," Yasib says. "Therefore, I want to change the subject."

"As you wish," Michel responds. "Do you think this is the palace? I cannot tell if anyone is living in it anymore."

"Look for guards, my boy."

They walk around to the front of the building. It has two imposing gates with one guard on each side.

"But where are the other guards?" Yasib asks. "It looks

to me they are guarding an empty building."

"Maybe their king is gone for a while. Well, I want to sit here and imagine my ancestor walking up and down this street and living in that palace," Michel says.

"Good idea. My bones are acting up."

The two magi squat on their heels across a road and a small plaza in front of the palace. One dreams of what might have been. The other dreams deeply enough to snore.

"Yasib, wake up I'm ready to go back into the city."

The two men walk back toward their rented domes.

"Hey, I see Kumar and Dushatra," Michel says.

"Where is Katazuli?" Michel asks.

"He's not with us. We thought he was with you."

"Well, let's go over to the market and find something to eat."

The four magi make their selections, then seat themselves on benches scattered around the city square.

"There you are," they hear.

"Katazuli. Where have you been?"

"I walked over to Urfa. I thought the city would be full of Hittites, but they were all Arabians. Don't know how they got here so far from home."

"You're really close to your people here, aren't you?"

"Yes, I am. Straight north of here a week's ride, is where the Hittite palace was. So, since we decided to stay a week, I am going to look around and see if I can find more of my people, and we can exchange what we know of whoever is left."

"You do know Harran is at the crossroads of the Silk Road," Kumar says.

"Yes," Dushatra says. "The Chinese bring it as far as here, then spread out going east to Greece and Italy, and north to Germannica, though I don't know why those barbarians would want to buy silk."

"That must be why our army fought Augustus here when I was a boy," Yasib says.

"Well, I could sure use some of that new silk right now," Michel says. "My clothes are starting to look terrible.

Michel: The Fourth Wise Man

And there are only so many times you can wash silk."

"Well, I'm tired. I think I'll go back to my room for a rest," Yasib says.

One by one, the magi disburse and retire for the night. As always, there are two guards standing on duty outside their door.

Morning comes.

"I think I'm going to go over to Urfa myself today," Michel tells Katazuli. "Care to go along and show me around?"

"No, I want to try another city. I'd like to go up to Malatya. It's much closer to where I was born."

"I understand you wanting to do this, but be careful. Don't go too far away."

"Oh, I won't."

"Besides," Michel adds, "I heard there are gangs of natives up in the foothills of those Taurus Mountains who make their living preying on travelers."

"Don't worry about me, Michel. You seem to forget I am one of the natives."

Michel smiles and pounds Katazuli on the back. "Okay, big man. Enjoy yourself today."

Michel spends the rest of the day in Edessa. He goes alone because Yasib is recovering from the day before, and Dushatra and Kumar decided to check out the library in Harran.

Evening comes, and the magi meet in the market again to pick up something to eat at the city square.

"Where's Katazuli?" Kumar asks.

"Not with me," Yasib says. "Wasn't he with you? How about you, Michel?"

"He wasn't with me either. But he did tell me he wanted to look around for any other Hittites who remembered the old language, and they could talk together."

"It must be hard to be away from home so long, then come back, but not quite close enough," Yasib says.

After a while, the men part and go to their rentals.

The next day they decide to do something together—

have a meeting with one of the local silk merchants and see if they can find enough tailors to make them each a new outfit before leaving.

"Then, when we present ourselves down in Jerusalem to the newborn king," Michel says, "we will be at our finest."

Once again, they go back to their domes to sleep for the night.

"I wish Katazuli would quit running around in those hills after his people and enjoy Harran with us," Michel says. "I think I'll go tell his guards to have him join us when he gets up tomorrow morning."

The next morning, the four magi walk over to the dome house Katazuli had rented, and knock on his door. No one answers. They call his name. "Katazuli, it's us. Let us in." Still, there is no answer.

"If you don't let us in," Michel says, "we are going to come in anyway."

Still, no answer.

The magi look at each other, then try to open the door. It is unlocked. They go in and see that it is in perfect condition.

"But where is Katazuli?"

They walk around the city checking with the merchants, the library, and anywhere else he may have gone. No one remembers seeing him since the first day they arrived.

They find Arshad. "Have you seen Katazuli?"

"No, I haven't. But his guards are always at his door." He checks with the guards.

"We just always assumed he was inside."

Arshad looks up at the sky and then to the magi. He grits his teeth. "I warned him not to go wandering around in those foothills by himself."

"I told him the same thing," Michel says.

"Now, I'm going to have to go up there and find him."

"Well, let me know when you do find him," Michel says. "We will be leaving in another couple days."

That evening, Captain Arshad reports to Michel and

the other Magi.

"We were unable to find him. He must have gone farther than we thought. Tomorrow we will take our camels so we can cover more territory."

The next day Michel and the other magi stay close to the market place so they will be easy to find.

Night comes, and still the soldiers have not found Katazuli.

"I am going to check with the local magistrates to see if they have any suggestions," Arshad says.

A little while later, Arshad reports to the other four magi. "He said there is a gang up in the hills toward Malatya that has been attacking everyone who they think is invading their territory. He told me where their hideout is."

On the morning of the third day searching for Katazuli, Captain Arshad takes all twenty of his men plus the five servants up toward the hideout.

At noon, the soldiers return. With them is Katazuli, on a camel being supported with a tall soldier sitting behind him. His chin is resting on his chest.

"He is barely alive," Anu tells Michel. "I will find a doctor."

Katazuli is lain on his bed in the dome house.

"Oh, Katazuli, what happened?" Michel asks, the other three magi kneeling by his pallet with him.

"I recognized that they were speaking...speaking Hittite," he groans. "So I...I tried to make friends...with...with them."

He stops and coughs, holding his side.

"What can we do for you?" Michel asks. "You've always been our doctor. Now we have to doctor you. What should we do?"

"Some opium tea would...would sure be...helpful," Katazuli groans, trying to smile.

"Did they break any of your bones?"

"They tried. But I'm pretty...pretty solid. Probably cracked some...though."

He closes his eyes and squints, pressing his lips

together.

"They beat me on...my front...my back, my head..."

The magi sit cross-legged now by their friend and colleague who had been through so much with them the previous year.

"Shhh. Anu will be here with a doctor soon."

They wait. They watch. They pray.

And Katazuli breathes his last.

When Anu arrives with the doctor, all the doctor can do is confirm what they already know.

They sit in silence the rest of the afternoon.

"He longed so much to be with his people again. We must bury him with them," Michel says.

"You are right," Yasib says.

"Kumar and I will check around town to see if there are any Hittite cemeteries nearby," Dushatra says.

Two hours later, they return.

"There is one on the other side of the palace."

The four remaining magi wrap their friend in the sheet he had been lying on.

"Captain Arshad, could we borrow one of your soldiers' shields?" Michel asks when the captain comes to check on them "We would like to carry him to the cemetery on it. He believed it was a sign of honor."

The captain organizes his soldiers into an honor guard. Four of the servants carry the shield. Katazuli's personal servant walks in front of it. The magi walk by two and two behind the shield. The honor guards walk on each side of the procession.

Slowly they walk.
With their friend.
Quietly they walk.
Michel sings a dirge written by his King David.

Oh, how the mighty have fallen.

The ground is hard because of the desert conditions, but their servants are able to dig through far enough they can bury their friend.

The magi wait while the servants complete their work.

Wait.

And watch.

And wonder why.

Carefully now, the four magi lower their friend into his grave.

They sit by the grave and push the dirt back over it with their hands.

Slowly.

Gently.

A little at a time

The dirt mingles with their tears.

Then it is done.

The magi walk back to their rentals and pack their things. Katazuli's servant packs his, and they allow the servant to return home with them.

The next morning, the caravan forms. Now only thirty-nine camels. One of their own is no longer with them. Nor his servant.

They cross the Bilikh River and head west toward Karkemesh.

Slowly they lead their camels.

Slowly they ride away from their friend.

Slowly doing what must be done.

They have also left behind the Tigris River. Now they head toward the Euphrates. A new river. A new part of their life. The former left behind. The unknown still ahead.

They camp for the night. They do not speak much. No one does. Arshad can be heard giving orders to his men. But that is all.

They mourn.

For five days, they travel toward the next city. Karkemesh is on the west bank of the Euphrates River.

When they arrive, they find an inn, eat a little, and go to their shared room. Guards stand outside their door.

The next morning, Captain Arshad leads the caravan southwest away from the Euphrates. They travel another day, and another, and yet another.

"Master," Anu says the night before they arrive at Aleppo. "Would it be all right if I played on my flute tonight? I do not wish to be disrespectful, but we are among strange people on the highway, and when we pull over to the side to put up our tents, we do not want them to become suspicious of us. Perhaps if I played my flute."

"Anu," Michel sighs, "of course you are right. Katazuli would not want us to mourn for him forever. Yes, Anu, play your flute."

On the fourth day out of Karkemesh, the caravan arrives at Aleppo.

When they enter the city, they are startled.

"This is like being in Athens," Dushatra says.

"Or Rome," Kumar says.

"What's that up there?" Yasib asks.

"Must be their acropolis," Michel says. "Let's go take a look."

They check in at an inn first to stable their camels and put their supplies in a locked room.

They meet on the portico of the inn, and walk to the high man-made hill with the moat around it, and find steps to the top.

There, they see an amphitheater and temple to Dionysius. They also see a temple to the god Hadad. The rest is barracks and a parade ground.

They leave and walk around the city. They see a few more temples, a palace, what looks to be a treasury building, baths, and a bazaar.

"I think this is a Roman province now," Yasib says.

"You know, fellows, I do not have the enthusiasm I did before...well, before. I am going back to the inn," Michel says. "Maybe I will feel better tomorrow."

Michel returns to his room.

Jehovah, I am tired. Give me strength so that, when we are through paying our respects to the child-king, I can get back to Eden and work on what is truly important. Jehovah, please walk the earth again with us.

And my father. Could you let him know somehow that I do love him? Somehow? Just in case something happens to me, let him know.

31 ~ EXHAUSTION

"How long have we been gone this time?" Yasib asks as their camels plod straight south on the long highway.

"Two months. We left toward the end of May, and now it is the end of July," Michel replies, taking his turban off and wiping his brow.

"We must be crazy, traveling through the hottest parts of the world during the hottest months of the year," Dushatra says.

"Perhaps we should call it dedicated," Kumar says, shading his eyes from the glaring morning sun.

"Did you realize we are back to our original four?" Michel asks.

"Hmmm. You're right," Yasib says. "We gained four who could lead us in their respective kingdoms. Now they're gone."

"Two dead because they were traitors. You just never know what is in someone else's mind. Or heart," Kumar says.

"Two dead because they were trying too hard," Michel says.

"Yes, I think you're right. They were trying to do the right thing, but out of ignorance. Hophni sucked the snake venom out of Borseen to save his life, but with a cut lip. Katazuli wanted to find his people to encourage them to carry on their ancestors' heritage, but approached the wrong

Michel: The Fourth Wise Man

ones."

"Are we doing the same thing?" Michel asks. "Are we seeking a newborn king with his own star and an eternal throne just to keep our king happy? Or do we really want to honor him ourselves?"

"What a question. That's one I'll have to think about," Dushatra says.

The magi are quiet the rest of the day. Their camels plod slowly along, ten soldiers and their commander in front, ten soldiers in back, four servants, and ten pack animals. All for the sake of four magi, their king, and a strange star.

That evening as the magi sit out in the evening breeze eating cheese and dipping bread in yogurt, they look up at the stars.

"Millions of them," Kumar says. "I've been taught by my Hindu priests there are as many gods as stars."

"I have been taught the same thing by my Buddhist monks," Dushatra says.

"Were you ever a monk, Dushatra?" Michel asks.

"Well, yes, I was. My schooling was at the feet of Buddhist monks in Taxila. Then I returned home to Kandahar and became a monk there for a while."

"Why did you stop?"

"I resented having to go around begging in order to help support the monastery. Besides, we Buddhists have to be perfect in order to stop the incessant being reborn over and over. I envy you Jews who believe in forgiveness."

"Dushatra and I agree on that, even though I'm a Hindu," Kumar says. "We have to be perfect too. Besides, our heaven is just being absorbed into the essence of the universe with no more identity. I want to keep being me. And I want gods that care about me. Your one God accomplishes more than all our thousands of gods put together."

"You mean, you fellows are actually listening to me sometimes?" Michel says with a grin. "I never thought you did."

"Well, you don't expect us to admit everything, do you?" Kumar responds.

The camp has grown quiet. The soldiers are through putting up the tents. The servants are through setting out needed supplies. The animals and humans have all been fed. The soldiers mustered for guard duty the first half of the night are in place.

The magi enter their large tent with the partitions in it, lie down on their pallets, and fall asleep.

During the night, the wind blows a little more. It is a cool wind. A refreshing wind. A good wind.

The next morning when they waken, one corner of the large tent is flapping in the wind.

"Sorry, sir," one of the soldiers tells Michel. "We did not attach that corner to the stake very well."

"Ah, it is a fine morning. I love that wind. Don't you?" he responds.

After breaking their fast with dried figs, cheese and bread dipped in yogurt, the magi remount their camels and once more head south.

"This is sure different than it has been the past couple of weeks," Kumar says. "The cool air feels good."

They continue on. The hair on top of their Bactrian camels' heads and each hump dances around in miniature waves.

As the morning progresses, the sky turns from deep blue to light blue to almost white

Still, the wind comes on.

They see the bushes and occasional acacia trees on each side of the road bend and sway one way and then another.

The sky turns a light brown. A sandy brown. The wind whips around the travelers. They put scarves around their necks, then up over their noses.

Still, the wind comes. Stronger now.

The camels close one set of eyelids. The men duck their heads and hump over.

"Look!" Anu shouts over the growing moan of the wind and pointing.

Captain Arshad signals for his men to break ranks

and make a run for it. He circles around to the magi. "Follow me."

The camels are put into a gallop as they rush to stay ahead of the bank of sand that reaches to the clouds above.

The soldiers, the servants, the magi all kicking their animals with their knees, raising their reins high with both hands and shouting hut-hut.

The wind howls around them. The bushes break free of their roots and tumble across the desert floor. Smaller animals scurry in circles ahead of them.

Hurry.

Nowhere to run to. Nowhere to hide. Nowhere to go for escape.

Captain Arshad raises his hand as his signal to stop. Though hard to see by now, the magi know what must be done. They bring their camels to a halt, form a circle, signal for them to kneel. The men climb down and huddle inside the circle, their heads down behind their camels who close their other set of eyelids and wait it out.

The wind howls and wails and shrieks around them. The sand blasts at them, whirling in circles to make sure it attacks everything in its way.

The men's eyelids squinted shut, scarves over their heads, and ducking almost all the way down to the desert floor, they wait.

Wait for the monster to do its worst. Wait for the monster's appetite to be satiated. Wait for the monster to move on to other prey.

Silence.

Only a distant reminder. Then gone.

One by one, the men raise their heads to view the damage. And each other.

One by one, they stand and let the sand fall off them. One by one, the camels stand and shake themselves free of the sand.

Sometimes someone can be heard. "You all right?"

"Whew!" Dushatra says. "I've seen worse."

"You have not," Yasib counters, still brushing the dust

off his shoulders and pulling off his robe.

"What's that?" Michel says.

The other three look in the direction Michel is looking.

"What?"

"That long stone. It wasn't there before. Nothing was out here before."

They walk closer and kick at the side of the long stone. More sand falls off the side.

"What is this?" Kumar says.

"Look over here," Michel says. "Here is another one."

They walk around the two slabs.

"I think they're connected."

"Here's a third one."

"I think we've found the foundation of an old building. Let's see if there are more out here. Get the soldiers and servants to help."

A little at a time, the caravan members find the foundations of several buildings.

"Hey, fellows," Michel calls out. "There is writing on this."

He holds out a small slab of clay with cuneiform etched into it. The others look at it.

"Where did you get this?" Yasib asks.

"Right over here. Do you think there are more?"

"One is over here," Dushatra. "It looks like an old receipt for grain."

"Mine looks like a receipt too," Kumar says.

"Well, whatever was here, it wasn't very important," Yasib says. "We need to get back on the highway now."

By this time, Captain Arshad has his men assembled for the caravan. The magi join them and resume their journey to the newborn king with his own star.

"It is certainly desolate over here," Dushatra says.

"My guess is that it hasn't always been desolate," Yasib says. "If we had stuck around back there, we might have discovered an entire city. This may have been important at one time."

"Remember what Borseen told us? About Mari? And

Michel: The Fourth Wise Man

another city to the west named Ebla?" Michel asks. "I wonder if that was Ebla. Well, we have more important things to do than fuss over an abandoned city buried under the sand."

On down the road. One day. Two days. Five.

"I see a city ahead," Dushatra says. "I wonder if that's Hamath. Did Arshad say anything to you?"

"All I know is that we got hit with a sandstorm when we left the Euphrates to get onto the Orodes River. Hopefully, the cities will be closer together now," Michel says.

"We will find out soon enough," Yasib replies.

They are led to the city gates. The soldiers stay outside while Arshad accompanies the magi and their servants to find an inn to spend the night.

"How long do you want to stay here?" the captain asks.

"I just want to get to Jerusalem and get this star business over with, so I can go back to more important things," Michel says.

"Are you sure this 'star business' as you call it is less important than your Eden project?" Yasib asks.

"What do you mean?"

"Just saying," Yasib replies. "Didn't it mean he is a god?"

"Michel stares in silence at the floor, trying not to acknowledge just what and who the child king really is.

"I don't know about the rest of you, but I just sent my servant over to the bazaar to buy some fresh food. Especially fruit," Dushatra says.

"I cannot wait to get out of these dusty clothes and get a bath," Kumar says.

The magi decide to spend two days in Hamath.

Refreshed, they resume their pilgrimage in answer to the beckoning of a strange star that had appeared in the spring over a year earlier.

After spending another night along the highway, the magi arrive in the next city at noon the following day.

"Where are we, Arshad?" Michel calls up to him.

Arshad turns his camel and guides it back to the magi.

"We are soon to enter Emesa. You will like it. Lots to do there."

Arshad leads the magi and their servants in through the vast gate into the city. Right away, they see a large market overflowing with every possible kind of food.

"This is a market city," Arshad explains. "And very wealthy."

He guides them to a section of the city with inns and selects the best one for them. He takes money provided him by King Phraates for the journey out of the pouch at his waist, and pays the innkeeper.

The magi settle in, then leave their room to walk around the city. They pass a temple to El-Gabal, the sun god. After that is a temple to Dionysius with a grand amphitheater on the other side.

"Seems as though we see Dionysius honored at nearly every city we go to," Kumar says.

"Well, to worship him, you must sing and dance and commit adultery, and get drunk, and anything else that brings you pleasure," Dushatra says, telling them what they already know.

"Of course, that is why he is so popular," Michel adds.

They return to the inn and order a meal full of their favorite delicacies.

As they eat, they overhear other customers speak of the mountains ahead.

"If there truly are mountains where we are headed, they are only going to slow us down," Michel says. "Let's skip a second day here and move on tomorrow."

The others agree. "We have been traveling nearly two months this time," Yasib says.

Morning comes, and the caravan reassembles at the gate of the city. Arshad confirms there are mountains ahead.

Once again, on the highway. Fewer camels. More mules and horses and donkeys and wagons and chariots.

"Who are those men?" other travelers ask.

"What are they doing here?"

People stare at the men dressed in colorful silk

turbans, long billowy silk pantaloons, and sleeveless wraparound vests.

"Where are they from?"

"Why are they dressed like that?"

More and more people stare at the caravan of camels that stretches itself along the road so far, it is hard to see the other end of it.

"Are they dangerous?"

"Are they our friends?"

The magi and their camels climb higher into the foothills of the Anti-Lebanon Mountains. The Orodes River ends. They keep going.

One day. Two days. Five more days, they travel through the amazing mountains.

Late afternoon on the fifth day, they arrive in Damascus. Damascus with long straight streets, but some winding and curving with the hills on which the city is built.

Drought conditions right now. The Baranda River bed dry. People carrying water. Not as much food in the markets.

But wares of pottery and brass and copper and cotton and linen are plentiful.

Everything for sale. Everything for either pleasure or survival.

"This is supposed to be a great city," Yasib says. "But I'm not impressed."

"It's old. That's why it is great," Dushatra says.

"The view is nice," Kumar says.

"Let's just spend the night here and be on our way tomorrow," Michel says. "We've got a lot more mountains to go through. And higher."

They leave out the stone Damascus gate the next morning.

"Arshad says the next city is Daraa," Kumar says, already sounding tired.

"I heard we were going to Bashan," Dushatra says. "That's the old name for it. Or something like that. I really don't care. I just want to hurry up and get to Jerusalem."

Three more days. Three days of climbing winding

roads through the mountains.

"Well, it's cooler up here," Michel says.

"I like the trees. Haven't seen trees like this in a very long time," Yasib says.

"My garden is going to have a lot of trees in it," Michel pronounces.

"Not that again," Kumar says. "Let's take care of one thing at a time. Forget Eden. We've got to get to Jerusalem."

"I hope he's worth it."

"Me too."

They ride on. Forever on. To find a child. A child-king. A star child. A child destined to rule from an eternal throne. A strange child who some of them call a god.

"What's that magnificent mountain up there?" Michel calls up to Captain Arshad.

"That is Mount Hermon," their leader calls back to them.

"Magnificent. Still has snow on it in the middle of August."

"There is a sanctuary there," Arshad adds.

"Watch out!" Michel yells.

The other magi look toward Michel, then in the direction he is looking.

It is too late.

Rocks tumble and fall onto the road. The largest one hits Yasib's camel. It honks and stumbles onto its knees. Yasib falls with it.

The soldiers see what is happening. Some jump down from their mount without waiting for it to kneel. They rush over to Yasib.

"Are you all right, sir?"

By now, Michel is there.

"Yasib. Yasib. Wake up. Yasib."

Another magus kneels by their friend.

"Yasib. Don't die. Don't die, Yasib."

"What condition is he in?" Captain Arshad asks.

"Yasib. Come back to us. Yasib."

One of the other soldiers stands behind them next to

the stricken camel.

"This animal is injured too much," he says, looking up at his captain. "He'll have to be killed."

32 ~ FINAL APPROACH

"Move the magus out of the road," Captain Arshad says.

Two strong soldiers take Yasib over to a grassy area. The other magi follow close and kneel by his body.

Yasib opens his eyes.

"Huh? What happened," he mumbles.

"We need Katazuli!" Michel shouts, looking up at his companions. "Katazuli always watched out for us."

"Sirs, if you can move aside, I can better determine what needs to be done." It is one of the soldiers.

The magi stand and move back.

Michel steps away, then sits on the road. He puts his head on his raised knees, and his shoulders shake.

Kumar sees and walks over to him.

"Kumar. I am so tired," he says, looking over at his companion. "Everything keeps going wrong. I just don't think we have God's blessings. Maybe the star didn't mean what we thought it meant."

"Arshad says we will be in the next city soon."

"But what about Yasib? He is so kind and never has harmed anyone in his life, and this happens to him. What if he dies?"

"He won't die," Kumar says.

"The camel died."

"Well, it isn't dead yet, but will be as soon as someone puts an arrow in him. But we can replace it with one of the supply camels."

"We cannot replace Yasib."

Kumar looks over at their wounded friend and sees Yasib sitting up. "Look, Michel. He is fine. The camel did not land on him. Yasib is small enough, he was thrown clear of the animal. See there. Your God is watching out for us, after all."

Michel sits and stares.

"Come on now," Kumar urges, pulling up on Michel's arm. "Come on. Yasib needs us."

Michel looks up at his friend, wipes his eyes, and stands. They join Dushatra kneeling next to the old man.

"What are you blubbering about?" Yasib says when he sees Michel and his reddened eyes. "I just had a quick nap. That's all. Help me up."

"Sir, you shouldn't be…"

"Yes, I should be," he says to the soldier. "Now we need to get going. Enough of these delays."

Michel and the others look over at Yasib's camel in time to see five soldiers tugging at it to roll it down a precipice.

Captain Arshad approaches with another camel. "Here is your new ride, Yasib, sir," he says. "Let me help you on."

"You are going to do no such thing," Yasib says. He orders the camel to kneel, climbs on, and rises.

"Well?" he says. "What's the name of the city we're coming to?"

"Paneas, sir," the captain says. "It is an old shrine and not really a city. It's a sanctuary where worshippers can come and meditate. That's all I know about it."

"Where are we?" Yasib asks.

"We have just entered Palestine."

"Well, I am riding close to you," Michel says. "Just in case…"

"In case what?" Yasib says. "We have better things to do than worry over me. We have a newborn king with a star of his own and an eternal throne who may be a god to worry over."

Two hours later, their road goes down a sharp incline. On the right side is a swamp. On the left side, they see cliffs. As they ride closer, they see a large cave with a stream gushing out of it and headed toward the swamp. On either side of the cave are worshippers.

The worshippers are naked except for goat skins around their waist. They wear leaf wreaths on their head. Some worshippers are dancing before the large cave. Others are strumming lyres and singing.

The worshippers stop and watch the long caravan of now thirty-eight camels snake its way past their holy place. One of them—perhaps a priest—approaches Arshad.

Arshad stops.

"May I help you?" the worshipper asks.

"We are travelers. We have come a long way. Where exactly are we? I do not see a city."

"You are at the Sanctuary to Pan. Who are you? I've never seen people like you before. Are those men over there kings? All your soldiers are guarding them."

"No, they are not kings, but they are on their way to meet one."

"Oh, King Herod?"

"Yes, I believe that is the present king. But we are going to see another one."

"There can be no other king as long as Herod is alive."

"This one is harmless. He is only a baby."

The worshipper grins. "Well, in that case..." and turns away.

The road through the sanctuary turns right and heads south once again. When Arshad is certain they are out of the bounds of the sanctuary, he holds his hand up and stops the caravan.

"This flat place right here is where we should stop for the night. There won't be many in these in the mountains. Besides, it is growing dark early up here among all the trees."

The next morning the caravan starts out again. An hour later, they realize the stream they had been following since Paneas is growing larger.

Michel: The Fourth Wise Man

The rest of the day, they follow the stream as it goes through tight gullies, sometimes falls with a rainbow around it, and winds its way down the mountain with them.

That night they sleep beside what is now a river. It is loud. They are too tired to care.

The next day they follow the river down farther out of the mountains. Just as the sun turns red, they see a large body of water below.

"It's beautiful," Michel says. "What is its name? Do you know, Arshad? No, wait. I think I have heard of it. It is Lake Galilee, isn't it?"

"I believe so," the captain replies.

"And that fishing village down there next to it?"

"Capernaum, sir. Capernaum. We should be able to find an inn there."

"Can you take care of that for us?" Michel asks the captain. "We want to walk along the lake."

He turns to the other magi. "Don't we?"

"Uh, yes," Dushatra says.

"Is Yasib up to it?" Kumar says.

"You don't have to make decisions for me," Yasib says. "I'm not dead. Yes, I'll walk with you a little way. Then I'll watch you young kids pick up sand shells."

The magi dismount from their camels and hand the reins to their servants to take on into the village.

Michel takes a deep breath and holds his arms out. He raises his face to the sky, takes off his turban, and lets his hair blow in the breeze coming off the lake.

"Now there is a happy man," Kumar says, grinning.

"I'm home, my friend. I'm home."

"Your home is in Parthia," Dushatra says.

"You know what I mean," he says, stooping to take off his sandals.

"Now I know what Katazuli felt like when he got among his fellow Hittites. That was the land of his ancestors. This is the land of my ancestors. I'm home. I'm home!"

"What are you going to do now?" Dushatra calls after Michel, who is running along the shoreline. "Go swimming?"

Michel does not answer. They hear him calling to someone in a boat not too far from shore.

"We may as well catch up with him, so he doesn't get us all into trouble with the locals," Kumar says. "You coming, Yasib?"

Michel waves his arms. "Hello out there. Is the fishing good?"

"The young man in the boat waves. "Not right now," he calls back. "They bite at night."

"Then what are you doing out there?" Michel shouts.

"Testing the boat. It had a leak in it. You people aren't from around here," the man shouts in return.

The magi watch as the young man in the boat rows to shore and climbs out.

"Hello there. Welcome to our country, wherever you are from. My name is Zebedee."

"My name is Michel, and these are my friends, Yasib, Dushatra, and Kumar. We are from Parthia."

"You are a long way from home. That is about the longest caravan I have ever seen. I see you brought soldiers with you. You haven't come to attack us, have you?"

"No, we have come as ambassadors of our king to your king. Is this your boat?"

"No, It's my father's. But he said when I am finished growing up, I can have it."

Zebedee looks up at the sky. "I guess I'd better get back out there. My father lives around the lake a little way in Bethsaida. If I'm not there ready to pick up the nets for tonight's fishing, no telling what he will do to me."

The four magi watch as the young Zebedee climbs back into his boat and rows away.

"Nice enough, young man," Yasib says. "Is everyone in your country that friendly?" he asks Michel.

"Of course. We Jews are noted for our friendliness."

"Well, I guess we'd better go on into the village. Arshad probably has an inn lined up for us," Dushatra says. "Besides, I'm hungry."

"We made it," Michel tells his friends as they eat at the

inn. "There were times I didn't think we would. I really didn't think we would."

"I know, Michel," Yasib says. "We all felt that way sometimes. It has been a long journey."

The following morning, the caravan with its thirty-eight camels reforms and works its way around the lake, going west a while, then turning south again.

That night, they arrive at the town of Salem.

"I'll be so glad when this trip is over," Michel says as they eat at the inn. "I know King Phraates needs to be on friendly terms with all the other kings. But I long so much to get back to Eden and do the important things."

People along the road move to the side to watch the strange regal-looking caravan of camels.

"Who are they?"

"Why are they here?"

"Does King Herod know about them?"

They stop at an inn.

"Uh, sir," Dushatra says to the innkeeper serving fresh, spring water for his guests to drink.

The innkeeper walks over to their table. "Yes? What do you need?"

"We were wondering about the celebrations."

"What celebrations? Oh, the harvest feasts down in Jerusalem? Everyone is getting ready for them, and will be heading down there in a couple weeks."

"Well, I don't think that's what we..."

"Oh, excuse me," the innkeeper says. "My wife is calling me. Must be having problems with one of the guests."

The next day, they resume their trek south. They remain on the west side of the Jordan River.

"How long have we been traveling now?" Michel asks.

"It must be late August by now. Perhaps it is September," Dushatra says. "What difference does it make?"

"The child-king must be nearly a year and a half old now," Kumar says.

"I hope he is really there," Michel says. "What if we read the prophecies wrong?"

"Michel!" Yasib says. "I am ashamed of you. These are the writings of the God you believe in. Either you believe it, or you don't."

"You're right. You're right, Yasib. I'm just...Well, my mind is here, and my heart is in Eden. It seems so much more important for me to be doing something so that perhaps my God will walk the earth again. Isn't that more important than going to see a child-king?"

No one answers.

"You yourself said he is going to sit on your David's eternal throne. That sounds pretty important to me," Kumar says.

"You need to get control of yourself," Dushatra says. "You convinced us. Now you'd better re-convince yourself."

"It's just jitters, I guess."

Night comes. They continue in the hills of Palestine. The Jordan River continues its fall and meanderings.

The soldiers spread the large tent out for the magi. The servants spread ornate rugs in front of the tent as well as inside. They place the usual pillows for them to sit on and set food on a low table for their convenience.

Other travelers who have stopped for the night eye the strange men in silk pantaloons, wraparound vests, and turbans.

As they eat, the magi look up into the sky as they always do in the evening.

"I wonder which star is his."

"And where are the celebrations?"

Morning comes. The caravan of strangers continues making its way through the kingdom of Palestine.

People on the highway stop and watch them pass.

"Where did all those camels come from?"

The strangers in the long caravan of giant animals with elegant tassels hanging from their bridles and saddles.

"What are they doing in our country?"

They stare at the soldiers and wonder if they should be afraid.

"Who are those strange men?"

They gawk at the fancy men in the middle wearing strange multi-colored silk turbans, pantaloons, and sleeveless wraparound vests.

On the magi go. Ever south. Ever toward a king they do not understand who had arrived with a strange star that had turned their world upside down.

One step at a time toward an unknown future. A future they have all figured out. But do not.

On the second night, they see ahead of them an imposing walled city. Arshad tells them it is Jericho and that they are very near their destination—Jerusalem.

"You will not have to order a bath at the inn here," he continues. "They have bathhouses. This is a very progressive city."

Arshad arranges the finest inn for them.

"Well, gentlemen," Michel says when they enter their room. "Tomorrow is the day. We shall don our grandest clothes so we may meet King Herod at his palace and pay our king's homage to his newborn son, the next king who will be sitting on David's eternal throne.

Michel is restless all night. He notices the others are too.

He sits up in bed. "Why?"

The other three magi, not being asleep themselves, groan back at him.

"That's a good question," Kumar says.

"Something is wrong," Michel says.

"It is indeed strange," Dushatra says.

"No one has said a word about any celebrations," Yasib says. "Of course, we do not know the customs of these Jews."

"But..."

"Michel, you have never been here before. You know Jewish customs as they exist in the land where your ancestors were exiled six hundred years ago. You have been out of touch with your people the way they really are."

Michel crawls out of bed and walks around the room barefooted, his hair down in his eyes.

He lies back down, and it is morning.

The day they had planned for nearly two years is here. The day Michel had lived and breathed for at last is here.

They dress in their most elegant and call for Captain Arshad.

"We shall enter Jerusalem this morning," Michel says. "Are your soldiers in their finest uniforms? Exactly how far is it from Jericho?"

"It will take us until mid-afternoon, sir. The road up to Jerusalem is steep."

"I see," Michel says.

"Do you know where we can stay while we wait for the king to respond to our message?"

"Yes. I have arranged for the finest inn Jerusalem has, sir."

"Fine."

"I have written a message and sealed it with the seal of King Phraates who gave me his signet ring before we left Ctesiphon," Michel says.

He hands the scroll to the captain.

"As soon as we are settled at the inn, we need you to deliver this to His Majesty, King Herod, requesting an audience with him."

"Yes, sir."

"We will remain ready to see him as soon as you return to us."

"Yes, sir."

"Is everything clear now?"

"Yes, sir. Your camels are ready now."

Captain Arshad salutes Magus Michel and the other three magi. He leaves the outer door open so the magi can follow him out. His soldiers are already mounted on their camels. Their servants are dressed in the colors of Parthia. The supplies of the pack animals have been covered with multi-colored tapestries with gold fringe and tied down with purple cords.

Michel, Yasib, Dushatra, and Kumar mount their camels, and the procession begins.

Everyone sits tall and proud in his saddle. Everyone looks straight ahead—not to the right nor to the left. This is royal business they pursue.

The caravan of strangers from the east moves slowly out of the city of Jericho and toward Jerusalem, the holy city of the eternal throne of David.

People from all over Jericho and nearby vineyards and farms and rock quarries have already gathered along the road. As the caravan passes them, some cheer, some shake their fists, some stand silently in awe.

Slowly they go forward.
Slowly.
The day has come. The day, and soon the hour.
At last.
At long last.
Finally.

33 ~ THE UNEXPECTED

"**W**ho are they?"

"They're not Jews."
"What do they want?"
"Why are they here?"
"Does King Herod know?"

The procession of strange men on tall, proud camels enters Jerusalem.

Camels with long necks adorned with beads and tassels. Legs covered with embroidered work of every color. Ornate tapestries covering the shoulders all the way to the rump. Tassels hanging from tails in the back and from tremendous noses in the front. Crowns of blue ostrich feathers blowing in the breeze.

Camel after camel after camel, the caravan stretching across the city. Traffic of mules and carts and horses and chariot and wagons all stop. Stop in the wake of the strange caravan.

Running now. Men running toward the palace. Does King Herod know? Warn the king? Praise the king?

The officer in charge is in the lead with the official standard of the Parthian Empire.

Ten soldiers dressed in blue uniforms with brass helmets behind him. Next, two blue-uniformed servants with matching turbans. Then the dignitaries in multicolored silk, precious stones on their turbans, around their necks, on their shoes, and adorning their fingers. Then two more uniformed servants. Then the ten supply camels decked out in Parthia's finest tapestries. Finally, ten more uniformed soldiers in their blue and brass. All looking straight ahead and proud.

The parade stretches out block after block of the holy city. People line the street on both sides. People in complete silence. And awe. And fear.

Only the steady clop, clop, clop of feet.

They arrive at the inn. The camels are stabled. The soldiers divide up to guard the camels, the magi, and to accompany their leader to the royal palace.

The magi go to their room and wait. They pace, sit, stand, lie down. They move around their room in silence.

Waiting.

Waiting.

Waiting.

It is nearly dark when the captain returns.

"The guard at the gate into the palace said His Majesty, King Herod, was not available this evening."

Michel sits on his bed and throws his turban off.

"Come now, Michel," Yasib says. "We cannot expect a sovereign, no matter how small his kingdom, to stop everything and allow us an audience."

"But we represent Parthia, with no equal except the Roman Empire."

"We were not expected."

"Tomorrow. We will be able to see him tomorrow."

Michel takes off his finery and lays them on a bench. He sits up in his bed with his hands behind his head.

"Are you thinking of the old king or the new one?" Kumar asks.

"Neither one. I am trying to figure out what to plant in my Eden."

"I shouldn't have asked. Can you never get that obsession out of your head?"

Michel's face turns red.

"God put that obsession in my head. I cannot control God!"

"Calm down," Dushatra says. "We are your friends. Remember?"

Michel stares at his friends, says nothing, scoots down into his bed, and pretends to go to sleep.

Morning comes.

Michel and the other magi dress in their finery and send for the captain.

"I have already been to the palace," he tells them. "I was told His Majesty had prior commitments all day today, and to come back tomorrow."

Michel takes off his shoe and throws it at the wall.

"We cannot go out," Kumar says. "It would not be seemly after our grand entry."

Dushatra goes to their door and tells one of the soldiers guarding it to bring them breakfast.

They spend the day playing dice and looking out the window taking bets on which cloud will float away the fastest.

Night again. Morning again. Once more, they rise and dress in their finery. The knock comes.

"He said he has a family emergency today and must tend to it. He can see you tomorrow."

Michel grits his teeth, grabs hold of the bench where he lays his clothes, and throws it at the wall.

"Out. Get out of here!" he shouts at Captain Arshad.

"Michel! What is wrong with you?" Yasib asks. "This is not like you. You know what kings are like. They enjoy playing games with their subjects. King Phraattes does it all the time."

Michel sits on the side of his bed and puts his face in his hands.

"I don't know what is wrong. Maybe I think he will never consent to see us. Then all we have been through will have been for nothing. And my garden…"

"You know what we should do tonight?" Kumar says with a grin. "We should borrow our servants' street clothes and walk around the city in disguise, just to get out a while."

"That's a brilliant idea," Dushatra says. "Even stodgy

me likes it."

"Come on, Michel," Yasib says. "It will be fun."

Three hours later, the four magi return to their room laughing.

"You should have seen their faces when I began spouting to them in the few Hittite words Katazuli taught me," Yasib says.

"And when Kumar chanted that Hindu song and pretended he was about to levitate, I thought they were going to run out of the room," Dushatra says.

"Ha, ha, ha. Thank you, fellows. I guess I needed that," Michel says.

"We all did."

"Now, let's get some sleep. Old King Herod may run out of excuses tomorrow and consent to see us.

The next day comes and goes. And the next.

"It's been a week. Perhaps we should change our tactics," Yasib says.

"What do you suggest?"

"I have more rings than my fingers can hold. I could send word that we have a special personal gift for him. If he's at all like King Phraattes, he will consent to see us.

The next morning, Captain Arshad knocks on their door.

"He has consented to see you."

"When?"

"This afternoon?"

"Finally."

"It will be in his garden, and only until the sundial has moved five degrees."

"Well, it's better than nothing," Kumar says.

"Once he finds out we have come to honor his son, the newborn king," Dushatra says, "he will invite us to be his guests in the palace."

The time arrives. The soldiers and servants are in place. They will march on foot to the palace.

Once more, the procession, but not so grand. Still, they have obtained what they had come for.

The inn is near the old Hasmonean palace. They take a street leading up a hill, at the top of which is Herod's grand palace.

The captain knocks on the gate into the palace. The guards open it but cross their spears in the way.

"Only the ambassadors themselves may come in. Everyone else must stay out."

Michel, Dushatra, Kumar, and Yasib step forward and are allowed onto the palace grounds. Before them is a large courtyard with round pools at each end. The courtyard is surrounded by columned porticos.

They cross the courtyard and are taken inside a building with red and green polished tiles on the floor and ceiling. The walls are covered with cedar paneling, much of which is decorated with miniature tiles of gold.

They walk through the building and to a second and much smaller courtyard.

"Well, well, well," says the man at the far end of the courtyard. "So these are my guests from Parthia. How is old Phraattes? You know he killed his father to become king. Same thing will probably happen to him."

Immediately the four magi drop to the floor in obeisance and wait.

"You may rise," Herod says.

The old king has a long beard, untrimmed. His eyes are small. What part of his face shows is wrinkled. He is holding a scepter with a hand that is equally wrinkled or more. He is wearing a purple robe and gold tunic with fringe on the bottom. Gold chains hang around his neck. His back is bent. He coughs.

"So, what have you brought me from old King Phraates?"

"Your Majesty, the great Phraattes, king of Parthia, sends his greetings to the greater Herod, king of Palestine," Yasib, as the eldest, begins. "If I may approach Your Majesty, I have his gift to you in this alabaster box."

The king motions to a guard standing nearby, and the guard takes it from Yasib.

The king looks at the ring, puts it on his finger, and holds it out.

"Well, thank you. You can tell your king I wish him health and good luck with his family. You may leave now. Your five marks on the sundial are up."

"But, sire," Michel says. "We saw his star?"

"Whose star?"

"Your son's star. The next king to sit on David's eternal throne. We have come to pay homage to him, your newborn son."

Herod stands.

"You what?"

"Your Majesty, what he means..." Dushatra begins.

"I know what he means. Get out of here. I have no newborn son. No one is going to steal my crown from me. No one. Now get out!"

"Uh, Your Majesty, we saw his star," Michel says. "We know he was born here because he fulfilled prophesies."

"What prophesies? What are you talking about? Leave before I have you put in prison, tortured, and executed."

Shocked, the magi back out of the private courtyard. Did they misread the prophecies? Did they come to the wrong kingdom? Will they live to return to Partha? Eight palace soldiers meet them in the adjoining room and escort them to the outer gate.

When they return to the street, Captain Arshad is waiting there with his men.

The soldiers flank the four magi and escort them back down the hill and to their inn.

They enter their room and close the door, the captain entering with them.

"He had no idea what we were talking about," Michel says. "The whole trip was a waste."

"No, sir," the captain says. "I will return to the palace tomorrow to find out what happened after we left. King Herod will not drop the matter. I will find out if you are in danger."

Another restless night. A night of wondering and

confusion and deep down darkness. A night of sitting and pacing and lying down to sleeplessness.

The next morning they hear a knock on their door.

"Has he sent his soldiers to arrest us as he promised?" Michel asks, staring at the door.

"If we do not answer it, they will break it down," Yasib says.

He answers the door and steps back. The magi stand motionless. They see eight palace soldiers.

"His Royal Majesty Herod requests that you return to the palace with us."

"Please stand out in the corridor while we get appropriately dressed," Dushatra says.

Some time later, Yasib opens the door, and the magi step out into the corridor.

The soldiers escort them back up the hill and to the palace. Once again, they are taken across the grand courtyard with the two round pools, through an elegant room, and out to a small, private garden.

Herod is seated in the same place as before. The magi drop to the pavement and wait for their arrest.

"You may rise, friends," Herod says.

They stand at attention.

"You will have to pardon my outburst yesterday. I have a lot on my mind these days and did not quite understand what you were trying to tell me. Now, did you say this child-king had a star?"

"Yes," Michel says, now emboldened.

"And when did this star of his appear?"

"A year ago last May," Michel says.

"Hmmm. So, he was born a year and a half ago. Well, by the time this child is grown, I'll be long gone out of this present world and its cares. I do want a chance to tutor the boy in the ways of kingship. I need to consult my priests. They understand these things better than I do. Can you wait another few days while I find out from my priests exactly where this child is? I will send someone to get you."

"Yes, Your Majesty."

"Dismissed."

The magi bow and walk backward to the door. They make their way out of the palace surrounded by the same guards as the previous day, and return to their inn.

"Much better this time, wouldn't you say, Michel?" Kumar says as they close to the door to their room.

Michel smiles. "Indeed. Perhaps things are going to come together now, we can pay our respects to both the new and old king, and be on our way."

"Yes, things are much better now," Yasib says.

"See there. You were right all along," Dushatra says.

The impatience of the previous week is not as acute now, but is still there, lingering in the shadows of Michel's confusion.

Three days later, Herod's soldiers are back. It is shortly afternoon.

"His Majesty, Herod, King of all Israel, requests your immediate presence."

"Kindly give us a few moments to dress appropriately," Yasib says, closing the door and leaving the guards to mingle with their own in the corridor.

Shortly, the magi walk out to the palace guards. "We are ready."

They are escorted out of the inn, out onto the street, and up the hill where King Herod has his palace.

Once again, through the gate. Once again, across the grand courtyard with the two round pools. Once again, through the ornate room and out into the private garden.

They see the king, drop to the multicolored marble tiles, and wait.

"You may rise," Herod says.

His eyes. Are they happy eyes or suspicious eyes? Michel wonders. *This man is an enigma. I do not trust him. Well, maybe it's just me. The others seem to trust him.*

"I have solved the enigma of the star king," Herod begins. "Well, I haven't; my priests have. At any rate, they informed me he was born in Bethlehem. They said that was one of the prophecies made about the special king. I believe them."

Michel shifts to his other foot.

"Now, this is what I need you to do for me," he continues. "I want to pay my obeisance to him. But all I know is the town. Bethlehem is a walled city with several thousand people in it. I need you to find exactly where he is and come back and tell me. Now that's fair, isn't it? I find the city for you, and you find the house for me."

"Yes, Your Majesty. That is very fair," Michel says. "Very fair."

The magi bow and back out of the garden. They rush back to their inn.

"Captain Arshad. We have found him. He is in Bethlehem, a city of about five *milles* as the Romans count distance. Get ready. Get everyone ready. We are leaving now."

"Everyone?"

"Yes, everyone. We are going to do this properly," Michel says.

"But it will be dark by the time we arrive."

"This can wait no longer. We go now."

The grand procession from Parthia forms and makes its way past the great white temple on a hill to their right, and arrives at the south gate of Jerusalem just as it is being closed. They leave the city.

A few more hours and their work will be done. A few more hours will seem as nothing.

Michel and the other magi become engulfed in their own thoughts and stare up into an empty evening sky. Wondering. Wondering about the star they had seen so long ago that had managed to turn their lives upside down.

What is it about this child-king? Why the star? Will he really be a god?

Still, they stare ahead along the darkened road between the holy city and the town of Bethlehem that they have never heard of. Staring. Wondering.

Why are we the only ones looking for the newborn king? Don't these people know what's going on? And the present king? Why the mystery?

Slowly.

The long majestic caravan.

Slowly.

"Huh?"

"What was that?"

They hear a snap. And what seems to be music.

They look up into the sky.

"The star! It is back!" Dushatra calls out.

"Just as we saw it that night," Michel says. "He really is going to rule from David's eternal throne!"

"He is going to be king of all kings!" Yasib says.

"The impossible star declaring an impossible king," Kumar says.

They stop their camels and stare with a strange understanding. Their excitement slips into awe.

At last, they continue on their journey. In silence. Deep silence that penetrates the soul.

They watch the star. The enchanted star. What does it really mean?

34 ~ DESTINY

*I*t is midnight when they arrive at Bethlehem. Captain Arshad shouts up to the guards in the tower.

"Open up! We are here from the Orient. We are ambassadors of the kings of Parthia and Indus. We have come to pay tribute to your newborn king."

"What king? We don't have any kings here!"

"The descendant of David," Michel calls up.

"Well, you've got the right city. King David was born here. And someday we'll have a great king born in this very town. But it hasn't happened yet."

"Don't you see the star? That's his star," Dushatra calls up.

"What star?" the guard responds.

"Man, can you not see what's happening tonight?"

"Oh, all that light? It's probably a reflection of campfires up in the hills."

"But don't you see the tail of the light?" Kumar asks.

"Yeah, but even if it is a star, it would be like the end of a rainbow. You don't ever really come to it. Are you astrologers or something?"

"Please! We have letters from the king of Parthia and the king of Indus. May we come in?" Michel shouts back to him.

The guard comes down from his post and walks through the smaller door in the larger gate in and out of Bethlehem. He looks at the letters.

"I don't read very well, but they look good to me. Where'd you find those beautiful camels?" He shifts from one foot to the other, looking at the grand way the men are dressed.

"Very well. You may come in. But you'll have to enter through the smaller door. No one comes in through the large gate at night. And you'll have to leave all your camels out here."

"That is agreeable," Michel replies.

Everyone dismounts. The four servants are left outside the city to watch the camels.

Gradually the four magi, along with their twenty-one guards, work their way through the door and into the town of Bethlehem.

"Now what?" Kumar asks.

"The star," Yasib replies. "Its beam seems to be pinpointing something."

"Stars don't do that, but we all see it," Dushatra says.

"Then let us proceed," Michel announces.

The procession of majestic magi and their guards march as quietly as possible through the darkened streets of Bethlehem.

Michel signals everyone to stop.

They know why. They have found it. The tail of the star. It is shimmering above the rooftop of a small home on a narrow street.

"Captain Arshad," Dushatra says quietly, "Stay out here. If this is the right place, we will send for you."

"Well, this is it, gentlemen," Yasib says softly. "The King of kings. The Priest of priests, the star god. The one predicted centuries ago."

"Gentlemen," Michel says with a rather shaky voice. "Shall we?"

The four slowly approach the gate. How does one greet a king with his own star? A knock. Nothing happens. They are forced to knock louder. One of the guards comes over to help. They wait.

Shortly, the gate creaks and is opened. A young man

with disheveled hair stands in the gateway in his night tunic, holding a small oil lamp.

"Yes?"

Michel comes right to the point. "We have come to honor the newborn king. We have traveled from Parthia and Indus. We saw his star on the night His Majesty was born."

"You saw his star?" Joseph replies. "You know about the star? You know he'll be the king someday? You know it all?"

"Yes, sir. King of all kings is what our Daniel said," Michel states proudly. *My father would be so proud if he saw me now.*

"Well, you don't look like King Herod's spies," the young man says.

He opens the gate wider and steps aside so the dignified magi may enter the small courtyard.

Michel notices Joseph staring at their silk attire, so different from the plain tunic and robe worn by the Jews.

"I will get him and his mother," Joseph whispers. "My name is Joseph. My wife is Mary."

"These are Dushatra, Kumar, and Yasib. I am Michel."

"Please wait out here," Joseph responds.

As acquainted as Michel is to regality, pomp, and the majestic, a lump rises to his throat. His heart beats faster.

They wait. They hear low voices in an adjoining room. Then shuffling. Moments later, a pretty young lady walks out with a toddler in her arms. They are both squinting from the light.

Mary is petite, has black hair with a little point at the top of her forehead, and a heart-shaped face. She stops and looks at the magi with a confused expression.

The four dignitaries immediately fall prostrate and bow their heads to the cobblestone.

They sense Mary is embarrassed, but remain where they are. After a long pause, they hear the cracking voice of the young man. "You may rise."

The visitors stand, and Joseph provides rough cushions for them to sit on.

Michel: The Fourth Wise Man

"Thank you, sire," Kumar says. "But we do not sit in the presence of royalty until they are seated."

The magi glance at each other with the knowing expression of delight in the midst of such plain people and their innocence.

"We saw His Majesty's star," Michel explains.

"His star? Jesus' star? You saw it? No one else seemed to notice. It didn't last long, you know," Joseph answers.

"Yes, we know," Kumar adds. "We instantly knew there was significance somewhere. We searched every way we knew how. We searched the heavens, we searched our archives, we traveled to famous sacred libraries throughout the world, and we finally found the answer."

Dushatra nods toward Jesus. "This little child will someday rule the entire world as the King of Peace? He will have the power of a god?"

"No, there is one God," Joseph explains. "He will have the power of the one and only God, Jehovah."

"Yes, he is a star-god," Yasib says. "Our king believes that, when a star is born, a god has been born."

Joseph smiles. "There is more truth in what you say that I believe you realize."

"We found the answer in your holy books," Yasib says.

"Yes, I showed them the prophecies in the Book of Beginnings, and of Isaiah and Jeremiah. But especially of our prophet, Daniel. I myself am Jewish, a descendant of Daniel."

"Then you understand our baby is also God's baby," Joseph says.

"We do not understand it completely, but yes," Michel says.

"Does he walk yet?" Yasib asks.

"Of course," Mary laughs, glad for the change of pace. "He's been walking for three months now. Would you like to watch him? Jesus, go see Daddy." Mary puts him down on the cobblestones.

The Son of God holds on to his mother's hand a moment to gain his balance, then toddles over to Joseph.

"Good boy, Jesus!"

Joseph sweeps Jesus up into his strong arms.

"Look at that," Michel says. "He is walking among us."

Michel jerks his head back, startled by his own statement.

It occurs to Yasib that this couple has not noticed the star is back.

"Look up," Yasib says. "Look. Your star is back."

"Star, Daddy! Star." Jesus points to the sky with little stubby fingers.

"Where did you learn that word, Jesus?" Mary asks with a broad grin.

His big eyes open even wider. A single tooth is displayed. Jesus repeats, "Star. Song. Star. Song."

"The angels announced it to some shepherds that night," Mary explains. "I think Jesus is referring to their announcement. I think he knows."

Michel stares at the boy. *He walks among us.*

"Do you think he'd walk over to us a moment?" Kumar asks, his voice a little shaky.

Joseph turns toward the magi with new understanding. "Jesus, would you like to go see the nice men who came to see you?"

Jesus smiles and tugs at Joseph's arms to let him down. His feet again touch the ground. Little Jesus toddles over to the great wise men from the Orient.

They grin. They're grinning at the god and he is grinning back at them.

He toddles over and pulls on Dushatra's square and tightly-curled beard. Then he toddles over to Yasib and tickles his wispy gray beard. The men laugh. Jesus laughs.

"He is destined to rule the earth on David's eternal throne, you know," Michel says.

"You understand much, but not enough," Joseph says. "He will not just rule on the eternal throne, but his rule will be eternal. He will never grow old and die. He will live forever."

Michel stares at Joseph, then at Jesus. He wrinkles

his brow. "What are you trying to say?"

"Think about it, Michel. Think about it."

Michel watches the magi reach out and take the hand of the eternal one and place it in their own.

Kumar kisses the eternal one. The eternal one giggles.

Mary, with a nervous smile, steps over and picks up her holy offspring and takes Jesus back to her seat.

"He is our holy child," she whispers.

"Holy?" Michel repeats. "He is holy? How holy?"

"All the way holy," she says, still looking at the boy.

With Jesus back on his mother's lap, the four men regain their composure.

"We have brought gifts as tokens of esteem from our countries," Dushatra announces. "Please give us a moment."

He excuses himself, bows, and walks backward the best he can to the gate and out onto the street. A few moments later, he leads Arshad and five other soldiers into the crowded courtyard.

Mary and Joseph stare at the soldiers in their puffy blue pantaloons and vests wrapped around their waist in matching blue, their brass cone-shaped helmets, and wide curved swords at their side.

The soldiers are carrying ornate chests.

"First," Dushatra explains, "may I introduce Kumar? He comes representing his country, Indus."

Kumar bows in respect before the mother and godchild.

"Please allow me the honor and privilege of presenting the child with this chest of frankincense," Kumar says. "Just as you burn incense in your temple to your god, and we burn incense in our temples to our gods, we offer it now to this child. On the day he declares to the world that he is a god, burn this incense to him and tell him it was from us."

Jesus reaches out and touches the pretty inlaid mother-of-pearl lid. Joseph takes it and sets it on his sturdy work table nearby.

"Next, may I introduce Michel, the Babylonian Jew who kept telling us we needed to read the writings of the

Jews."

"Your Highness. Your honor." Michel stumbles over the words as he addresses the child-king. "Your Majesty. Young sire," he continues. "Please allow me to present you with this chest of the finest myrrh in the world. Save it for his coronation day. The day when he will be anointed priest and king, not only of your small country but of the entire world. Remind him that Indus and Parthia came and honored him. We pray he will give special honor to our two countries as a result."

Jesus plays for a moment with the amethyst knob on the lid of the chest. Joseph takes it, too, and sets it on the table near the other gift.

"Last, there are Yasib and myself, Dushatra. I am from Indio-Parthia, and Yasib is Median, what people today call Xiongnu Mongol."

Old Yasib steps forward. Two soldiers step around him to present another grand chest, though smaller than the others.

"There is enough gold in this chest to make the grandest crown in the world. There will also be enough gold for a scepter. As your own prophets predicted, the scepter will never leave him. He will have a kingdom of peace that will reach the entire world. And he will reign on earth and in heaven forever. For, even though he was born, he will never die. He is a god and cannot die. And he will create a holy kingdom that will never die."

Michel stares at Dushatra. *Does he understand something I do not?*

Joseph motions to the soldiers where to place the small chest on the cobblestones. Little Jesus crawls down from his mother's lap, goes over to the chest, and playfully sits on it. But it is cold, and he jumps up and giggles.

"We must leave now," Michel announces. "We have fulfilled the mission. We have found the celestial secret of the star. Are there any inns in town?"

"Actually, one," Joseph explains. "We were planning to stay in it the night he was born, but it was full and bulging.

I hear it is nice, but probably not as nice as what you are used to."

"It will be fine," Michel says.

Joseph tells them how to find the inn.

Once more, the four magi bow with heads touching the cobblestone. Then they rise halfway and back out of the courtyard one at a time to the narrow gate.

As they leave, Joseph says, "God has come to walk the earth and bless the whole world."

Michel hears, but the voice seems far away. *Who did he say?* Michel asks himself as they make their way down the dark street to the inn.

The star is now gone.

"Uh, Arshad, take your men outside the city gate and wait for us there. In the morning, we will return to King Herod to tell him which house the newborn king is in."

"Are you certain you will be safe without guards?"

"We are certain."

Kumar knocks on the gate of the inn and manages to obtain the attention of the proprietor. They rent their room and get settled for the few hours that are left of the night.

They prepare to bed down.

"Why do you think no one paid attention to the star light but us?" Kumar asks.

"Have they quit learning?" Dushatra adds.

"All along, these people have had their own documents to read and recognize him." Yasib tries to find a comfortable spot in his bed. "It is as though the whole country is blind. As though that's not the king they wanted."

"But he was sent by God," Michel responds with a groggy voice.

The four fall asleep. They all four dream. The same dream...

Laughter. A face appears out of blackness. It is King Herod's face, King Herod's hideous laughter.

Soldiers come. The laughter is replaced with crying. Strange crying. Screams. Pitiful screams of babies. And blood.

Now a divine voice is heard.

DO NOT RETURN TO JERUSALEM.

In their sleep, they stir restlessly.

**LEAVE THIS COUNTRY THE
OPPOSITE WAY FROM WHICH YOU CAME.
STAY AWAY FROM JERUSALEM.**

All four wake up. Simultaneously.

"We must leave immediately!" Michel declares, grabbing his clothes.

Back out in the street. The night barely lingers before a new dawn. A dawn of terror.

The foreigners make their way down narrow streets. They arrive once more at the gate of the city. They do not try to explain. They give four silver coins to the guards and quietly make their way back out through the door within the larger gate.

"Wake up," the magi call to their servants and the soldiers. "Hurry. Saddle the camels. Load them up. Hurry."

"Where to?" Arshad asks.

"South. South through the desert. Hurry."

Back out on the road, they whip their camels into a gallop. Stretching their long legs, eyes wide, mouth open to fill strained lungs with air.

By daylight, the magi are at Hebron. They continue around it, then farther south to Beersheba. They turn east, still racing to evade horror.

Still galloping, they see ahead of them the Dead Sea and the end of the Jordan River.

Still galloping, they work their way to the salty plain at the south end of the sea.

Then beyond to the desert. The barren desert of Arabia.

Camels panting, muscles straining, lungs gasping.

Still galloping.

Still escaping.
What has just happened?

35 ~ MELTDOWN

Once convinced they are out of the kingdom of Palestine, they slow, then stop.

"Where is Michel?" Yasib asks Kumar.

The magi dismount and call up to the captain.

"Do you see Michel?"

"Oh, no! Did they kill him?"

"Men, spread out," Arshad bellows when he sees one of his charges is missing.

"Did Herod's army follow us?" the captain asks the rear guard.

"No, captain. No one followed us."

"You're sure."

"I'm sure."

They hear Dushatra call out. "He's over here. He's okay."

The magi rush to Michel while the servants and guards assemble near the captain.

"Michel, what's wrong?" Kumar asks.

Michel is on the ground, kneeling with his head under his hands, rocking back and forth.

Yasib catches up with them. He kneels.

"Michel. Talk to us."

Still, Michel huddles in his own darkened world, lost in a black hole that no one understands, especially Michel himself.

"No! No! No!" he mumbles.

He stands. He looks up into the morning sky and shouts at the clouds.

"No! It cannot be. I could not have been wrong. No, God, no!"

He walks in circles, stumbling, and peering into a sky he does not see.

Dushatra goes to him and grabs his arm.

"Michel!"

Michel struggles free and stumbles up an incline of barren rocks with a sand dune on the other side.

Still, he runs.

And runs.

The magi try to follow him.

"Stop. Stop running!"

"No. It cannot be!"

"Herod's soldiers did not follow us. We are safe," Kumar calls out. "You do not need to run from them."

Still, Michel runs and stumbles. In a circle in the dry, dry desert. A circle of nothingness going nowhere.

He stops. He crumbles in place. Once again, the rocking and sobbing.

Kumar and Dushatra kneel next to him. They say nothing.

Yasib catches up with them, kneels in front of Michel, and takes him into his arms.

"My boy," he moans. "My poor boy. Shhh."

He brushes the hair out of Michel's eyes and holds him close, one hand around his shoulders, the other hand on his wet cheek.

"Shhh. Shhh."

Michel's sobs lessen. He grows quiet.

"Shhh."

Michel breaks free, stands, and runs again.

"Why?" he cries out to the sky. "Why?"

Stumbling again. Falling again. Now crawling. Crawling like a criminal begging for mercy. Crawling before his executioner.

The other three magi stay where they are.

Captain Arshad stands back with his men, startled but trying not to show it.

Anu leaves the soldiers and walks in Michel's direction.

Yasib shakes his head at him, and Anu stops where he is. He sits on the barren ground like the others. All watching as the man they love and admire, the man who led them to solve the mystery of the star, crumbles.

Once more quiet.

Michel looks up and sees them watching him. All watching and wanting to help, but beyond being able to.

Michel crawls over to Yasib. He looks up into Yasib's eyes. The eyes of the man who had always understood him when everyone else did not.

"I was wrong. Oh, Yasib, how could I have been so wrong?"

Yasib reaches over and touches Michel's hand in the sand. "No. You were right. You were the only one who was right."

Michel jerks his hand away. It lands on a piece of rock, mostly buried, but sticking up far enough, it can cause pain.

His eyes are red, his face streaked with dusty tears that have buried themselves in his short beard. No more proud turban. Lost in the sand like Michel is lost. Hair back down in his eyes. Lips parted and sucking in defeat and humiliation.

"Tell me, son," Yasib whispers. "I want to share your pain."

"No!" Michel shouts, trying to stand again. "You cannot share my pain, my loss, my utter failure. You must not, Yasib. You could not bear it."

Yasib reaches up, takes Michel's hand, and gently pulls him back down.

By now, Kumar and Dushatra have joined them.

"We're here for you," Kumar says.

"We admire you more than you know," Dushatra says.

"No you don't. Not after what I have done."

"Shhh," Yasib says. "You have done nothing wrong."

"Oh, but I have. I have shamed you, I have shamed God, I have even shamed my father."

"That is not true," Dushatra says.

"You do not know what you are talking about," Michel says, back on his hands and knees.

"What is it? Is it the star? The child?" Kumar asks.

"Is it your father? Your wife? Your Eden?" Yasib asks.

Michel stands. His arms stretched wide, he screams again at the sky.

"It is all of it! Don't you understand? All of it."

He crumbles again. "I have failed everyone."

They remain quiet.

"I thought I had it all figured out. I thought God was telling me what to do, and I was being the obedient son, so he would not be ashamed of me."

Silence.

Michel puts his face in his hands. "I thought if I did not do it, it would not get done."

"What wouldn't get done?" Dushatra asks.

"I thought I was the only hope for the world. Me whose ancestors were cowards and wouldn't go back to rebuild Jerusalem when given the chance."

"That was nearly five hundred years ago," Kumar says.

"You are smarter than to blame yourself for that," Dushatra says.

"Smart? Important me shows you the meaning of the star, but I was too dumb to see it."

"No, you had it all figured out and led us to the child."

"Yes, I led you to the child, but I didn't understand. Eternal. I told you his throne would be eternal. But I missed it. It was not his throne. It was him! He is eternal."

"Well, that could mean a very long time," Dushatra says.

"No! No! No!"

Michel stands and walks away from them. After a few steps, he turns back.

"Don't you see? He will never die! Never!"

He looks over at Dushatra. "You said it yourself.

Though he was born, he will never die."

He waits.

"Didn't you hear what Mary called him? Holy."

Michael groans from deep in his throat. A sound they had never heard before. An otherworld sound. He looks up into the sky, shakes his head, and crumbles once again to his knees.

"Only one is holy."

The other three stare at Michel in a way they had not before.

"What does he mean?" Kumar asks Yasib.

Yasib sighs, shakes his head, and walks toward Michel. He kneels and embraces him.

"What just happened?" Dushatra asks Kumar.

Yasib pulls back from Michel and looks at the other two magi.

"He said only one is holy. Think. Who is holy?"

Kumar looks at Dushatra.

"God?"

Michel crawls over to Kumar and Dushatra. He looks up at them. "Yes," he moans. "God."

Yasib stands and walks back to the three.

"Remember what Joseph said just as we left?"

Michel answers for them. "God has come to walk the earth again."

Silence.

For a long time, silence.

The soldiers, still at a distance, watch, not quite sure what they are watching. The servants. And Anu. All watching and not understanding.

Michel stares into his nothingness. "I have sacrificed everything. I have nothing left. No wife. No father. No home. Just a piece of worthless land underwater and a dead dream that should have never lived."

Silence.

Michel stands and whips around, jabbing his finger at his friends.

"Big me! I had to jump up and declare God wanted me

to do something no one else could do—restore the Garden of Eden so he could walk the earth again." He groans.

"Oh, yeah. Big, important me. Me, who was so brave, I could stand up under ridicule and persecution. Me, who was now at God's right hand, doing his work for him."

He takes a step forward and jabs his finger at his chest.

"Big me who thought God couldn't work things out for himself. Big me, who am just a big nothing."

Michel walks away from them, his arms raised.

"Strike me dead, God," he shouts at the sky. "Just do it and get it over with."

He turns and looks at the magi again. "He tried to tell me. He sent the star, and I only thought of it as an interruption. How I hated that star."

"No, Michel, you did not hate the star," Yasib says.

"Oh, I may not have said so. But I did."

"No, Michel," Kumar says. "Yes, you saw it as an interruption to your other work, but you respected the star. You respected it."

"Not until last night. Until then, even when I suspected, I was not sure."

"Oh," Kumar says. "The voice."

"Yes, the voice," Michel says.

"You heard it too?" Dushatra asks. "Both of you?"

"I heard it too," Yasib says.

"I thought someone knocked on our door last night and warned us," Dushatra says.

"No, we all heard it, and it was not at our door."

"You mean..."

"Yes. God himself. It took God speaking directly to me to snuff out the final embers of my stubbornness," Michel says. "The star alone didn't do it. God had to speak to me directly."

"It was more than that," Yasib says. "We were mean to you, Michel."

"Yes, we were," Kumar says, "and I was the worst of all. I teased you incessantly. And I refused to check out the

Jewish holy writings just like everyone else."

"I didn't want you to be right," Dushatra admits. "I didn't want a dreamer like you to be right."

"Yes, your Jewish writings convinced us of what the star meant; it revealed the meaning of the star," Yasib says. "But, to us, it meant a god—any kind of god—had been born. Not the God. I still don't understand it, but I'm trying."

"So, you see, Michel, you were not the only stubborn one among us. It took the voice of God—your God—to convince us that we really had been in the presence of holiness when we met that child. We were all guilty."

Michel sits down with his friends. His voice more normal but still strained.

"Now that my egotistical dream is dead, what do I do?"

"What do you want to do?" Dushatra asks.

"I don't know. I guess get rid of the land I bought."

"You mean the land that is underwater," Kumar says, daring a slight grin.

Michel returns the grin briefly. "Yeah, the land that is under water."

"Well, who did you buy it from?"

"A sea captain. He said he won it in a bet with some military man he hadn't known very long.

"Do you think you could sell the land back to him at a discount?" Dushatra asks.

"What about giving it to the swamp people you hired to drain it?" Yasib asks.

"That sounds like a superb idea," Dushatra says.

Without saying more, Michel stands and stumbles once again toward the rocks with the sand dune on the other side, his head in his hands.

"Well, that didn't last long," Kumar says.

"Fellows, this man has opened our eyes to something we, too, had not faced or admitted," Yasib says.

"That God of his," Kumar says.

"Yes, that God of his."

Michel sees Anu sitting halfway between the soldiers and the magi. Anu understands what Michel is silently telling him, and walks toward him.

They speak a moment, then Anu walks over to Captain Arshad.

"All right, everyone," the captain calls out. "We're stopping here the remainder of the day to let the camels rest. We will resume tomorrow."

Anu returns to Michel.

"Master, what else can I do for you?"

"I need you to look in my supplies and see if you can find some pieces of parchment that have not been written on yet."

Michel rejoins the magi but does not say anything more. He has a calm about him they do not understand. Nor does he.

The soldiers and servants come to the magi and set up camp. The tents are erected, carpets laid out, low tables put in place, food prepared.

"Anu," Michel says, standing outside the circle of the camp. "I need you over here."

Anu understands, picks up the carpet used by his master, and spreads it out in a private place away from the others.

Michel sees Kumar, Dushatra, and Yasib watching what his servant is doing, but does not try to explain.

The rest of the day, Michel talks to Anu, and Anu writes. The others try to keep track how many scrolls they have gone through.

Late in the afternoon, Anu walks back to the tent and gets something out of Michel's section. As he does, he overhears the other magi. He smiles and reports it back to his master.

"You really have them going in circles, Master," he tells Michel when he gets back to him. "Yasib thinks you have dictated three scrolls to me."

"Is that so?" Michel responds, half listening.

"Then, Kumar accused Yasib of having bad eyes because Kumar saw you dictate four scrolls to me."

Anu does not notice Michel is looking away from him.

"Then Dushatra claimed you had dictated seven scrolls of something. Then they started arguing over what you were dictating."

"Uh, huh," Michel replies when Anu pauses.

"Kumar thinks you had a vision like your ancestor Daniel used to have. Dushatra thinks he might be right. Yasib thinks he had a vision once.

"Well, I brought the last of the grapes we bought in Jerusalem. They need to be eaten. They'll be…"

"I don't really want to eat anything, Anu."

"Oh."

Michel looks east toward his broken dream and broken everything else. No father, no wife, no home, no dream. "I don't deserve to live."

"Don't talk like that, Master. You are the best person I know."

Michel looks back at his servant. "I have appreciated your loyalty all these years, Anu. I really have. If you ever see my wife and father, would you tell them I never meant to be a burden to them, and that I always loved them?"

Anu does not reply.

"And I appreciate my friends putting up with my silliness these past two years. Will you tell them that?"

Anu wrinkles his brow. "You are going to tell them yourself, Master." He stands, walks away, then back to Michel. "You are going to tell them yourself."

Michel pulls out his gold-handled dagger and toys with it.

Anu kneels next to Michel. "Oh, Master, what is happening to you?"

"This dagger. Dushatra always admired it. Will you give it to him for me?"

He pulls off his amethyst ring. "Give this ring to Kumar. And my favorite turban with the blue topaz stone on it that is in my luggage? Would you give that to Yasib?"

"Master!"

"Moses. I don't think I ever thought much about Moses. He had a broken dream, you know," Michel says, looking now west toward Egypt. "He gave up everything to try to help his enslaved people, and they turned against him. He ended up away from the country where he was born, away from his people, away from his family."

Michel looks back over at Anu. "He ended up with nothing."

"Master, don't do this."

Michel stands and looks up at the sky. "Well, I guess that's not so bad. He survived."

"Yes, Master. Moses survived, and you will too."

"And my camel. I want you to have my camel. Oh, and these contracts you wrote for me. Take them to Captain Arshad and tell him not to open them until he is back in Parthia."

Anu does not respond.

"I'm tired now. I think I'll go to bed early." Michel walks to the large tent where his pallet is.

The next morning, when everyone rises to resume their journey back to Parthia, Michel has disappeared.

36 ~ MOSES

Moses. Is this how you felt after you lost everything? How did you go on living?

Michel walks south. All he knows for sure is that he is in a desert with some kind of mountains to the west.

Walking, and not knowing where he is walking to. Walking and not caring.

Now in a world that is not a world. Existing. Just existing. Perhaps a living death. A life with no purpose. A life with no meaning. A life void of everything but just existing.

He shifts the pack on his back and double-checks his water supply – one on each side of his belt.

Stay alive. For some reason, stay alive. Defeated, but not down. Destroyed, but not gone. Devastated, but not void.

Keep going. And keep going. And keep going.

But into what? Another nothingness? Another emptiness? Another place of wondering.

Is that a village over there? Among the rolling hills? Among the shallow valleys? Among people who are alive?

Pass the village. Go over the hills. Into the valleys. Down, down, down. Then up a little. Back down.

He sees a low place to his immediate right.

I wonder if the Jews' Jordan River used to flow down here. It looks like a wadi, but I don't guess it is.

It is not important. Nothing is important. Not any more.

Michel: The Fourth Wise Man

Just exist and keep walking. Exist and keep walking. One day. Two days.

Keep walking and treading, stumbling, and getting up again.

Small rocks. Great rocks.

Small valleys. Great hills.

Brown and stark and red.

Three days.

Moses? Moses? Is this how it was with you? Did you ever cry?

What about shouting and stabbing the air, Moses? Did you ever fight what you could not see?

Michel stops, takes a small draw of water, and puts the skin back on his belt.

How long will the water last? And life? And death?

Walking again. Walking up hills that are higher now. Hills that are redder now. Hills that are less inviting.

Keep going anyway. Challenge those hills and cliffs and drop-offs. Dare them. Become invisible so they cannot stop you.

Four days.

The sun a little warmer today. It is November now, isn't it? Warm sun, but not too warm. More rocks, but perhaps not too many more.

Hills and valleys.

Cliffs and drop-offs.

Boulders and pebbles and everything in between.

Little bushes. Sometimes an Acacia tree. Scampering scorpions looking for prey.

Five days. What is that?

So tired. Time to hide. Hide between those rocks. Crawl behind them. Stay unseen. Stay invisible. Stay in a world of half-existence.

Michel walks between two high red cliffs. The path they form is narrow. He turns sideways sometimes to continue on.

When it deadends, it will be time to stop. Stop what? Stop the world? Stop time? Stop existence.

The cliffs do none of that. The cliffs open up for him. Wide. Welcoming. Smiling.

He stands still, beholding a whole new world. A hidden world. An enchanted world.

"Welcome to Petra."

Michel turns and sees a man in a plain brown tunic walk toward him.

"There is a village back here?" Michel asks.

"Well, we are fast becoming what we would call a city. King Aretas has ordered three temples to be carved out of the cliffs you see ahead. Also, of course, a decent main street which he plans to have columned on both sides."

The man looks at Michel and interrupts himself.

"Oh, forgive my manners. You have traveled a long way, haven't you? Coming from the north or south? Hungry? Of course, you are."

The man turns and walks over to the right. Michel follows him.

"Welcome to my tent. No, I do not live here all the time, but I work here a lot, so have my own tent. My servants take good care of it. Have a seat, my friend. By the way, my name is Zabin."

He pushes a large silk cushion toward Michel, then sits on a cushion across from it. He crosses his legs and smiles.

Nothing.

"Well, maybe you want your privacy. I shall call you Gurab. That means stranger in my native tongue. So, Gurab, where are you from? Oh, there I go again. Prying."

A young lady walks up with a tray of fruit on it and sets it on a low table.

"Here, have some fresh grapes. Yes, you would not think anything could grow here, but we have our gardens near the wadis. Even have a few fruit trees. Here, have some figs."

"Thank you, sir," Michel finally says. "I really do thank you. I just have not been around anyone for close to a week, and well, I am having to bring my attention back to my surroundings."

"There for a while, I did not know if your tongue had been diseased or something, but I am glad it was not," Zabin says. "Regardless, you do not have to talk. I can tell you are tired. I think, by your strange clothes, you came from far away. Perhaps Parthia?"

"Yes, I believe I am tired," Michel replies. "By the way, sir—Zabin—you said I am in Petra. If I keep going south, will I be at Mount Sinai?"

"Oh, you're searching for Moses. Everyone knows about Moses."

"You too?"

"Of course. You're on the northern edge of what they used to call Midian. That's where Moses was a shepherd for forty years. But that's not what you want, is it?"

"No. Not really. I want to find Mount Sinai. Or did it ever exist?"

"Oh, it exists, all right. It is west and south of here, but I wouldn't go west quite yet. You're on the edge of King Herod's kingdom, and you do not want to tangle with him. He is a snake."

"Yes," Michel says, remembering just a week earlier when he was beholding God walking on earth—albeit small steps—then protecting him.

"Yes," Michel says again. "I do not need any snakes in my life."

"Well, you just keep going south. Look for the seagulls and follow them. Now and then, one gets lost and wanders up here. But, anyway, you will arrive at the shores of a gulf."

Michel watches the stranger.

"That's where it will be safe for you to start going west. Just follow the mouth of that gulf west. Then follow it south. It will take you to Moses' Mount Sinai.

For the first time in a week, Michel feels hope. That elusive hope that had been crushed to death by the feet of a terrible fate. Crushed and killed and buried.

Michel smiles. It is faint, but a smile.

"God has sent you to me. You have become my savior,

my guardian, my leader."

Zabin clears his throat. "Well, not quite all that. I am just being hospitable to a stranger. Now, it will be dark soon. It gets dark earlier here among all these cliffs. I must make the rounds of my men to find out what progress they have made today and give them directions for tomorrow."

"Yes, sir," Michel says.

"I want you to spend the night here. So take whatever food you did not eat and put that in the basket you had on your back. And refill your water skins. And over here is a pallet you may sleep on. Feel free to roll it up and take that with you too. It is needing replaced anyway."

When Zabin returns to his tent at dusk, Michel is asleep. At dawn the next morning, Michel is gone.

Now back out in the open, Michel makes his way south in the first rays of the sun. It is a cool morning. Michel pulls his full robe with the billowy sleeves tighter around him.

Walking again. Walking to what? Walking from what? Walking. Existing.

Desert again. But a smoother desert. Mountains still on the right. The rest sand dunes.

Walking and plodding and trudging to somewhere, anywhere, nowhere.

Warmer now. No clouds. Heat.

Keep going. Keep going to Moses. Moses? Where are you, Moses?

Mushrooms. Mushrooms in the desert. Giant mushrooms. Food. No. Poison. No. Just mushrooms.

Rock mushrooms. Mushrooms to shade a person, a multitude. Mushrooms to shade a village.

Protection. Protection from the heat. The cold. The sun. Clouds.

Another day of walking. Two. Three.

Where did the clouds come from? Rain. No rain. Desert. Hot desert.

Nothing. Just sand and more sand. Mountains in the distance. Mountains and rocks and barriers.

Stepping and stepping and stepping.

Four days.

Sea Gulls. White seagulls. Squawking. Arguing. Belittling.

Looking for food. For themselves. For their young. For the others.

Heat. Steam. Humidity in the air.

Billowy pantaloons now clinging to the calves, the thighs, the hips. Silk pantaloons fit for a king.

King of Parthia. King of the Jews. King of the World.

Six days. Eight.

Water.

Michel hears water and shouting and gonging of bells. Ships. There must be ships. He does not see ships.

He sees a city gate.

No. No city. No buildings and bridges and streets. No people and wagons and camels.

Camels. Where's your camel, Michel? Did you forget your camel? Gone.

Michel remembers Zabin's instructions. He turns right at the city wall and walks until he can see the water. The gulf. The way to Moses.

On he walks, the gulf now on his left.

Safe. Safe now in Egypt. And the gulf. And Moses.

Hills. Higher and higher the hills.

Michel walks to the west a little and finds the desert again. Now south again. South at the top of the hills where the gulf flows far below.

Where is below? What is below? What does below mean?

Walk. And keep walking. And Walking.

Another day. Another week. Two weeks of walking.

Death above. Vultures hovering and circling and wanting their due.

Looking for the dead. Looking for what once was. Looking for that which was alive and now is no more.

A wadi. Stroll across the sand of a wadi. A river that surges and swirls and destroys whatever is in its path. A river that lives a while, then dies.

Life and death. Death and life. And all that is between. Another day.

Moses. I'm coming, Moses. Wait for me.

Climb now. Climb into the mountains.

Now down. A valley. A valley that promises everything, but hides it all.

Up again. Up into the mountains. Higher and higher.

Another day. Another night.

Cold. It's getting cold. So cold. So very cold.

Pull the billowy coat around. Tuck it under the arms against the wind.

Cold and wind and something white.

Floating. Something floating and playing and dancing.

Moses. I'm coming, Moses. Are you still here? Did it help? Did the mountain help? Did the mountain show you the way to live again?

Another step. Another. Each one higher and harder.

Stretch the legs. Stretch and reach and grasp.

Use the hands now to help. Higher now. And higher.

Reach for the mountain, Michel. Reach for the mountain. And Moses. And God.

God, are you up here? Help me find Moses. And you.

The wind. So cold. Grasping and clawing and paralyzing.

Stop the wind. Stop the cold. Stop the snow.

Four days. Five.

Wading. Wading through the white. Where did the white come from? Is the white pure? Does the white sin? Will the white ever go away?

Leaning. Leaning into the wind. Into Moses. Into God.

Lift your eyes, Michel. Lift your eyes. Look for it.

Eden. Is that you, Eden? Adam? Eve? Where are you? Where are the flowers and gentle streams and sweet, sweet fruit?

Adam, don't go away. Eve? Not you too. The garden. Floating away into nothingness.

Moses? God?

Where is everyone?

Michel: The Fourth Wise Man

I need you. I don't want to die. I don't want to die.

Come back, Meira, my beloved. Come back, Father, my hero. Come back, Eden, my broken, broken dream. All gone. All deserted.

So alone. All alone.

No one left.

No Adam.

No Eve.

No Meira.

No Father.

No Moses.

No...

God? Is that you, God? Have you come back for me? Moses? God? Help me.

"Shhh, Master. I'm here now."

"Moses?"

"No, Master. It is I, Anu. I'm here. Shhh."

Warm. Warm again.

Michel opens his eyes. He is on the ground, cradled in the arms of his servant.

He tries to speak. But his lips. They hurt so much. And his tongue. So swelled and dry. "Wha..."

"Shhh, Master. You are going to be okay now."

Michel holds up his hand to Anu's face.

"Mo...?"

"No, I am not Moses, Master. But I am sure he is looking down on you right now."

Anu reaches into a pouch and brings out a piece of cheese. He puts it in his warm mouth a moment, then puts it in Michel's.

He scoops some snow into his hand and trickles a few drops into Michel's mouth.

"Master, I have come for you to bring you home."

"Home?" Michel whispers, blinking against the snowflakes still coming down gentle like feathers.

"Heaven?"

"Well, not yet, Master," Anu says with a hint of laughter. That will come later. Can you sit up a little more now?"

Anu supports his master and helps him sit. Michel realizes patches of snow are falling off his clothes. "How long?"

"Oh, not too long. I have been following you ever since I caught up with you in Petra."

"Petra?"

"When you disappeared, the whole caravan wanted to turn around and look for you. I told them they were still in danger. Besides, I had a pretty good idea where you would be headed."

Anu puts another small bite of cheese in his warm mouth, softens it, and puts it in Michel's.

"Yes, I knew you talked of ending your life, but I kept praying to your God to keep you alive. Isn't that cheese good? I'd give you a grape, but it is ice. You don't need any more ice right now."

Michel hears honking and neighing and whistling.

Anu laughs. "No, I did not take your camel. Well, I did take it. But only behind the one I have been riding. They want to get out of this cold. They tolerate cold weather but prefer hot. Let's get you on your camel so we can get out of here."

Michel looks around.

"Oh, Moses?" Anu asks. "He has been here and gone. I suppose your God is here like he was before, but he is planning to go with us. Now, try to stand. That's right. That's right. You can do it."

Michel takes a step forward and stumbles. Anu catches him. "Koosh," he calls out to Michel's camel. "Koosh, koosh."

By the time they arrive, the animal is seated and waiting. Anu helps Michel swing his leg around, then ties a rope around Michel's waist and to the camel's saddle.

"Hang on now, Master. As soon as I get on my camel, they will both stand and get us out of here. Hang on, Master. I have the reins."

Now down the mountain. Down Mount Sinai. And

Michel: The Fourth Wise Man

Moses. And the dream. But not God.

Down. Down. Down.

The snow eases. Not many feathers anymore. Just a few floating lazily down here and there. It stops.

The sure-footed Mongol Bactrian camels with their big, hairy feet wend their way down the mountain.

God, are you still here?

37 ~ RECOVERY

Step by step, the camels take their passengers back to the living. Step by step down the mountain. South and East.

A beach. A sandy beach. Just beyond the rocks. And water.

Down off the rocks. Down onto the sand. Toward the waves. The salty waves.

Ships. Ships coming and going, to the north and from the north. East. West. Bells and seagulls and heavy footsteps on planks.

"Sir," Michel hears Anu say off in a distance in a land he does not quite remember.

"This is my master. He is one of King Phraattes' magus. He has been on a pilgrimage and needs to go home now. How much is passage across the Indus Sea under Arabia and up the Parthian gulf?"

"I'm sorry. I am not going that way. Are you sure that's where you want to go?"

"I am sure."

"Well, then, try that ship over there."

Anu leads Michel toward the other ship.

"Sir, this is my master. He is one of King Phraattes' magus. He has been on a pilgrimage and needs to go home now. How much is passage across the Indus Sea under Arabia and up the Indus gulf?"

"Not many ships headed for Parthia these days. I'm

certainly not going there. Are you sure that's where you want to go?"

"Yes, I'm sure," Anu replies. "Any suggestions?"

"Well, if you insist, try that ship over there."

Anu and his master work their way along the docks.

"Sir. This is my master. He is one of King Phraattes' magus. He has been on a pilgrimage and needs to go home now. How much is passage up through the Parthian gulf?"

"You have certainly picked a bad time to go by ship. The weather is too unpredictable this time of year," the ship captain says.

"Sir, I am becoming desperate. As you can see, my master is not feeling well. He nearly froze to death on Mount Sinai, and…"

"What was he doing up there this time of year?"

"Well, it was something he had to do. But it's done now, and he needs to go home."

"I don't know. No one is allowed to die on my ship."

Anu stares hard at the captain but does not reply.

The captain stares back.

"Sir, I believe I have enough for passage. I sold a camel and many fine clothes and, well, I have five pieces of silver. Will you accept that as passage?" Anu asks.

"Number one, that will not get you as far as Parthia. However, that does not matter because I am not going there anyway. Number two, it is not enough to get you even to Indus."

"Sir."

"Huh?"

Both Anu and the captain look over at Michel, who is still on his camel.

"I can write out any documents you would like to have prepared for you," he says with a weak, gravelly voice. "If your ship's log is any behind, I will help you update it. If you…"

The captain holds his hand up for Michel to stop talking.

"You don't look strong enough to write anything. Well,

okay. But what about these camels?"

"We were hoping the silver I offered you would include the camels."

"What about meat? We could use some fresh meat on the voyage."

"Uh, sir. We would have nothing to ride on to get us through Indus. But one of them had a calf several months ago. Would fresh milk satisfy your table?"

The captain stares at Anu, then Michel, then each camel.

Anu pulls his coat with the billowy sleeves closer around himself, still trying to warm up.

"Oh, all right. Five pieces of silver, plus free scribe services, plus fresh milk, plus your other camel."

"What? No. We need both of our camels."

"Then stay here. I don't want to sail up there anyway."

"Uh, Anu. It's okay," Michel says with a loud whisper.

The captain looks at Anu, grins, and shrugs his shoulders.

"Okay. Okay. Here are your five silver coins."

The captain calls up to the deck for a crewman to put down extra gang planks next to the single one already there.

"Your master needs to get off his camel. They handle easier without passengers."

"Koosh, koosh," Anu says.

The animal kneels, Michel climbs off, teetering a little when he does, and his ride stands again.

A crewman lays down four more planks, and Anu walks the camels up. He sees stalls along one side of the ship and leads them in that direction.

"I hope you have your own food for them. I don't feed animals, and I don't feed people on my ship."

"Them? You want us to feed the camel you bought too?"

"The captain smiles and shrugs. "What can I say?"

"Well, when are you setting sail?"

"In two days."

"Two days?"

Michel: The Fourth Wise Man

"Yes. And it's going to take us two weeks to get you to Karachi or where ever I deposit you. Now go on. I'll see you in two days."

"Uh, sir. Could we sleep on board the ship until then?"

"First, I have a name: Captain Zeno. Second, my ship has a name: The *Kymaata*. Third, the answer is no."

Anu leaves the ship and takes Michel's arm. "There is a tavern over there, Master. You need to sit down."

They turn in the direction of the tavern.

"Do you have any money left, Anu?"

"No, Master. I gave him all I had."

"That's okay. I have some. Just get me to that inn and give me a chance to finish warming up."

"They tell me this is an unusual wind for this time of year. It usually doesn't get very cold until January. Perhaps tomorrow will be back to normal."

They settle in the tavern and order cardamom tea.

"I'll be okay tomorrow," Michel says.

"Well, you're much more alert than you were when I found you this morning."

"How did you find me?"

"As I said, I have been following you since Petra. I knew you had to work things out for yourself, so stayed back as long as I could. But, when that snowstorm hit up on Sinai Mountain, I knew it was time to step in."

"Anu, I want to set you free."

"Master, where would I go? What would I do? Let us discuss that at another time."

"Hey, you! Boy!"

The tavern keeper shouts at a ragged boy running through the inn and back outside.

Anu jumps up and runs after the boy. He catches him outside. Michel stands and follows them out.

Hanging on to the boy's torn tunic, Anu forces him to stop running.

"Let me go! Let me go!"

"What's in your hands?" Anu demands. He grabs the boy's hands from behind his back and sees two large pieces of flatbread. The boy has tears in his eyes.

Anu looks over at Michel. Michel has already pulled out a coin from his pouch.

Anu tugs at the boy to follow him to Michel.

"You stand here while I go back in and pay the man."

The boy shakes his head, tears still in his eyes.

"You either stay here, or I take you back in to face the tavern keeper. Now, promise me you will stay here. Promise."

The boy says nothing.

"I may have a warm place for you to stay tonight," Anu adds.

"Okay. I promise," the boy says.

Anu disappears inside the tavern and is back moments later. He looks at Michel.

"Now what?"

"You lied to me," the boy says. "You don't have a warm place for me tonight. I'll bet you don't even have a warm place for yourselves. I'll bet you are thieves like me."

"Well, it's for certain we cannot take him on board the ship with us tonight," Anu says to Michel. "And we need to get you to bed before you collapse."

"Well, if you're nice to me, I know a place," the boy says. "It's where my mother and me used to live."

"What do you mean?" Anu asks, now kneeling in front of the boy.

Tears return to his eyes.

"Oh. Your mother has died."

The boy nods his head. "They're coming tomorrow to take it away from me so someone else can stay there."

"Well, if it isn't very far away, we would be grateful to stay tonight where you and your mother did, and figure out something else tomorrow."

The boy wipes his eyes and forms a small smile.

"Will you take this man's other hand so we can get him there? I hope it isn't too far."

"Oh, it isn't far. See that shack over there at the end of the dock? That's my home."

The men walk to the end of the dock, the boy holding

Michel: The Fourth Wise Man

one of Michel's hands and Anu holding the other.

When they go in, they see a single pallet on the floor and some baskets in one corner.

Michel gives his backpack to Anu. "Use what you need." He lies down on what apparently had been the boy's mother's pallet and falls immediately to sleep.

Morning comes. Michel sits up and sees Anu on the old pallet his host had given him in Petra, and the boy asleep at his feet.

He lies back down and sleeps some more.

"Hey, you bums. Get out of here. Boy? What are you doing? This is no longer your shack. Get out of here and take your bum friends with you."

A big man with a wild black beard and heavy brown robe stands in the doorway.

Michel, Anu, and the boy stand, gather up their pallets and backpacks, and leave. Once out in the street and back on the docks, they look for a place to sit.

"Over here," the boy says. He leads them to the edge of the dock where he sits and dangles his feet over the water below. "Come on. I do it all the time."

Anu and Michel look at each other, smile, and sit with the boy, dangling their feet also.

"I'm okay now, Anu," Michel says.

"Were you sick?" the boy asks.

"I was caught in a snow storm. See those mountains up there?"

"Woah, you were up there?"

"Yes, and I have Anu to thank for getting me safely back down here."

Anu smiles. *Welcome back, Master.*

The boy looks at Michel a moment. "Mister, are you rich?"

"Well, I used to be. I don't guess I am any more."

"You look rich."

"My name is Michel. This is Anu. What is your name?"

"I am Sanjar."

"That is a very nice name, Sanjar," Michel says. "And

how old are you?"

"I do not know."

"Well, you look eight or nine years old to me," Michel says.

"Master," Anu interrupts, "we need to buy enough food for us for three weeks on board the ship, and for the camels for three weeks."

"You're going on a ship?" Sanjar asks, his eyes wide.

"Indeed, we are."

"I could tell you aren't from around here. You dress funny."

"Us? Funny? What's so funny about our clothes?"

"You've got those billowy whatever you call it that you wear around your legs. How do you move in them?"

"Oh, we move very well in them."

"And that thing on your head."

"Oh, our turbans? At least they stay on in a wind. When you Arabs are in a wind, your hoods keep falling off."

"Master, we must take care of our business. What if the captain decides to leave today instead of tomorrow?"

"You are right, Anu."

"If you have camels, I know where you can find lots of barley for them to eat, and it's squooshed together real tight so you can carry it."

"Ha, ha! You are our good luck," Michel says. "Lead on."

Sanjar stands and takes both Michel's and Anu's hands and walks between them up past his mother's shack at the end of the dock, and up a hill where there is a bazaar. He leads them down two different streets and stops at a corral.

"Sir, my friends want to buy food for their camel."

"Two camels."

"For how many days?"

"Two weeks, at least."

"Then you will need thirty-five bundles. That's one bronze coin per bundle, so thirty-five bronze coins."

Michel looks in his pouch and hands the merchant the

money.

"Now, how are we going to get it to the ship?" Anu asks.

"I will stay here and guard your bundles while you make as many trips to your ship as you need. Would that be helpful, Master?" Sanjar says.

"Well, I am not your master, but that would be satisfactory. And I will pay you for your services."

"Master, are you sure you are up to it?" Anu whispers.

"There is something about that boy," Michel whispers back. "He has brought life back into me. I do not understand it."

"Yes, Master, you do have a gleam in your eye I have never seen before," Anu says aloud.

Carrying five bundles at a time, the men have all the food for the camels on board the ship in three trips.

"Now where to, Master?" Sanjar says, taking Michel's hand.

"Stop calling me that. I am not your master."

"Yes, Master."

Michel sighs, rolls his eyes heavenward, and lets Sanjar take his hand.

"Well, if you insist on following us around, I guess we need to feed you."

"And you too," Sanjar says. "Come with me. I know where the best baklava is."

"Not for breakfast, young man," Michel says. "Fruit and cheese. That's what you need."

They buy their food and take it back to the dock to sit and swing their legs over the water while they eat.

"Well, we have had an enjoyable day with you, Sanjar," Michel says. "But now we need to go onboard our ship. We do not want it to leave without us. We had hard enough time buying passage from that captain. He was very hard to please. So, goodbye."

Sanjar lets go of Michel's hand and backs away. Tears form in his eyes. "You lied to me. You lied!"

With that, he turns and runs up the docks and does

not look back.

Michel looks at Anu. "What just happened?"

"Master, that boy loves you."

"No, he doesn't. He doesn't even know me."

"You have become a father to him."

"What are you talking about? He has only known me a few hours."

"It does not take long, Master. When you are a boy, everything is in slow motion. To a child, a moment is like an hour, and an hour like a day."

"Well, I cannot help it. I got along without a father growing up, and I grew up fine. He can too. Let's go."

"Master, think about what you just said. Think about it."

Michel has already turned toward the ship.

"Uh, Master, you're forgetting something important."

"What now?" Michel replies over his shoulder.

"We have not bought food for us to eat on the ship."

Michel stops. "Oh, that. You are right."

The two men go to the bazaar, buy two baskets each, then work their way around the booths, filling their baskets with three kinds of cheese, dried figs, dried, dates, dried grapes, fresh green apples, fresh green pears, flour to make their own bread, and three skins of yogurt.

"Why three?" Michel asks Anu.

"I like yogurt. You owe it to me for saving your life up on Sinai."

"Are you going to hold that over me for the rest of our lives?"

"I plan to."

"Okay, do we have everything we're going to need?"

"No, Master. We need something to do for two or three weeks."

"Like what?"

"Like parchments and blackener. Captain Zeno may not have enough on hand. Plus, you may want some extras to write down whatever you like to write. I have never seen you miss an opportunity to observe the stars, and they say the stars at sea are especially..."

Michel loses his smile.

"Oh, Master. I am sorry. Your special star. Well, why don't I pick up a few things for us to do on the ship and I will join you there."

Michel walks back to the ship. As he does, he notices a shack at the end of the docks. He walks close to it. He thinks he hears a boy inside. Crying.

Michel keeps walking.

38 ~ THE SEA

"Weigh anchor! Hoist sails! Cast off!"

The *Kymata* slips slowly away from the dock at the narrow strait separating the Arabian Peninsula from the Red Sea.

Michel and Anu stand at the rail near the ship's stall for their one remaining camel.

"Did you find what you were looking for on Mount Sinai, Master?"

They look to their west at the mountain, still with snow on its top.

"I'm not sure. Maybe," Michel responds.

"Were you looking for Moses or those Ten Commandments?"

"I don't know. I was looking for a man who had lost everything for his dream, even to being exiled from his country. I needed to know how he survived."

"And how did he survive, Master?"

"I guess he had to see for himself that what God says is written in stone and will happen God's way."

"Anything else, Master?"

Michel looks over at his loyal servant. "I don't know, Anu. I just don't know. I still feel lost."

"You didn't seem lost yesterday, Master."

Michel says nothing for a few moments. "I guess so. But that was yesterday." He walks away.

"Michel, I need you," Captain Zeno says the next day.

"I need to catch up on my ship's log. Then I need to write a letter to my wife. Oh, and I need you to translate a document a Parthian gave me."

For the following two days, Michel stays busy with the captain, while Anu sits with their one remaining camel and talks to it.

"Let go of me!" Michel hears through the captain's cabin door.

He and the captain jump up and rush out to the bridge.

"Let go of me!"

He looks down and sees Sanjar struggling with a crewman.

"What's going on down there?" Captain Zeno bellows.

"Cap'n, we have a stowaway."

"Throw him overboard."

"No! Don't kill me. I promise to be good."

"Uh, captain, sir," Anu says. "Didn't you say you were short of help in the mess? Perhaps the boy could earn his fare."

"No! Throw him overboard," the captain says, turning back toward his cabin.

"I make good baklava," Sanjar shouts up to the captain.

"You do?" the captain says, turning back around. "Well, I suppose we can keep him. But he cannot eat any of our food."

"Uh, sir," Anu says. "We have enough food for the boy, also."

Michel glares down at Anu.

"He's small, Master. He doesn't need much," Anu replies.

Michel points at Anu. "Then he's yours. You are responsible for him."

"Yes, Master."

It has now been a week. The captain orders the rudder on the *Kymata* to head the ship northeast through the Indus Sea toward Indus itself.

So far, the wind has remained in their favor.

"I don't like those dark clouds up there," Captain Zeno tells his first mate at the helm.

"Sir, I thought it never rained down here," Anu calls up from his spot by the camels. "Isn't Arabia all desert?"

"The rains come in January," the captain responds, "then that's it for the year. It's not January yet."

Afternoon arrives.

"Do you ever think about the boy?" Michel asks, sitting next to his servant.

"What boy? Oh, you mean Sanjar?"

"No, not him. The boy. The boy."

"Huh?"

"The eternal boy. The boy who will never die. The boy God materialized into so he could walk the earth again."

"Yes, I suppose so. But it's hard to understand."

"When he takes over, according to my ancestor Daniel's prophecy, he will be thirty years old. That will make me over sixty-five. I wonder if I'll still be alive then."

"Perhaps you can visit him in Bethlehem sometimes through the years."

"I don't think they're in Bethlehem. I think they are in hiding somewhere."

"Oh, the dream you said you and the others had."

"Yes, the vision. God warned us that people were planning to kill him that night. I wanted to take our twenty-one soldiers over there and protect them."

"But you said God ordered you to go home. How long do you think he will stay in hiding?"

"Until he is grown, maybe. I don't know. All I do know is that I had to step aside. Once again. I didn't like it. Why won't Jehovah God let me help him?"

"I don't know, Master."

"All I wanted to do was help the boy."

"Master, I made extra baklava in the mess. Here is a piece I made, especially for you for saving me."

"You mean, you made it for Anu for saving you."

"You are his master. You allowed him to save me. He

does your will."

Michel tries not to pay attention to Anu, putting a hand up to his mouth to hide a large grin. He reaches out and takes the baklava.

"And quit calling me master," Michel says.

For twelve days, the ship *Kymata* sails under Arabia, heading east toward Indus. The winds have been steady.

Michel has spent half of every day with the captain. Both are grateful.

As Michel works, the captain makes sure there is plenty of oil in the lamp when the sun does not come directly into his cabin. He orders the best food for meals. He presents Michel with a basket of silk in deep red.

"If there is anything you need," the captain says at least twice a day, "just let me know or let my first officer know."

Michel is grateful for the work for a different reason. A far different reason.

I don't know what I would have done without all this to take my mind off...

Evenings are the hardest for Michel. *My mind is scrambled and jumbled as though I have thrown a hundred grains of rice up into the air, and what landed is all my thoughts going in different directions.*

"We should be in Karachi in a couple more days," Captain Zeno tells Michel on the twelfth night.

"I'd like to hire you permanently to stay on the ship with me. I will have to get approval of the shipowner, but I know he will go along with it."

Michel does not reply.

"I need you to help me keep the ship's log up to date, make entries of what cargo and passengers we take on board, how much we earn from them both. I need you to decide what supplies and equipment and foodstuffs we need before each voyage."

Michel still does not reply. Instead, he continues to look out the port side of the ship at the stark Arabian coast.

"You would have good pay."

Still, Michael says nothing.

The captain and the magi stand side by side in quietness for a while.

"Well," the captain finally says, "you haven't said no yet. Does that mean yes?"

Michel looks at the captain, stares a moment, then looks toward Arabia again.

More silence.

"I cannot do it all myself," Zeno resumes. "I have tried. But business has picked up so fast, I cannot do it all anymore. You know why I gave you such a hard time about your passage back there? I'm behind on my ciphering and am not really sure anymore if I am going to have enough to pay my crew. I think I have enough but am never sure. And that's no way to run a business. I have evaded the ship owner's questions and gotten by with it for longer than I thought I would."

Michel says nothing. He walks away and slips into the tent Anu had set up for them on the upper deck.

"Anu," Michel says, "remember I told you I would like to set you free?"

"No, Master. I would have nowhere to go."

"I am going to hire on with Captain Zeno and work for him permanently."

Anu sits up, crawls out of the tent, and stands by the starboard rail. Michel follows him.

All is quiet. The moon is out. The ship is slipping silently across the surface of the Indus Sea, followed by a small wake shimmering in the moonlight.

"Master, you cannot desert everything and everyone so you can run away."

"I wouldn't be running from anything or anyone. I have no wife anymore. No father anymore. No home any more."

"But, Master."

All I own is a worthless piece of land that is underwater. I am the laughing stock of Parthia. I do not know what the king will do when he finds out what I have done. He may dismiss me as insane."

"He wouldn't do that, Master. Besides, what about the boy?"

"Which boy?"

"You know what I mean? Sanjar. He has no mother now."

"I grew up no father. I survived."

"But, Master. What about the king? No one leaves the service of the king without his permission, and he never gives it."

"Are you jesting with me?" Michel says. "I am an embarrassment to him. He will want no part of me. My mind is made up. When the ship docks in Karachi, I am going ashore to pick up what I need to live aboard the ship, and return to Egypt, then on to Greece or where ever the ship goes. You cannot talk me out of it. The subject is closed."

Michel crawls back into the tent and goes to sleep.

Morning comes. Michel hears the first bells of the day and rises. He reports to the captain and does translating for him the rest of the morning.

The cook brings them something for a mid-day refreshment. They pause to take a bite of fresh bread with raisin sauce.

"Michel, I would give you good pay. And the ship's owner will provide you with a house of your own. He lives in Athens. Wouldn't you like to live in Athens?"

"Yes."

"Huh?" the captain says, jerking his head back. "You would?"

"Yes, I will go to work for you."

Captain Zeno's eyes brighten. "You would?"

He slaps Michel on the back. "Fine. Fine. Fine. Now, the first thing we're going to have to do is get you out of those strange clothes and into a decent tunic. Also, you need to shave that beard off. That will make you look dignified. I have friends at each major port and will introduce you to all of them. They have the most marvelous feasts and amazing entertainment. Oh, you will love life aboard my ship."

"Yes, sir. I'm sure I will," Michel says.

The following day, Michel rise and goes to the captain's cabin as usual. He sits at a bench, opens up a jar of blackener, checks where he had left off making entries in the ship's cargo manifest, and dips his pen to make the next entry.

A loud bang. The ship lists to the left, and Michel slides off his bench along with his work. Then the shouting.

He rushes out to see what is happening.

The *Kymata* has been rammed by another ship with no standard on it. The enemy ship does not back up. It continues to push the *Kymata* in the direction of the Arabian coast.

Michel immediately runs below deck to the mess. He grabs Sanjar, putting one hand over his mouth and the other around his wrist. He crouches with Sanjar against the back hull. And listens.

Aboveboard, he hears the pounding of footsteps, rushing in every direction. He hears shouts. He must decide what to do.

If I stay onboard the ship, it may sink. If it doesn't everyone on board will kidnapped by the pirates.

"Now, Sanjar. Now!"

He stands and pushes his way through the crewmen who have rushed down to escape and hide. He rushes up the ladder and briefly looks around. He catches the eye of Anu amid the chaos. Once on the upper deck, he grabs Sanjar around the waist, runs to the edge of the ship and jumps overboard.

Down into the water. Down and down and down.

Fight. Fight to return. Fight to breathe again.

He sees daylight. He sucks in air, looks around, and swims.

He realizes Sanjar is not with him. He looks around in the water, but he is not there. He dives under the water but can see nothing but seaweed and sand and loosened planks, and bubbles from the pirate ship pushing the *Kymata* where it does not want to go.

He looks again toward the shore of Arabia and swims

as hard as he can. He does not know if arrows are being shot at him. He does not know if someone with a dagger is nearing him. He does not know if he has the strength to swim that far.

Michel begins to weaken. The tide is coming out. For every two strokes he takes, he is pushed one stroke back out to sea.

Still, he swims, struggling once again as he has his whole life to live and do the right thing.

He feels something around his waist. A rope? Have they caught him? He looks.

Sanjar grabs Michel's hand. "Come with me, Master. I am a good swimmer."

Together, they kick and claw and fight the tide. Together they see the beach come closer.

Something scrapes Michel's knees. He tests it and finds he can touch the bottom. He stands and wades the rest of the way in, then collapses at the edge of the water.

"Master, we have to hide," He hears Sanjar say. "Those boulders. Hurry."

Michel struggles up to his knees, then stands. He runs for the boulder and crouches behind it.

The rest of the day, they watch the fighting aboard the two ships. Arrows, daggers, fires. Shouting, threatening, dying. Just before the day ends, the pirate ship with its copper front hull backs away from its prey, floats on down the Indus Sea, and leaves the ghost of the *Kynata* gutted and dead on the outer shoal.

Morning comes. The morning of another day shrouded in defeat. Michel stands and comes out from behind the boulder. Bodies on the shore. The skeleton ship still protesting its own death out on the shoal.

"Master!"

Michel turns and looks to the east and sees two people headed in his direction.

"Master," Anu says. "Sanjar told me where he had left you. We have been looking around to figure out where we are. Come. Look at this"

Michel follows Anu and Sanjar to an eastern tip of land and looks across a narrow strait to another piece of land.

"Are we on an island?" Anu asks.

Michel runs his hands through his hair. "I have no idea."

"I will find out for you," Sanjar says.

He runs into the water and swims toward a rowboat with a small sail on it. He stays with the fisherman a few moments, then swims back.

"The man said we are on the eastern tip of Arabia, and that village on the other side is Gwandar. He lives there."

"Gwandar?" Michel says. He squints. "It sounds familiar. I think I have been there before. Did he say what kingdom it was in?"

"He said it is on the border with Parthia."

Michel looks north and stares. "We're nearly home."

"We are, Master?" Anu says. "That's wonderful."

"We also have no way to get there. My money pouch is gone. We have no money."

"That's okay, Master. I will go diving. We can get some planks from the ship and go to the other side of the water to the village. How much will it cost to go home?"

"More money than you can make diving for fish, Sanjar. Just stay out of this while I figure something out."

With that, Sanjar dives back into the water and swims out to another boat.

"What is he doing? Well, I'm not responsible for him. Let's go, Anu."

"Go where?"

"Anywhere from that boy. It is hard enough trying to figure out how to get two of us rescued. I don't need three."

Michel and Anu walk back in the direction of the wrecked *Kymata*.

"Master. Master. The fisherman said he would take us home."

"Sanjar, go away."

"I said I would go divine for him. I know how to dive for pearls. That is how my mother and I got by. I dove for pearls, she cracked the shells to get them out, then sold them to special merchants."

"You did?" Anu says.

"You did?" Michel says.

"He has agreed to take us up the gulf to the Karkeh River and all the way to Susa for three pearls." Sanjar stands before them, a broad grin on his face.

"Three pearls? One pearl alone is worth enough for him to take a whole village up there," Michel says.

"He even said he would throw in something for us to eat," Sanjar adds.

"How long do you think it will take you?" Michel asks.

"I do not know. But he said there are many pearl shells right out there."

For the next two days, Michel and Anu wait as Sanjar dives over and over with no success.

At night, they lie down on the sand, and wrap their robes tightly around them.

"It's not sweltering hot like it was when we traveled through here over a year ago," Michel says. "But it is still hot. I do not think it is ever really cold here. Well, the nights are cool."

Still, they wait.

"Perhaps the fisherman was wrong," Michel finally tells the boy.

"He said the storm probably blew them to a different spot. I shall keep looking for them."

Two more days.

"I found one, Master," Sanjar calls out, running toward them, waving. "I found one."

He arrives where the men are and hands Michel a shell.

"I do not see a pearl."

"Of course not, Master. The pearl is inside the shell. You'll have to break it open and look for it. You can now be my helpers," Sanjar says, still grinning.

By the next day, they have their three pearls.

"He is ready to take us home, Master," Sanjar says.

"I am not your master, and this is not your home."

Sanjar glances over at Anu, who shrugs his shoulders and smiles.

It takes another week. Though the boat has sails, all three help the fisherman row. They arrive at the mouth of the Tigris River, which shortly is joined by the Karkeh River.

Anu watches Michel when they take the turn northeast.

"I know what you are thinking, Anu, and it is no. I do not wish to go up there where Eden used to be."

As they continue on up the Karkeh, they notice people watching them from the shore.

"What are they looking at?"

"I do not know."

They pull over to the shore. Anu climbs out and asks if anything unusual is going on at the palace. People stare, then walk away without answering.

"Something is wrong," Michel says. "We must hurry. King Phraates will need me."

When the sun is low in the sky, they draw close to the palace. Soldiers in blue uniforms march out to them fully armed, their camels in a full gallop.

Michel stands up in the boat, and an arrow flies over his head.

"Over there!" he shouts at the fisherman.

At the shore, Michel jumps out, hanging on the Sanjar's hand. Anu follows close. It is desert, but they see boulders. They run for protection and duck behind them. When they do and look up again, the soldiers have turned around and are headed back to the palace.

"I guess it is too dark for them to see us now," Anu says.

"What is going on?" Michel says. "There is some kind of upset at the palace. They seem to be attacking anyone who gets close to it. We have no choice but to head west back to the Tigris. Maybe we will see someone on the way willing to talk to us."

"Remember, Master, when we were in Arabia?

Michel: The Fourth Wise Man

Everyone said they weren't about to go to Parthia now. Did something bad happen while we were gone?"

Michel, Anu, and Sanjar begin walking. They walk all night. The following morning, they see a cart with an ox pulling it. They stop the farmer.

"Sir," Michel says. "We have come a long way to see King Phraattes."

"Which King Phraattes?"

"Old King Phraates, of course," Michel responds.

"Not any more."

"What do you mean?"

"The young Phraattes has killed his father, and he and his mother—Ther Musa—have married. Now they are King and Queen of Parthia."

Michel stands where he is, staring.

"Filthy, isn't it? Filthy wrong," the farmer says.

The farmer snaps the reins, and his ox continues on down the road.

"What do we do now, Master?" Anu asks.

Michel sits in the middle of the road. He stares. He says nothing.

"Master, what do we do now?" Anu asks again.

Sanjar kneels, then snuggles into Michel's arms. No one says anything more for a very long time.

39 ~ EDEN

*T*he sun goes down on the three.

"Why?" Michel finally says.

"Everything has gone wrong. I have lost my wife, my father, my estate, my Eden, my dream, and now my king and job." His voice is now a whisper. "Everything that I was and had is gone."

"Come, Master," Anu says. "Let's go over to those boulders and sleep. We need to rest so we can think."

Michel allows Anu to lead him to the boulders. Sanjar holds Michel's hand.

During the night, Michel groans with a sound that comes from deep in his throat and deeper in his soul.

Sometimes he stands and looks up at the stars.

"Jehovah, I made it right. I did what you wanted. But..." He turns in circles and raises his hands to the hosts of heaven.

"What do you want, God?" he bellows. "What is it that you want from me? I have given you everything."

Silence. He slumps back down to the desert floor and sleeps again that sleep, which exists in a land of empty questions.

Dawn comes.

"Master, the Tigris is just ahead of us," Anu says. "If we cross it tonight and keep going, we should be in Nippur two days after that. Isn't Meira there? Isn't your wife there? Perhaps this is where your God wants you. Let us go to

Michel: The Fourth Wise Man

Nippur."

Once again, Michel obeys his servant. All day they walk. Sometimes Michel stumbles, but Anu is always nearby.

"Sing something," Anu whispers to Sanjar. "We cannot let him get depressed. He is a good man. Sing a happy song."

Sanjar sings a song his mother used to sing.

They continue on toward the Tigris. That night they sleep on the other side of the river.

Michel is quieter now. In his sleep, he still groans in an almost otherworld groan. But no more outbursts. No more questionings. Just fitful sleep in a world he no longer recognizes.

Morning and evening again.

"Master, we should be in Nippur by the time the sun is down tonight. Your wife will be there. Meira is a good woman. She still loves you. Let us go to your wife."

In late afternoon, they arrive in Nippur. Michel remembers his mother-in-law lives near the southern gate. They have entered through the east gate. Anu gets directions. They work their way around the city until they find the house with the gate Michel had watched over a year earlier.

"Let me," Michel says when Anu reaches up to knock on it. He knocks on the gate and waits.

Oh, Jehovah, let Meira take me back. Let Meira love me again.

He hears the creaking of hinges. The gate slowly opens. Michel tries to smile.

The smile does not stay.

"Yes, may I help you?" the stranger asks.

"Uh, I am looking for Meira," Michel says, still trying to smile.

"I'm sorry. I do not believe I know her."

"What about a woman named Atossa?"

"That name I do recognize. We bought this house from an Atossa."

Michel struggles to not panic. "Do you know where

they went?"

"She said something about going south of here."

Michel says no more. He turns to his servant but does not see him.

Anu smiles broadly. "She has planned a surprise for you, Master. She has gone down to Uruk, where your father lives. What a grand surprise that is."

"We are playing a wonderful game," Sanjar says. "This is fun."

They leave out the south gate of Nippur and get on the highway down to Uruk.

Michel looks straight ahead now. He has nothing left. No will of his own.

Has my life been a mere dream?

Am I really here?

What is life anyway? Coming into being, then dissolving into nothingness?

Sometimes Anu and Sanjar sing Sanjar's mother's song together.

They see a merchant on the highway. Sanjar stops the merchant.

"I will sing a song to you in exchange for that bread you are taking to market,"

The merchant smiles. "Well, aren't you a cute little boy. Is that your father over there?" The merchant waves at Michel, then sits back on the seat of his cart, his arms folded. "So, sing me a song."

Sanjar stands, his feet apart, his arms stretched out on both side, and launches into the happiest song he can think of.

At the end, Sanjar bows.

The merchant applauds and hands the boy three pieces of flatbread.

"If I ever see you anymore, boy, I expect you to sing to me again."

Sanjar rejoins Michel and Uruk, hands them each a piece of flatbread, and skips ahead of them, though sometimes he walks backward so he can tell a story about the biggest pearl he ever found.

That night, they sleep by the side of the road. Michel now is completely quiet.

When they rise in the morning, Michel once again follows directions. No more will. No more being Michel. No more being a husband, a son, a magus. No more of being anything.

Tears do not come. Shouts do not come. No groans or whimperings or otherworld sounds.

"Let's rile him a little," Anu whispers to Sanjar. "Let's get him good and mad."

Sanjar looks at Anu and grins. Anu winks in return.

"You are the best father in the whole wide world," Sanjar says, tugging on Michel's hand. "I am the envy of everyone I know. I cannot wait to tell all my friends."

"You have no friends," Michel growls.

Sanjar looks over at Anu, and Anu silently applauds.

"When we get to where ever we are going, we are going to do all kinds of father-son things together. Remember, you promised to teach me how to ride a camel."

"I promised you no such thing," Michel barks.

"Okay. It was a horse. Didn't you say you were going to teach me to ride the best horse in the world? The kind your father rides?"

"I have no father," Michel rumbles.

"That's not what Anu told me. Anu told me your father was a war hero."

"He was not my hero, and stop calling me your father. He was not my father, and I am not yours. He never spoke a decent word to me."

Sanjar looks at Anu, who holds up a finger to his lips.

They continue down the highway in silence. For a long time in silence. No one speaks the rest of the day.

Another night beside the road. Another new day. Down the road toward Uruk.

"My father was a fisherman," Sanjar says, holding Michel's hand. "He was always gone. When he was home, he yelled at me all the time. He never let me hug him."

Michel looks straight ahead. The three walk in silence another hour.

"Good," Michel finally says. "Never let people get too close to you."

Mid-afternoon. Michel wipes his nose. They walk on. He stops in the middle of the road, then walks over to the side. He looks down at Sanjar.

"Father, why are you crying?" Sanjar says.

Michel draws the boy close to him. "I never realized. I never understood," he whispers.

Sanjar looks up at Michel. "If I had a father, I would have everything."

Night again. then morning.

They walk into Uruk. Michel finds the street where he grew up. He finds the house he had shared with his mother and occasionally with his father. He takes a deep breath and knocks.

They hear the scraping of a bar on the inside. It opens.

Michel stares.

The man in the gateway stares.

"Michel?"

"Captain Tefnak?" What are you doing at my father's house?"

The two men stare at each other more.

"Nebo is your father?"

"Of course. How do you know him?"

Captain Tefnak leans his head back and lets out a guffaw that echoes around the courtyard.

"Come in, my boy, come in," he says to Michel.

Michel, Anu, and Sanjar enter the courtyard of Michel's childhood home.

"Have a seat, my boy. You are going to love this."

"What?" Michel asks.

The sea captain leans back and roars again. "You remember that passenger I had the bet with when we were becalmed that time? Ha, ha, ha. He, he, he."

Tefnak wipes his eyes. "That was...that was...ha, ha, ha...your father. Nebo! Ha, ha, ha."

"My father owned the land where Eden used to be?"

"Ha, ha, ha. He owned it, he cheated me with it, then I cheated you with it, and the land ended right back where it started. Ha, ha, ha."

Silence.

Michel's head swirls, trying to comprehend.

"What are you doing here?"

"I retired. So, he sold me his house. You are not wanting to buy it now so it can go right back to him, are you? Ha, ha, ha. Wouldn't that be something? Ha, ha, ha."

"Then, what happened to my father? Did he go back to war? Did he join forces with the young King Phraates? Where is he?"

"Ha, ha, ha. He is down at your Eden."

"He's where?" Michel asks.

"He, he, he." Captain Tefnak bursts out in laughter again. My boy, I think you need to get down there where your father is. I will take you in the morning."

"No, I want to go now. Maybe my father needs me."

"Very well, the captain says. I will get the horses ready. I have two. Will your servant mind riding behind me?"

"No, Anu will not mind. Then your son or whoever he is can ride with you."

Tefnak disappears in his stable and comes out with two large black Niseans.

"They look just like my father's Niseans," Michel says.

"They are your father's Niseans. He sold me half his herd."

"I cannot imagine what he could do with them down in the marshes."

Within the hour, the four are out of Uruk and headed south on the broad Parthian highway. They put their horses into a trot the rest of the afternoon.

"We have made enough progress tonight," Captain Tefnak says, "that we should be there tomorrow."

Michel lies awake a long time.

My father has gone into the boating business down there. Or fishing. Or selling water buffalo. Why am I in such a hurry? He has only gone away so he can disappear from my life again. This time, he did not plan on me finding him. This time, he thought he would be rid of me for good. Well, after this time, maybe it will be for good.

The next day, the strong Niseans take their passengers once again toward Eden.

As they draw closer, Michel notices there aren't as many marshes. Closer they come to where the Tigris and Euphrates Rivers meet. The ground is dryer. He sees a canal over on the left. Captain Tefnak leads them off the highway to another road.

"Remember that deed you sent me by your caravan captain, signing your Eden back over to me? I burned it."

"Why?"

The old man does not answer. Instead, he grins.

Michel sees two men ahead walking toward him. They are talking to each other in animated conversation.

Who are they? They look familiar.

Michel brings his horse to a halt and stares. The two men realize something is in their way, and look up.

"Huh?"

"Kumar?"

They stare.

"Dushatra?"

Still, they stare.

"Michel?"

Michel dismounts, and the three men rush toward each other. They embrace. They laugh. They cry. They pound each other on the back.

"We thought you were dead," Kumar says.

"What happened to you?" Dushatra says. "We thought Herod's soldiers had found and killed you."

"It's a long story," Michel replies. "Is Yasib with you?"

"Of course. Of course," Kumar says.

"Walk back with us. We will take you to him."

Michel continues to turn in every direction. "They got it drained. They actually got it drained."

The three old friends walk together as they had done

so many times before, while Tefnak and Anu follow them still on their horses.

Sanjar takes hold of the reigns of the horse he had been sharing with Michel and looks over at Anu. "See, I told you he said he would teach me how to ride a horse."

Shortly, they see an old man sitting in the doorway of a small mud-brick building.

"Buildings out here in my Eden? What has been going on?"

"Hey, Yasib," Kumar calls out. "Look who we found!"

Yasib looks up, pushes the scroll off this lap, and walks as fast as his old legs will carry him to the arms of Michel.

Laughter once again. Tears once again. A reuniting once again.

"We thought you were dead," Yasib says.

"Well, as you can see, I am not dead."

"What happened to you?"

"That's a long story," Kumar, Dushatra, and Michel say in unison.

Michel looks at his friends, still in a huddle with them, then at the surroundings, then back at his friends.

"What is going on around here? I am gone two years and..."

"There is someone else you need to see," Yasib says.

"In this building?" Michel asks.

Yasib points back toward the road.

"Oh, that's Tefnak. He has already told me everything he knows."

"Let's just go see that old man he is talking to," Yasib says.

Michel notices Tefnak pointing to him. The old man he had been talking to turns and faces Michel.

Michel runs toward the old man. The old man runs toward Michel. They embrace as they had done on Nebo's rooftop two years earlier.

"I see you two have kissed and made up."

Michel looks toward the gentle voice that had touched

his life and heart for so many years in Ctesiphon.

He stands and holds out his arms. "My darling. Can you ever take me back?"

"Well, if old Nebo can take you back, I suppose I can too."

Meira moves into the arms of her husband. They embrace, kiss, embrace again, and whisper things no one else can hear.

"We certainly are having a jolly old time," Sanjar says from his big horse.

Anu climbs down from his and goes over to Sanjar. He helps the boy down, takes his hand, and walks him over to Michel and Meira. Sanjar takes hold of Meira's hand.

"Dear, I think you and I have inherited a son," Michel says.

"If you will have me," Sanjar says. "I will sing for you, and I make real good baklava, and I can find pearls for you, and..."

"How charming," Meira says, interrupting. She looks over at Michel. "However, I think he is going to take a little taming."

"Ha, ha," Michel says. "Good luck."

"Come, my son," Nebo says. "We have been waiting for you."

"You have?" Michel says, standing in the middle of a lot of grinning people with his hands on his hips. "Just what is going on here?"

"Your dream, my son," Nebo says. "It is a reality. Now walk with me."

Nebo puts his arm over his son's shoulder while Michel puts his arm around the waist of his wife on the other side, and Sanjar clings to her other hand.

"Come up on this little hill, and you should be able to see what we have accomplished," Nebo says.

They walk up the hill. Michel takes off his turban and runs his hands through his dark hair.

"Is that them?"

"Yes, that is where the Tigris and Euphrates meet.

Michel: The Fourth Wise Man

They are now meeting in sweet harmony. Now, do you see those saplings over there? Those are fruit trees that we have planted. Now over there..."

"But that building. And I see a few more buildings. And isn't that a farm? Who are those people hoeing?"

"They are the marsh people. They are still pagans, but they will come along. They get to keep one-tenth of what they produce at the farm. The rest of the produce will go to the school."

"What school?" Michel asks, trying to absorb everything at once.

"Well, if it isn't Michel. We thought you were dead."

Michel turns and sees Captain Arshad walking toward him. They clasp hands and forearms.

"What?" Michel can say no more.

"After the young Phraates and his mother killed our old King Phraates, we all lost our positions in the kingdom. Your magi friends learned what your father had accomplished with your Eden, so decided to come down here and start a school."

Michel remains speechless.

"I and my men came down to build what buildings you needed for your school and then be guards."

"That includes classrooms as well as small houses for your future students and their young families," Nebo says.

"But money. Where are you getting the money to do all this?" Michel asks.

"I cheated my old friend, Captain Tefnak, out of enough money for my house and horses to get the school built," Nebo says with a grin. "After that, the farm will provide for some of our needs, and tuition will provide the rest."

"And what are we going to teach besides mathematics and science?"

"We are all going to teach about the one true God, Jehovah," Yasib says. "After seeing the eternal child, we knew you and your Daniel were right."

"We have become believers in Jehovah," Dushatra

says.

"Pagans everywhere will come to Eden and learn about the one true God, just as you dreamed," Kumar says.

"Tomorrow," Captain Arshad announces, "I propose that we have a parade, a celebration."

That night, Michel prays. *I am so ashamed. I thought if anything got done, I had to do it. That was not true. If anything got done, you had to do it. My God, forgive me. I will spend the rest of my life making it up to you.*

The next morning when Michel wakes up, he enjoys breakfast with his wife, his father, his new son, and his magi friends.

"We are ready for the parade," Arshad announces. "All the pagans who lived in the marshes have lined up along the road to honor you."

The parade begins. Arshad first. Then his soldiers, all dressed in blue. Then servants in their uniforms, Anu among them. The three magi next—Yasib, Dushatra, and Kumar. Then the heroes.

Once again, as he had done in his childhood so long ago, Michel rides a big Nisean horse next to his father. Nebo is waving a copy of the Torah as the pagans along the road clap and shout and sing. Only now there are three—grandfather, father, son. Proud and united at last in a dream come true through a star.

40 ~ THE ETERNAL CHILD

"Rabbi," a student asks, "how long have you been teaching at the School of Eden?"

Michel smiles. His hair is now grey. His eyesight not as keen. His voice weaker.

"Thirty years," Michel replies.

"Is it true you saw a great star predicting the birth of a god?"

"Oh, no. It predicted the birth of the God. God put a part of himself in a child. Just as in the days of Adam and Eve on these very grounds thousands of years ago, God came back to walk with us again."

"Is he still here?"

"As far as I know, he is."

"How long has it been since you saw him?"

"A long time. Too long. He must be thirty-two or three years now."

Michel pauses, squints with a glint in his eye, then points at the young man, shaking his finger for emphasis.

"You know, I think you have a good idea there. I think it is time I go see him. I need to do that before I die."

As soon as the class is over, Michel walks down the hall to a small office.

"Sanjar, go with me."

"Certainly, Father. I just need to be back in time to teach my next class."

"You won't be. It will take us a year. Perhaps longer."

"What are you up to, Father?" Sanjar says, setting down the scroll he is reading.

"I need to go see the eternal child."

Sanjar is now taller than Michel with olive skin, dark eyes, and oval face with dimples that sometimes show from behind his short beard and mustache.

"He is still here? Well, I suppose he would be, being eternal and all," Sanjar replies. "But that's a long time to be gone. What will happen to my students?"

"Don't go thinking everything depends on you. I thought that when I was your age, and I paid dearly for it."

"Well, do you know where he is?" Sanjar asks.

"He was predicted to be the Jewish Messiah. We will go to Jerusalem. Perhaps he has taken over the palace and temple. The eternal throne was to be his."

"I don't know, Father. I really don't want to be gone that long."

"Then it's settled. You and I will be onboard a ship no later than a week from today."

"Father, it is not settled."

Michel squints and gives Sanjar one last piercing look before leaving.

"What about Kumar? Cannot he go with you?" Michel hears out in the hall. He keeps walking.

He arrives at another room and knocks on a door.

"Come in, Michel," the gravelly voice says.

Michel walks into the small studio and seats himself.

"I'm going to do what we should have done a long time ago."

The former magus of King Phraattes is holding a brush and leaning over a sheet of papyrus. "Wait a minute. I've got to get this flower just right."

That done, he looks over at Michel. "I've got better eyesight than you, old friend," Kumar says.

"Well, you've also got more gray hair, and you stoop when you walk," Michel replies, a glint in his eyes.

"So, you're going to do it," Kumar says. "I wish I could go with you."

"I wish you could too. But I will tell you all about it when I get back."

"Where do you think he is?"

"Jerusalem. Definitely Jerusalem."

"Which route are you going to take? The one straight there across that dratted desert, or the north one up and around it like we took when we went to see him that time?"

"Neither. I'm going by ship. Sanjar is going with me."

"Too bad Dushatra isn't going. But he's too far away."

"Yes, back where he grew up in Kandahar. Well, he is doing a good job over there since becoming a rabbi."

"Poor Yasib. How I miss him."

"He was a good man. Everyone liked him. How long has he been gone now?"

"Died five or six years ago, seems like."

The two old magi sit together and let their minds drift back to all they had been through together, trying to find the meaning of the star, and then going to Bethlehem as their kings' ambassadors.

Michel sighs. "Well, I need to send a messenger down to the gulf to arrange for passage."

A week has come and gone.

Michel and Sanjar have just boarded the *Asteri*.

"Do you have our money, food, a tent that will fit on the deck, and some scrolls to read while we're at sea?"

"Yes, Father. And our changes of clothes, don't forget."

"Remember the last time we were here, Son?" Michel says as the ship slips away from the docks.

"You sure weren't letting me call you Father yet," Sanjar says, poking Michel's arm.

"I was afraid I would grow attached to you, then you would disappear like my father did so many times while I was growing up."

"What you were really doing was acting like your father."

"Yes, I guess you're right. Well, everyone got over that, and I got my father back and a son thrown in."

"So, I was thrown in, was I?" Sanjar teases.

For six days, the *Asteri* works its way down through the Parthian Gulf to the Indus Sea. It veers west to travel under Arabia.

"I wish the other magi could be here with us. How I miss them."

"Well, you don't miss Kumar much because you see him every day. But, Dushatra and Yasib have not been around for a long time," Sanjar says.

"Didn't you say there were eight of you magi looking for the meaning of the star to start with? You never told me anything about them."

"Hophni was a dear man who was part Cushite—you call them Ethiopians—and part Egyptian. Died of snake bite trying to save someone else. Demetrius was Roman and turned traitor. Katazuli was Hittite and was killed by his own people. Borseen was Syrian and turned traitor also—worshipped power. Sad what happened to them. Sad."

Michel sighs. "But four of us were loyal. Loyal to our king and loyal to our star."

Another four days pass smoothly. The wind has been favorable. It is spring. A good time to travel.

Finally, the *Asteri* veers north.

"Do you have any memories of where we are now?" Michel asks, standing at the rail facing east toward the Arabian coast.

"Not really. Is this it? Is this where I was born? I only remember living in a shack on docks and diving for pearls."

As the ship begins the final part of the journey up the Red Sea, Michel wanders over to the other rail and looks up at the mountains on the Egyptians side of the water.

"I met Moses up there," he tells Sanjar. "Well, not literally. He got the Ten Commandments up there on Mount Sinai. It was the lowest point of my life. If it hadn't been for ole Anu. Did you know I tried to set him free, but he wouldn't go?"

Sanjar does not answer. He knows Michel has transcended time and only sees and hears yesterday.

Michel: The Fourth Wise Man

Five days later, the *Asteri* docks at Ezion Geber.

"Shall I purchase two camels for us, Father?"

"No, people around here ride mules. See if you can find a dealer in mules."

Michel sighs and smiles. "Oh, it will be so good seeing him again. So good. He will have everyone living in peace, and life for the Jews in their homeland will be good. You will see, Sanjar. You will see."

Michel and Sanjar work their way up the Wadi Arabah between the Red Sea and the Dead Sea. They pass Avith, Teman, Petra, Punon, Bozrah, Zalmona, and finally, come to the Zered River. On the other side, they pass Kir, then cross the Arnon River. They go through Dibon, Medeba, and Heshbon. It has taken them three days.

"We will be in Jericho by tomorrow noon. It is very near Jerusalem. Two days from now, we will be visiting with Jesus, the eternal star child, now all grown up and spreading peace everywhere. Ah, it will be so good seeing him again after all these years."

They arrive in Jericho and rent the last room in the last inn available.

"What's going on here?" Michel asks.

"It's Passover time. A lot is going on in Jerusalem. You'd better hurry. You will miss out on the fun."

Michel smiles at Sanjar. "Then we will not wait until tomorrow. We will go now."

As they draw nearer to Jerusalem, the more people they see on the road. Some are on carts with their animals in a trot. Some are on mules that are galloping.

"Look at the excitement. What a celebration," Michel says.

"No, Father. They are angry. They are shouting curses. Are you sure we should enter Jerusalem right now?"

"Oh, you are just imagining things. People have different ways here."

"Look, Father."

"Where?"

"Up on that hill."

Michel looks up and sees three crosses. He squints, furrows his brow, then looks back at Sanjar. "That doesn't concern us."

"But, Father, did you read the signs on their crosses? You cannot see that far, but I can."

"What signs?"

"The Romans always nail a sign with their offense to the crosses. Father, let's stop here."

"No, I don't want to stop here."

"Please. Just a little while. Do it for me."

"Well…"

"Come, Father. There are hitching posts along the road here. Our mules will be fine."

Old Michel slides off his mount and stands with his back to the hill with its crosses.

"Come, Father. Let's walk up the little hill."

Magus Michel sighs.

Slowly they make their way up. Sanjar takes Michel's arm and supports him as they draw close to the cross in the middle.

"No. No! He was supposed to be eternal."

Michel looks up into the bloodied face of the boy, the God Child now grown.

"He was supposed to bring peace on earth."

He stares. Tears run down from his old wrinkled cheeks and through his grayed beard.

"They cannot do this to him."

Sanjar continues to support his old father.

"Oh, Jehovah. We weren't wrong. I know we weren't wrong. What is happening? Jehovah?"

Michel kneels at the foot of Jesus' cross. His old shoulders shake.

Then, he hears it.

"Father. Father! I give you my spirit."

The earth rumbles. Wind whips in circles. People scream.

"Hurry, Father. We have to get off this hill. It's an earthquake."

"Is he dead?" Michel asks. "He's dead, isn't he?"
Slowly, Michel and Sanjar go back down the hill.
"I'm not leaving."
"You have to."
"I left him in danger once before. I will not leave him now."
"It is too late, Father."
"It is never too late."

Eventually, Michel and Sanjar are back in nearby Jericho. Michel does not speak. The rest of the day and the day after and the day after that.

"Father, we need to be thinking of going back to Eden."
"No. No! I will not go and desert him. Not again."

Michel lies down on his bed. "Moses. Oh, Moses," he whispers sometimes.

He sits up and stares at the floor.

"Father, I got some broth for you. Please take some."

Michel lies back down and turns his face to the wall. Sometimes Sanjar hears him whisper.

"My elusive star. Don't disappear again. Come back. Come back. We could not have been wrong."

Early on the third day since arriving, Michel puts on his robe.

"Where are you going, Father?"
"Back to Jerusalem. Check out of the inn. Passover is done with now. I want to get an inn there."
"Father, we need to be going home."

Michel stares at Sanjar and pounds his fist on the door frame. "No! You can go home if you want to, but I must stay."

Back on their mules, they ride near Jerusalem. They pass by the hill. The crosses are still there. They see some women coming up from a valley garden nearby. "He's gone. He's gone."

Michel directs his mule over to the women.
"Who's gone?"
"Jesus!"
"Disappeared?"

"No! He came back to life!"

The women hurry on up the road. Michel directs his mule down the little valley from whence the women had come. He climbs down and walks the rest of the way on the narrow garden path. He stops.

"Father, what are you doing?"

Michel stares at the tomb. He looks in. He turns toward Sanjar.

"I knew he was eternal. You cannot kill God. I have to find him. I need to find him."

They go on into Jerusalem and find an inn. The wait begins. Each day, Michel leaves the inn and looks to his right, where he sees the palace on a hill. "He was a sly one, that old King Herod," he always tells Sanjar.

He looks over in the opposite direction and walks up to another hill, the one with the temple on it. He goes in and waits. And listens.

"Surely, this is where he will come."

Days later, he hears what he had been listening for. "He's up in the Province of Galilee."

"That's where we're going, Sanjar."

"No, Father. We're staying right here in Jerusalem. You yourself said he would be here."

"Well, I was wrong. He is not. He is in the north province, and that is where we are going."

"You won't know where to go once you get there."

"I will figure it out."

Three days later, they arrive in Galilee. Michel asks people on the road if they know anything about Jesus coming back to life and where he might be. All laugh at him. One does not.

"Yes, sir. He was seen by his apostles just outside of Capernaum."

Michel spurs his mule into a gallop.

"Father, you're going to fall off."

That night, they arrive in Capernaum.

"My, it has grown. It was just a small fishing village when we were here last time."

Michel: The Fourth Wise Man

"You've been here before?"

"Oh, yes. We had been traveling two months by then. Maybe three. We had just come out of the Lebanon Mountains north of here. I wonder if Zebedee is still around. He was just a teenager fishing from his father's boat when we met him."

Michel hurries on into the city. He heads for the city square, where he hears the name of Jesus being spoken by several people hurrying up into the hills on the other side of the lake.

"Let's go, Sanjar. He's up in those hills. He's waiting for me."

"No, he isn't, Father. Why would he wait for you?" Sanjar says, following his father back out of town.

They arrive at a meadow with a cliff overlooking it. "I'll bet there are five-hundred people here," Michel says.

He slides off his mule and walks it through the crowd.

"I was there after he was born," he says now and then. "I saw his star," he adds.

More and more people take notice of the old man. Someone stops Michel. "Sir, were you really there?"

"Yes, young man. I was one of the magi, one of the ambassadors of King Phraates, who sent us to make sure we were on friendly terms with the new eternal king. He was so cute, toddling over to us. And he already knew the word 'star.'"

"My name is Philip. Come with me."

Michel hands the reins of his mule over to Sanjar and takes faltering steps up the rocky hillside to the top of the cliff.

Stopping to rest, Michel sees a hand full of men who are gathered around someone.

Philip leads Michel over to the small group and whispers to one of them.

"I am so thrilled to meet you," Andrew says. "Come with me."

Michel follows. He knows. He knows.

The small group of men step aside. Michel is led to the

man in the middle. He knows.

Michel looks into the eyes of the boy he had seen over thirty years earlier. The star child. The eternal one. They smile at each other.

"You're the one who brought my parents the sweet-smelling frankincense."

"Actually, that was Kumar. He is still alive, but his health is poor. He could not come."

"Then, perhaps you were the one who brought the gold."

"No, that was Yasib—he is dead now—and Dushatra, who is over in northern Indus now."

Jesus smiles. Michel knows what Jesus is doing, and likes it.

"I am the one who brought you the jar of anointing myrrh."

"I played with the amethyst lid. It was my favorite lid."

Michel grows serious. He stares into Jesus' eyes again, bends his knees, and touches his forehead to the ground.

Jesus reaches down and helps Michel back up.

"Next?" they hear.

Michel turns and sees there is a long line behind him. Philip walks over and helps him back down the hill.

"Back to Jerusalem," he tells Sanjar when he rejoins his son.

"Did you see him?"

"Yes, I saw him. He is going to start a different kind of kingdom soon—a spiritual one for the hearts of mankind. It's all in the scriptures. And it's going to go forth to all the world. We must return to Jerusalem."

Three more days on the road. Three more days of chasing Michel's star.

"Are you sure, Father?" Sanjar asks every day as they go to the temple and wait for something they do not understand.

"I am sure, Michel. I am as sure as I was of the star."

"Fourteen days later, on their way to the temple, they hear a wind like a cyclone. They follow the sound and see a large building near the temple.

"Hey, that's Andrew up on that roof. I remember him. Oh, and there is Philip."

For the next two hours, Michel hears the amazing news. The news that today is the first day of the kingdom of the eternal star.

"Repent of all the bad you have done," Peter calls down. "Repent and be immersed in water so your sins will be forgiven and you will receive the Holy Spirit."

That night at the inn, Michel takes his extra clothes off the peg and puts them in the large leather pouch they had brought with them from Eden.

"We must hurry home, Sanjar. We must spread the word. We must give them a chance to be baptized, have their sins completely forgiven, and become citizens in the kingdom. We have work to do, Sanjar."

Four days later, Michel and Sanjar are back at Ezion Geber at the headwaters of the Red Sea. They board the ship and watch the shoreline move along as the captain takes them down toward the Indus Sea and home to Eden.

"Father, you are not eating again."

"I will, after a while, Son. You know we have a lot of work to do when we get back to Eden. We must teach our students that Jesus really was the eternal King, the eternal star. We've got to encourage our students to go out from Eden and spread the word everywhere."

"I know, Father. I know. But will you eat something now?"

"I will take a few sips just for you, my son."

Michel manages to consume half the bowl.

"Take me over to the railing now," he says. "I think we're nearing Mount Sinai again."

Just as the sun touches the horizon and turns gold, they see it.

Michel smiles. "It has snow on it again. I wonder if Moses got cold up there like I did."

"I don't know, Father," Sanjar says. "Maybe he was there in the summer."

"Maybe so."

"Moses survived it all, didn't he?"

"Yes, he did, Father. Just like you have."

Michel grabs hold of Sanjar's arm and clings to it hard.

"A kingdom was started there two thousand years ago." His hand slips a little. His knees grow weak.

"It did, indeed, Father."

"Now the new kingdom begins. And, Son, we must…" Michel slips down to the deck.

Sanjar sees what is happening and holds him in his arms. "Father? What's wrong? Father? Don't leave us. Father?"

"…we must…tell them."

Michel closes his eyes for the last time.

With tears of pride and anguish and hope, Sanjar whispers. "Yes, Father. We will tell the world from your Eden."

THANK YOU

Thanks for reading my book! I'm so honored that you chose to spend your precious time with my characters. You are appreciated. I'm an independent author who relies on my readers to help spread the word about stories you enjoy.

Would you take a few minutes to let your friends know on Facebook, Pinterest...wherever you hang out online? Also, each honest review at online retailers means a lot to me and helps other readers know if this is a book they might enjoy.

I welcome contact from readers. At my website (below), you can do so. You can also sign up for my monthly newsletter (below) for half-price paper, and 99c ebooks for the whole family - novels, non-fiction, storybooks, and first peek at my newest release.

Katheryn Maddox Haddad

GET ALL 8 BOOKS IN THE HISTORICAL SERIES
INTREPID MEN OF GOD

Novel 1 ~ Lazarus: The Samaritan
Novel 2 ~ Paul: The Unstoppable
Novel 3 ~ Luke: Slave & Physician
Novel 4 ~ Mefiboset: Crippled Prince
Novel 5 ~ Joseph: The Other Father
Novel 6 ~ Michel: Fourth Wise Man
Novel 7 ~ Stephen: Unlikely Martyr
Novel 8 ~ Titus: The Aristocrat

HISTORICAL BACKGROUND

CTESIPHON was the capital city of the Parthian Empire and on the east bank of the Tigris River. Its remains are 20 miles south of Baghdad (which did not exist then). The ruins of the great veranda arch still stand, though it continues to crumble.

KING ORODES II was King of the Parthian Empire BC 57 to BC 37. He was murdered by his son, Phraates.

KING PHRAATES IV was King of the Parthian Empire BC 37 to BC 2 (2 years after Jesus' birth in BC 4). He was murdered by his wife, Ther Musa and their son, Phraates V.

QUEEN THER MUSA was a slave girl Augustus gave to Phratees IV. She was the mother of Phraates V. She and her son poisoned the king and assumed the throne in 2 BC. They appear together on their coins and were apparently co-rulers. Josephus alleges that Musa married her son.

CHEBAR CANAL has been located near the ruins of Nippur in Iraq. It was part of a complex network of irrigation and transport canals that also included the Shatt el-Nil, a silted-up canal toward the east of Babylon.

GONDOPHARES I was the founder of the Indo (Indian)-Parthian Kingdom in what is now Afghanistan and Pakistan. (Pakistan was part of India until the 20th century.) Some say he was king BC 20-10, and others say he was king AD 20-40.

MAGI was a priestly tribe of the Medes (later absorbed into Babylon and Parthia). They were the "wise men" of their nation. Other ancient historians say they were priests of Zoroaster, the religion held to by Phraates.

TURBAT is a city in SW Pakistan with ancient tombs carved out of rock which have never been identified.

HINGLAJ has a Hindu cave temple of Hinglaj Mata is located in a narrow gorge in the remote, hilly area of Lyari Tehsil in Pakistan's Balochistan province. It is situated 160 mi. from the north-west of Karachi, 12 miles inland from the Arabian Sea, and 80 miles from the west of the mouth of the Indus. It is located at the end of a range of Kheerthar hills, in the Makran desert stretch, on the west bank of Hingol River.

GONDRANI CAVES have small rooms with hearths and wall niches for lamps, along with verandahs or front porches. It is believed to have been a Buddhist monastery.

CANDACE was the Ethiopian title for queen.

CANDACE AMANISH AKETO was a warrior queen of Kush (today's Sudan, which was formerly part of Ethiopia) BC 10 to AD 1, known for her lavish gold jewelry and having successfully kept the Roman Empire from taking over her kingdom. NATA KAMANI, her son, was king after her.

EDFU LIBRARY was an extension of the Temple of Horus and exists today. The walls of this chamber are filled with engravings and captions depicting numerous receptacles filled with manuscripts of papyrus as well as scrolls bound in leather.

ALEXANDRIA LIBRARY was founded by Ptolemy, and was said to have amassed an estimated 400,000 manuscripts and was considered the leading intellectual metropolis of the Hellenistic world. It fell into the Mediterranean Sea during a 4th-Century AD earthquake.

MILOS, a Greek Island, was a favorite haunt of pirates and their slave trade during the height of the Roman Empire.

LIBRARY OF ARISTOTLE in was a private library and the earliest one reported on by ancient chroniclers. It is not known what books nor the number of books that were included in the library. It was destroyed in 86 BC, but it is thought it was refounded in the first century by Andronicus and again flourished.

LIBRARY OF APOLLO was part of the Roman Forum and associated with the temple of Apollo Palatinus.

PERGAMUM LIBRARY of Anatolia on the west coast of today's Turkey had a collection of over 200,000 volumes. It was also in Pergamum parchment made of hides was invented, thus replacing the more fragile reed papyrus.

HATTUSA LIBRARY in Anatolia constituted the largest collection of Hittite texts discovered with approximately thirty thousand inscribed cuneiform tablets.

ANTIOCH LIBRARY in Syria (where the Apostle Paul lived sometimes) along with the city itself was considered by some to be the cultural capital of the ancient world, even more prestigious than Pergamon.

MARI was an ancient Semitic city in Syria. Its remains are on the Euphrates river western bank. It had been abandoned centuries before our story.

AI, EMPEROR OF THE CHINESE HAN DYNASTY, ruled 7 BC to 1 BC and was known for his hot temper.

ECBATANA was the capital of Parthia under Darius I and Cyrus. Herodotus describes it as a magnificent city fortified with seven concentric walls. In it, the royal archives were kept.

FORT BIRTHA was located where today's Tikrit, Iraq, is. The ruins of the castle are on a perpendicular cliff over the Tigris River.

ASHUR, at one point, was capital of the ancient Assyrian Empire. It was still occupied in the first century through not as important then.

HARRAN of Abraham's time is a small village in southern Turkey. Ruins of the city include the unique beehive houses.

MOUNT SINAI is believed by some to be at the southern tip of Egypt's Sinai Peninsula, which is at the north part of the Red Sea. Others believe it is at the southern tip of Arabia, which is also the southern part of the Red Sea. In this book, it is represented as being in the Sinai Peninsula.

GARDEN OF EDEN. The Tigris and Euphrates Rivers meet in today's southern Iraq just north of Basrah, then flow into the Persian Gulf. They come within a few miles of meeting in Turkey/Armenia near Mount Ararat.

BUY YOUR NEXT BOOK NOW
Check out what they are about and a buy link.

HISTORICAL NOVELS FOR ADULTS

THEY MET JESUS Series of 8
http://bit.ly/TheyMetJesus

INTREPID MEN OF GOD Series of 8
http://bit.ly/IntrepidMen

HISTORICAL STORYBOOKS FOR CHILDREN

A CHILD'S LIFE OF CHRIST Series of 8
(Parallels Adult *They Met Jesus*)
http://bit.ly/ChildsLifeOfChristSet

A CHILD'S BIBLE HEROES Series of 10
http://bit.ly/Bible-Heroes

A CHILD'S BIBLE KIDS Series of 8
http://bit.ly/bible-kids

A CHILD'S BIBLE LADIES Series of 10
http://bit.ly/BibleLadies

DISCUSSION QUESTIONS

CHAP. 1:
*Why do you think Michel blurted out to his friends what his plans were to restore the Garden of Eden.

CHAP. 2:
*Meri judged what her mother should be doing, and Michel judged what his father should be doing. At what age should parents of grown children give up making their own decisions?

CHAP. 3:
Do you have a love-hate relationship with someone? Or do you know people that do? Do they even remember why they argue so much? What can be done to help them stop arguing?

CHAP. 4:
Do you have a dream? What is it? Are you willing to do whatever it takes no matter how long it takes for your dream to become a reality? Why?

CHAP. 5:
Michel has agreed to do something deep down he knows he cannot do. Have you ever gotten yourself into something like that? What?

CHAP. 6:
How successful were you when you starting trying to find someone to help you with your dream? What things did you try as incentive to help you?

CHAP. 7:
We now see that Michel tends to have mood swings. Do you

think his sudden singing of songs and praising the sky was forced? Was it good for him or not?

CHAP. 8:
Although we usually deny it, most people believe what is in print or on the radio or television.
Is there something you believed because you read or heard it on the media? What was it? When did people begin to doubt it?

CHAP. 9:
Michel sees the "star of Bethlehem" as an interruption to his dream of restoring Eden so God can walk the earth again. He has lost some of his influence with the other magi, and they are not willing to search the Jewish scriptures to find the meaning of the star. Have you ever set up a large project and been interrupted so much, you ended up using all your time for the interruption?

CHAP. 10:
In order to be thorough and not leave any gods out, the magi decide to go to all the large sacred libraries known to man. But is it possible? Things keep getting more complicated. Do you know anyone who gets carried away and won't do anything halfway, sometimes interfering with the lives of others in their family or among their friends?

CHAP. 11:
Michel has a mind of his own and doesn't always agree with the other magi. He goes down to the docks instead of to the market for food. What do you think he was looking for among the ships?

CHAP. 12:
Rather than form a committee, the magi are taking turns being in the lead. Which do you think is most efficient—the committee method or the lone-leader method?

CHAP. 13:
Obsessive, compulsive Michel who marches to the beat of a different drum, is so convinced the star is a waste of time, he slips away to go back to his Eden project. Are you sometimes obsessive and compulsive? Do you sometimes judge things different from other people?

CHAP. 14:
So far, Michel has caused more problems to the other magi than solved. All he is doing is slowing them down. Do you recall being the one who throws a chink into plans of family or friends with a sudden accident? Have you ever taken a short cut and ended up going farther?

CHAP. 15:
Recall a time when you thought you were in trouble, and it turned out you were just being told something helpful. Have you ever ridden a strange animal? What was it like?

CHAP. 16:
As ambassadors of the king of Parthia, the magi use that fact to butter up the kings and queens of lesser kingdoms. What are some situations you have been that could only be handled with diplomacy?

CHAP. 17:
Travel in ancient times was dangerous, especially ship travel. Travelers had to be prepared for any kind of disaster. Was there ever a time when someone was injured, and you were the only one around besides the injured person? Or perhaps you were the injured person. How did you handle it?

CHAP. 18:
The average lifespan in ancient Egypt was around 35. Much was due to accidents and diseases. If you had been given the chance to travel the world to search for the meaning of the "Bethlehem star," would you have gone with them?

CHAP. 19:
Do you personally know anyone who has been or is being cheated by unscrupulous people? Is there anything you can do to rescue them?

CHAP. 20:
Have you ever had a friend a long time who turned out to not be what you thought? Do you think the change was gradual, or s/he was always like that in secret?

CHAP. 21:
Do you recall doing something everyone warned you not to do? And that something turned into a disaster. How did you feel? How did those who had warned you treat you?

CHAP. 22:
After all the misfortunes they have encountered on both land and sea, they can go no farther. They have been stricken with the final blow. Recall a time you worked a long time to accomplish something, and at the last minute, it broke. Did you give up or start over?

CHAP. 23:
In this story, Borseen is in his twenties, the youngest of the magi. He thinks he can restore a deserted city and become its king. Sometimes young people do not understand reality. When you were young, what great and stupendous thing did you think you would do someday?

CHAP. 24:
You might say that four of the imprisoned magi formed a committee while the fifth one tackled the problem alone. Why is it that often committees get a lot less done than a single person?

CHAP. 25:
The men ate what they had to in order to survive. They

followed the animals who knew where to find sustenance. The Bible says, "And a child shall lead them." Recall a time when you were led by someone who knew far less than you did about your situation.

CHAP. 26:
Daniel 9:25 predicted the year Jesus would come and begin preaching, Daniel 12:34 says good wise men will shine as the stars and lead others. Numbers 24:17 says a star representing a king's scepter will come out of Israel someday. Has anyone ever made you face the truth and, even with the facts, you would not believe? Why?

CHAP. 27:
Isaiah 9:2 says people saw a great light, and in verse 6, it explains why: "Because unto us a child is born, a son is given," and he shall be called God. In the story, even Michel has trouble with this one. So much so, that he quickly puts it out of his mind. Are there scriptures you do not want to be in the Bible. Here's one: Love your enemies. What other scriptures do have a hard time accepting?

CHAP. 28:
The commander of the fort bragged that he had been a cataphract in the army. Michel saw through it because he knew his horse would have to be powerful enough to carry its own heavy armor as well as his rider and armor. What do you tend to exaggerate about yourself? Why do people do that?

CHAP. 29:
They got lost, then had an impromptu camel race. When you are on a long trip, do you force yourself to get there as soon as possible, or do you allow yourself a little "me" time?

Since Michel's ancestor, Abraham, lived there two thousand years earlier. About a hundred miles north of there, Katazuli's ancestors ruled much of today's Turkey. Both wanted to stay there a few days. Do you ever want to "connect" with your ancestors? Why?

CHAP. 30:
Injuries, shipwrecks, highwaymen continue to plague the travelers. Now they lose Katazuli. After so much bad luck, why wouldn't they just stop, go back home, and give up the chase?

CHAP. 31:
Though Michel is a believer in the one true God and sometimes tries to convert his companions, he has his own inner struggles, especially when they refer to the child-king as a god. Why do you think Michel is fighting it?

CHAP. 32:
Michel's mood swings are more prominent now. Do you sometimes plan something very important for week, and when the day finally comes, you get jittery? Why do we do that?

CHAP. 33:
Christmas songs say the wise men followed the star all the way from home. But the Bible says after they left Jerusalem, "the star appeared again" and they rejoiced. Have you caught yourself with other misconceptions from the Bible? What?

CHAP. 34:
Just as the other magi have been forced to admit the newborn king was a god, Michel struggles to understand just who this child walking on earth is. What do you think it is like for people of other world religions to be told God is one, but Jesus was the Word of God?

CHAP. 35:
Michel finally admits to himself that Jesus was the Word of God walking on earth. He had given up everything to do what God never told him to do. Have you ever given up more than

most people for something that turned out to be wrong?

CHAP. 36:
There are sometimes people around us who feel empty and worthless. All ambition is gone, though some people call it laziness. What can we do for someone in this state?

CHAP. 37:
Michel is befriended by a boy. Who does his back-and-forth attitude toward the boy remind you of?

CHAP. 38:
Sometimes in life the servant becomes the master or the child becomes the parent. Roll reversal. Have you reversed rolls with anyone?

CHAP. 39:
Do you know someone with a broken dream? What was the dream? How can you help that person turn it into a better dream and reality?

CHAP. 40:
Through all the years of Michel struggling with his faith, it just was growing stronger. Have you had a dream that collapsed, and something much better rose up in its place?

ABOUT THE AUTHOR

Katheryn Maddox Haddad spends an average of 300 hours researching before writing a historical novel—ancient historians such as Josephus, archaeological digs so she can know the layout of cities, their language, culture, and politics.

She grew up in the northern United States and now lives in Arizona where she doesn't have to shovel sunshine. She basks in 100-degree weather, palm trees, cacti, and a computer with most of the letters worn off.

She is author of 77 books, both non-fiction and fiction. Her newspaper column appeared for several years in newspapers in Texas and North Carolina ~ *Little Known Facts About the Bible* ~ and she has written for numerous Christian publications. For over twenty years, she has been sending out every morning a daily scripture and short inspirational thought to some 30,000 people around the world.

She spends half her day writing, and the other half teaching English over the internet worldwide using the Bible as textbook. She has taught some 7000 Muslims through World English Institute. Students she has converted to Christianity are in hiding in Afghanistan, Iran, Iraq, Yemen, Uzbekistan, Somalia, Jordan, Tajikistan, Sierra Leone, Pakistan, Indonesia, and Palestine. "They are my heroes," she declares.

With a bachelor's degree in English, Bible and social science from Harding University and part of a master's degree in Bible, including Greek, from the Harding Graduate School of Theology, she also has a master's degree in management and human relations from Abilene University. She is a member of American Christian Fiction Writers, Historical Novel Society, International Screen Writers Association, and is also an energetic public speaker who can touch the hearts of audiences.

CONNECT WITH
KATHERYN MADDOX HADDAD

Website: **https://inspirationsbykatheryn.com**

Facebook:
bit.ly/FacebooksKatherynMaddoxHaddad

Linkedin: **http://bit.ly/KatherynLinkedin**

Twitter: **https://twitter.com/KatherynHaddad**

Pinterest:
https://www.pinterest.com/haddad1940/

Goodreads:
https://www.goodreads.com/katherynmaddoxhaddad

GET A FREE BOOK
Sign up for Katheryn's monthly newsletter with half-price books for the whole family and insider tips on what's coming next.
http://bit.ly/katheryn

JOIN MY DREAM TEAM
Members get the first peek at my newest book and have fun offering me advice sometimes. I have a point system of rewards for helping me get the word out. Check it out here: **http://bit.ly/KatherynsDreamTeam**

www.ingramcontent.com/pod-product-compliance
Lightning Source LLC
Chambersburg PA
CBHW020035120526
44588CB00031B/449